2004

BATTLING DEMONS

THE MAGIC IN HISTORY SERIES

The Magic in History series explores the role magic and
the occult have played in European culture, religion, science, and politics.
Titles in the series will bring the resources of cultural, literary, and social
history to bear on the history of the magic arts and will contribute to an
understanding of why the theory and practice of magic have elicited fascination
at every level of European society. Volumes will include both editions of
important texts and significant new research in the field.

MAGIC IN HISTORY

BATTLING DEMONS

WITCHCRAFT, HERESY, AND REFORM IN THE LATE MIDDLE AGES

MICHAEL D. BAILEY

THE PENNSYLVANIA STATE UNIVERSITY PRESS
UNIVERSITY PARK, PENNSYLVANIA

Library of Congress Cataloging-in-Publication Data

Bailey, Michael David, 1971-
   Battling demons : witchcraft, heresy, and reform in the
late Middle Ages / Michael D. Bailey.
      p.   cm. — (The magic in history series)
   Includes bibliographical references and index.
   ISBN 0-271-02225-6 (cloth : alk. paper)
   ISBN 0-271-02226-4 (pbk. : alk. paper)
   1. Witchcraft—History—to 1500.
   2. Nider, Johannes, ca. 1380–1438.
   I. Title. II. Magic in history.

BF1569 .B35 2003
133.4′3′09409024—dc21   2002010394

To the memory of my mother

nos qui onus belli contra iras demonum portavimus
—Johannes Nider, *Formicarius* 3.3

CONTENTS

ACKNOWLEDGMENTS

My work on this book and the subjects with which it deals stretches back many years now, and I have incurred numerous debts. I must thank first of all my teachers. At Duke University, Charles Young introduced me to the study of the Middle Ages, and it was in his seminar that I first began researching late medieval magic and witchcraft. Thomas Robisheaux then helped to guide my early explorations of these topics, and he has continued to take an interest in my work to the present day. At Northwestern University, Richard Kieckhefer, Robert E. Lerner, William Monter, and Edward Muir taught me, through their classes and through the example of their scholarship, about late medieval and early modern religious and cultural history, and how to be a student of it. Above all Robert Lerner, my *Doktorvater,* and Richard Kieckhefer, who at the very least is my *Doktoronkel,* have provided me with unstinting support at every stage of my work on this project, both while I was their student and in the years since. I am glad to be able to acknowledge my gratitude to them here.

Many other people—colleagues and friends—have lent me their advice, expertise, or assistance in various ways. I am grateful to Martin Steinmann, who oversaw my work during a year of research in Basel, and to Stefan Weinfurter, who welcomed me into his seminar while I was in Munich. Brigitte Degler-Spengler, Franz Egger, and Kathrin Utz Tremp all took the time to speak with me about heresy and witchcraft while I was in Switzerland. H. C. Erik Midelfort and Edward Peters read the manuscript for Penn State University Press with great care and provided me with numerous valuable suggestions. Others have helped me by reading full or partial drafts of my work, by sharing their own work with me, or simply by discussing aspects of late medieval religious history, of academia in general, and of the broad world beyond. For their help, their support, and not least their friendship I thank Karl Appuhn, David Bachrach, Jim Brennan, Louisa Burnham, Christine Caldwell, Sabine von Heusinger, Samantha Kelly, Jennifer Kolpacoff, Lillian Lee, Jimmy Mixson, Marc Rodriguez, Brett Shadle, and Werner Tschacher. My thanks go also to all the members of the GAF *Stammtisch* in Munich, some of whom have raised their glasses with me not just in Germany but, astoundingly, on four continents now.

My initial research, done in Chicago, would have been impossible had I not enjoyed access to the special collections of the Newberry Library, as well as to the general holdings of the Northwestern University Library. In Europe I relied mainly on the rich resources of the Öffentliche Bibliothek of the University of Basel and of the Bayerische Staatsbibliothek and Monumenta Germaniae Historica in Munich. I am grateful especially to the staffs of the manuscript departments in both Basel and Munich, and to the staff of the Monumenta and its library. I am also pleased to be able to thank my former colleagues in the history department of the University of Cincinnati and at the Medieval Institute of the University of Notre Dame, where much of the final work on this book was done. For financial support I am grateful to the J. William Fulbright Program, to the Swiss Federal Scholarship Commission for Foreign Students, and to the Deutscher Akademischer Austauschdienst.

Finally, I thank the Benedictine monk who ran the elevator in the bell tower of San Giorgio Maggiore, Venice, on the afternoon of August 10, 1996. Ecclesiastical history is my favorite, too.

ABBREVIATIONS

WORKS BY JOHANNES NIDER

Contra heresim	*Contra heresim Hussitarum,* Basel, ÖBU, MS E I 9, fols. 386r–453v.
De abstinencia	*De abstinencia esus carnium,* Basel, ÖBU, MS B III 15, fols. 249r–264v.
De lepra morali	*De lepra morali* (Cologne, c. 1467/72).
De paupertate	*De paupertate perfecta secularium,* Basel, ÖBU, MS B III 15, fols. 22v–54r.
De reformatione	*De reformatione status cenobitici,* Basel, ÖBU, MS B III 15, fols. 186v–248v.
De secularium religionibus	*De secularium religionibus,* Basel, ÖBU, MS B III 15, fols. 1r–22r.
Formicarius	*Formicarius,* ed. G. Colvener (Douai, 1602).
Preceptorium	*Preceptorium divine legis* (Milan, 1489).

OTHER WORKS

Aquinas, *Opera*	*S. Thomae Aquinatis opera omnia,* ed. Roberto Busa, 7 vols. (Stuttgart, 1980).
CB	Johannes Haller et al., eds., *Concilium Basiliense: Studien und Quellen zur Geschichte des Concils von Basel,* 8 vols. (1896–1936; reprint Wiesbaden, 1971).
L'imaginaire du sabbat	Martine Ostorero, Agostino Paravicini Bagliani, and Kathrin Utz Tremp, eds., *L'imaginaire du sabbat: Edition critique des textes les plus anciens (1430 c.–1440 c.)* (Lausanne, 1999).
Mansi	Joannes Dominicus Mansi, ed., *Sacrorum conciliorum nova et amplissima collectio,* 36 vols. (1758–98, 1901–27; reprint Graz, 1960–61).
MC	F. Palacky et al., eds., *Monumenta conciliorum generalium seculi decimi quinti: Concilium*

	Basileense scriptores, 4 vols. (Vienna/Basel, 1857–1936).
MOPH	Monumenta Ordinis Fratrum Praedicatorum Historica
ÖBU	Öffentliche Bibliothek der Universität Basel
QF	Quellen und Forschungen zur Geschichte des Dominikanerordens in Deutschland

INTRODUCTION

WITCHCRAFT, HERESY, AND REFORM
IN THE FIFTEENTH CENTURY

Sometime in the mid-1430s an unknown author, certainly a cleric and most likely an inquisitor, recounted the errors of a new and terrible heretical sect. He described a secret nocturnal gathering, which he termed a synagogue. Presiding over this assembly was the "enemy of all rational creatures," the devil, who appeared "sometimes in the form of a man, although imperfect, or in the likeness of another animal, but generally in the likeness of a black cat." Before this figure, new members of the sect were required to renounce their faith and to swear oaths of loyalty both to the devil and to their fellow heretics. The author then described the following scene:

> After having sworn and promised these things, the poor seduced person adores the presiding devil by giving homage to him, and as a sign of homage he kisses the devil, appearing in human or in another form, as noted above, on the buttocks or anus, giving to him as tribute one of his own limbs after death. After which all the members of that pestiferous sect celebrate the admittance of the new heretic, eating whatever is around them, especially murdered children, roasted or boiled. When this most wicked feast is completed, after they have danced as much as they desired, the presiding devil then cries, while extinguishing the light, *"mestlet, mestlet!"* After they hear his voice, immediately they join together carnally, one man with one woman, or one man with one man, and sometimes father with daughter, son with mother, brother with sister ... scarcely observing the natural order.

After this depraved ritual, the author continued, the devil would instruct his new minions in various magical arts and would give them certain magic potions, poisons, and unguents, as well as magically anointed staves on which they were to ride to all future synagogues. Indeed, all the members of this sect were described as possessing terrible magic powers and being able to work powerful and destructive sorcery. They could raise storms and cast down hail, kill children, wither crops, and cause death and disease among both animals and human beings. In short, these people were not merely heretics, they were witches.[1]

Although the notion that certain people could perform harmful sorcery was extremely ancient, the full stereotype of European witchcraft—that is, the idea of a diabolically organized and conspiratorial cult of maleficent sorcerers bent on harming faithful Christians and subverting the order of the Christian world—actually developed quite late in the medieval period, appearing only in the early fifteenth century. Mostly within the space of a single decade, the 1430s, several important documents were written describing this phenomenon in detail for the first time.[2] The source quoted above, *Errores Gazariorum* or "Errors of the *Gazarii*" (a common term for heretics), is perhaps the most lurid of these early accounts. This anonymous work is also relatively brief, however, and the immediate circumstances in which it was written remain entirely unknown. It thus serves to illustrate one of the major problems confronting scholars seeking to understand the rise of witchcraft in the late Middle Ages. Just as the *Errores* is an immediately, if gruesomely, captivating document but provides virtually no larger context in which to situate the horrors it describes, so too witchcraft as a whole evokes a certain dark fascination but remains largely isolated from other major aspects of European history. Although a great deal of scholarly attention has focused on this subject, a tendency still prevails among many historians to regard anything to do with witches as, in the words of one expert, "somehow peculiar and historically unassimilable," and a survey of the history and historiography of fifteenth-century Europe has aptly noted that "research has still not yet integrated the problem of witchcraft in a meaningful way into the overall development of Christian religiosity."[3] Witchcraft, however, was not an isolated phenomenon; nor, for all its seemingly fantastical and horrific elements, was it a concern only to certain particularly paranoid minds. Although the extent of actual witch-hunting has often been exaggerated, belief in witchcraft quickly became nearly universal in late medieval and early modern Europe, and the image of the witch that first appeared in the early 1400s endured as a figure of fear and persecution for many centuries.

Of all the sources dealing with witches and witchcraft from the early fifteenth century, some of the most valuable, particularly in situating this new phenomenon in an understandable historical context, were produced by one man, Johannes Nider. A German Dominican theologian and religious reformer, Nider presented long accounts of magic, superstition, and witchcraft in several of his theological and moral treatises, but significantly, in none of these works did he deal solely with witches. He wrote also about other heresies, religious crises, questions of morality, and general matters of faith. His most important work, for example, titled *Formicarius* (The anthill), although best known today as a treatise on witchcraft, was not solely, indeed not even primarily, about witches. Rather it was a work of what I shall call spiritual reform, decrying a supposedly widespread laxity of belief among the Christian laity and aiming at a general rejuvenation of faith among all believers. Thus the detailed and in many ways seminal accounts of witchcraft contained in this work can be fully understood only in relation to these larger reformist concerns. This book explores the rise of witchcraft in the early fifteenth century primarily through the writings of Johannes Nider. But it explores several of the other subjects he dealt with as well. The breadth of Nider's writings provides a unique opportunity to understand witchcraft not as an isolated or historically aberrant phenomenon but as one significant aspect of a larger world of religious thought and spiritual concern. My goal, therefore, is not just to examine one of the earliest and best witnesses to the emergence of witchcraft in late medieval Europe, but through him to help integrate that dark new phenomenon more fully into the overall religious, intellectual, and cultural history of the period.

Johannes Nider was by far the most important single authority to treat the subject of witchcraft in the early fifteenth century, in respect to both the amount of material he produced and the influence his writings would have. Taking up this notion at almost the very moment it first appeared in Western Europe, he played a key role in its construction, codification, and spread. His major work, the *Formicarius,* survives in over twenty-five manuscript copies from the fifteenth and early sixteenth centuries and went through seven printed editions from the 1470s to 1692, thus covering the entire period of the great European witch-hunts. His writings also served as an important source of information for what is today the most infamous of all late medieval treatises on witchcraft and witch-hunting, the *Malleus maleficarum* or *Hammer of the Witches,* by the Dominican inquisitor Heinrich Kramer (Institoris in Latin), first published in 1487. Kramer drew heavily on the earlier accounts of his fellow Dominican Nider, reproducing large sections of Nider's texts virtually verbatim in the *Malleus* and referring to him at one point as "the most eminent doctor." Moreover, the fifth book of the *Formicarius,* dealing primarily with witchcraft, was often printed along with the *Malleus* in later editions.[4]

Writing at the very beginning of the so-called witch craze in Europe, Nider is a critical source for understanding the early development of this new phenomenon. During the early fifteenth century, the crime of witchcraft no longer entailed just the practice of harmful sorcery against others, but took on terrible demonic and indeed diabolic overtones. Ultimately witches were accused of worshiping demons, renouncing their faith, and surrendering themselves completely to the service of the devil. Thus they were guilty of idolatry and apostasy, and, believed to be in league with Satan, they were regarded as a serious threat to the entire order of the Christian world. Certainly this new conception of witchcraft was by no means solely the creation of clerical authorities such as Nider, later imposed on the rest of European society through propaganda and persecution. Many aspects of the witch stereotype arose from common conceptions of magic and popular folklore widely held by the laity, and belief in witchcraft fed to a large degree off common social structures and interactions, not extraordinary waves of official persecution.[5] Still, it has long been known that many theologians and other clerical authorities became increasingly concerned with notions of superstition and sorcery in the late Middle Ages, particularly in the early fifteenth century, and their concern did much to facilitate the witch-hunts that were to come.[6] Among such men Nider was a figure of overarching importance, and his descriptions of this new and dark form of magical practice and demonic activity offer some significant insights into how and why the concept of witchcraft emerged and spread so rapidly across Europe.

In approaching the origins of witchcraft primarily through the writings of Johannes Nider, this book focuses on witchcraft as an idea, not as a social reality or object of institutional persecution.[7] The principal story told is of the emergence of this new concept in the mind of a single important authority. But witchcraft alone is not the sole element of the late medieval religious world discussed here. I consider numerous other issues that figured prominently in Nider's thought—concern over the threat of heresy, which was a significant force in the early fifteenth century; debates among clerical authorities about the questionable status of semireligious lay people such as beguines; and above all the pervasive late medieval desire for reform *in capite et membris,* in head and members, both within the church, its institutions and its orders, and more broadly in Christian society as a whole. The figure of the witch did not exist alone or in isolation in Nider's thought. For him witchcraft was but one aspect of a larger religious world that he saw to be in turmoil and crisis. Any attempt to understand his view of witchcraft, to grasp his understanding of that new idea and the anxiety it aroused in him, would fail if it did not set witchcraft within the larger context of his other religious concerns.

Although Nider is known today (when he is known at all) almost exclusively as an authority on witchcraft, he was actually an important figure in many areas of late medieval religious history. Trained as a theologian, he served for several years as the Dominican professor of theology at the University of Vienna. Within his own religious order, which was undergoing a movement for reform throughout his lifetime, he was a leading figure in the so-called observant movement (as the reform party was known), and he directed the process of reform for the entire Dominican province of Teutonia, which stretched from the Rhine to Vienna and from the Alps to the Low Countries. He personally reformed several important Dominican houses, and he wrote the first and only extended theoretical treatise on religious reform to emerge from the Dominican observant movement—*De reformatione status cenobitici* (On the reform of the cenobitic status). A contemporary, the observant Dominican chronicler Johannes of Mainz, praised him as "the greatest zealot of the order and the greatest propagator of the reform," and a generation later his reputation remained so high that the chronicler Johannes Meyer, also an observant Dominican, could write, "Even today in the reformed houses of our order one can hear the brothers say, 'Thus did Master Johannes Nider act, thus he taught and commanded and forbade, and thus he himself lived.'"[8]

Nor did Nider limit himself to affairs within his own order. His writings on the subject of reform, for example, extended to other religious orders as well. He wrote these works while participating in the great ecumenical Council of Basel, and it was here that he surely achieved his greatest influence and importance in the larger religious affairs of his day. The council convened in 1431 as a gathering of ecclesiastical leaders from across Europe. It soon became entangled in a protracted struggle with the papacy, which feared (rightly) that such a body would limit papal authority over the church. This conflict progressively drained the council of its energies, until it finally dissolved itself in 1449.[9] During the early years when Nider was present in Basel, however (he departed for a post at the University of Vienna probably at the end of 1434 or very early in 1435), the council was extremely active in many areas of ecclesiastical concern. Indeed, for a time Basel became virtually the center of the entire Western Christian world, and Nider was one of the most active and important men in Basel. Not only was he an official representative of the Dominican order at the council, but he also served as prior of the local Dominican convent, which during these early years was a principal center of the council's activity. The initial general sessions were held there, and several deputations, the various standing committees in which most of the council's work was actually done, met within its walls.[10]

While he was a member of the Council of Basel, Nider undertook crucial negotiations with the most threatening heretical sect to confront the church in the early fifteenth century, the Hussites of Bohemia, and he also found time to consider the questionable status of beghards and beguines, lay people who chose to live a quasi-religious life and whom, for a variety of reasons, many clerical authorities found suspicious or even heretical. Although he does not seem to have taken much interest in issues of conciliarism per se—that is, the

ecclesiological debates over whether the council or the pope should wield
supreme authority within the church—he was clearly involved in such matters at
least insofar as they affected the other issues that held his attention at Basel.
Matters of ecclesiastical reform, for example, were entangled in complex ways
with the issue of conciliarism. It was also at Basel that Nider became interested
in the matter of witchcraft. Although the council does not appear to have engaged officially in any discussion of this new phenomenon, scholars have long
recognized that Basel was an important center for the codification and diffusion
of the idea of witchcraft from lands in and around the western Alps, where some
of the earliest true witch trials were beginning to take place at this time, to the
rest of Europe.[11] Nider was one of the most important figures in this process.
Although he actually wrote most of his influential accounts of magic and witchcraft after leaving Basel, many of the stories he related focused on lands in western Switzerland, and he obviously collected much if not all of his material on
these subjects while at the council. Here the matter of witchcraft would have
been raised and discussed amidst many other religious issues and concerns, and
Nider would have seen this new phenomenon as but one aspect of a larger crisis
facing the Christian world.

Despite his significance in so many areas of late medieval religious history,
however, Nider has until recently remained a remarkably understudied figure.
The only general account of his activities, the biography written by the German
parish priest Kaspar Schieler, is now over one hundred years old, and was hardly
serviceable even when it was new, offering more eulogy than critical historical
analysis. More recent scholarship on Nider (what little there is) has generally
focused on specific categories of his writings or on individual aspects of his
thought.[12] Broader studies of the major issues and events with which he was
involved rarely do more than mention his name, if that. His treatise on the
Hussite heresy (which admittedly survives in only two incomplete copies) goes
unmentioned and unexamined in all scholarship on that topic. His attacks on
the heresy of the Free Spirit have been noted, but his two far more positive treatises on lay poverty and the semireligious way of life led by many beguines,
although labeled by one expert as "fundamental" to any discussion of the subject in the fifteenth century, have remained "almost completely ignored" by
modern scholarship.[13] Even in the area of witchcraft, in which he clearly made
his most enduring contributions to the later history of Europe, he has until
recently received far less attention than was his due. As recently as 1991, Carlo
Ginzburg was still able to note, quite aptly, that Nider's major work on witchcraft, the *Formicarius,* remained "more quoted than analyzed."[14]

I do not aim here at a complete study of all aspects of Nider's thought. Quite
simply, he wrote too much and his religious concerns were too catholic.[15] Any

full examination of all his writings would quickly become encyclopedic, both in volume and in thematic coherence. Such a work would doubtless prove fascinating, shedding light on many areas of the late medieval religious world, but it is, to use the hackneyed phrase, simply beyond the scope of this book. The focus here is on witchcraft, yet still not witchcraft solely. Other factors and other concerns must enter into consideration, both for their influence on Nider's approach to witchcraft and his understanding of that new phenomenon and for their influence on my approach to the same subject. In reality, this expanded focus could well serve as a license to enter into all areas of Nider's thought, but two areas in particular stand in close relation to witchcraft. The issues of heresy and reform, both broadly understood, do much to clarify how Nider approached the issue of witchcraft and how he conceived of the threat that witches represented to the Christian faith.

At first glance, the elements of witchcraft—extreme diabolism, gruesome cannibalism of infants, and secret nocturnal conventicles filled with orgies and other depravities—appear entirely irrational, and such authorities as Nider who accepted and propounded these notions appear either mad, naive, or ridiculous.[16] One might expect, given Nider's deep concern over witchcraft, to see his fears in this area paralleled by other anxieties about possible assaults on the church and Christian faith, and that his lurid accounts of demonic sabbaths would be matched by shrill denunciations of the major heresies of the late medieval period, the Hussites and the Free Spirit. In fact, while he obviously opposed these movements and regarded them as utterly condemnable, he seems to have been far less concerned about heretics than about witches. In his writings on heresy, and especially in his broad defense of the semireligious beguines, who were often accused of heresy, he appears much more restrained, moderate, and (to modern minds, at least) "rational." Moreover, in these works he begins to reveal the degree to which all other areas of his thought were influenced and shaped by his profound commitment to reform. His support for beguines in particular was based on his conviction that these devout lay people, whom other clerical authorities often viewed with grave suspicion, followed an entirely laudable way of life and might provide a model of spiritual reform for the rest of the laity. A careful examination of his reformist treatises then reveals how wide-ranging his concept of reform was, not just encompassing institutional change within the church but, even more important, entailing a moral and spiritual regeneration within individual believers. In this spiritual sense, Nider firmly believed that religious reform could and must extend to the laity as well as to the clergy, and should encompass not just the institutional church but ultimately all of Christian society. In this spiritual sense, too, his ideas of reform shaped and fed his fear of witches.

Only when viewed from the perspective of these larger reformist concerns will the phenomenon of witchcraft begin to appear to us as I think it must have appeared to Nider—as but a single terrible aspect of a world degraded by sin, assailed by demons, and desperately in need of reform. In tales of witchcraft Nider the reformer found ideal material with which to propel faithful Christians who had become somewhat lax in their beliefs back to full piety. To a large extent, he used accounts of the relatively new phenomenon of witchcraft just as moral reformers within the church had for centuries been accustomed to use stories of demonic power and demonic possession, to instruct and encourage proper belief and to warn of the dangers of moral and spiritual lapses. That such men should have been attracted to the fantastic horrors of witchcraft and have proved more than ready to accept and employ this new concept is hardly surprising. Scholars have long noted a connection between the growing desire for reform and the rise of witch-hunting in the late Middle Ages.[17] Yet the specifics of this relationship have never been fully articulated, let alone explored. Nider provides exemplary insight into this connection. His entire concept of witchcraft was shaped and colored by his particular understanding of reform.

Although I see a strong connection between witchcraft and reform, particularly for Nider, I do not wish to suggest that the emergence and the acceptance of the idea of witchcraft in even a single mind, let alone by an entire society or culture, is an easily explained or monocausal process. The alchemy involved was far more complex than just a matter of reformist concerns transmuted into diabolical fantasies. Indeed, the rise of witchcraft remains so fascinating and still so difficult to fathom, despite the vast array of scholarship devoted to it, largely because it was such a multifaceted and "multifactoral" phenomenon,[18] drawing on and feeding off many other aspects of late medieval religious culture. When the inquiry is limited to one man who left an extensive record of his thought on such matters, and whose writings then had a significant influence on the thoughts of others who followed him, some sense of order, however constrained, should emerge. What follows is a cultural history of ideas and concepts, however, and not an intellectual history in the usual sense. That is, Johannes Nider was himself never aware of consciously developing or constructing the idea of witchcraft. It was instead, for him, a reality that he merely accepted, described, and sought to explain. Thus he leaves no clear passages that might allow us to trace with absolute certainty the development of his thought in relation to this matter. Never does he write, "I saw witchcraft as a means toward reform," or "My concern over heresy caused me to turn to witchcraft." The reader will understand, then, if I more often suggest and attempt to demonstrate rather than to prove definitively the connections that I see between various areas of his thought.

Given that the overall focus of this book is on the emerging idea of witchcraft, particularly as described in Nider's writings, I considered whether I might not interweave a discussion of his writings on other subjects such as heresy and reform into the chapters on witchcraft per se. To do so seemed to me, however, to suggest too great a unity in his thought and concerns where I see only continuities, influences, and overlaps. I also worried that such a structure would necessitate digressions so long and unwieldy as to disrupt the flow of the central arguments about witchcraft. I decided, then, to keep the various areas of witchcraft, heresy, and reform more or less distinct in separate chapters, although with obvious overlaps and linkages between those chapters. The present structure turns out to reflect almost exactly how I myself initially worked through Nider's thought. I began with the problem of witchcraft, and then moved on to what I saw as the closely related area of heresy. I soon realized, however, that in his treatment of heretics Nider appeared in a far different light, far less credulous and fearful, than in his accounts of witches. Through his writings on heresy I came to understand that reformist concerns formed the basis of his approach to most other issues, so I moved next to his treatises on reform and then returned to his magnum opus, the *Formicarius,* and his stories of witchcraft recorded there, attempting to understand them in the context of reform. The story that follows here thus opens and closes with witchcraft, moving through other matters in between. I find this approach essential. The insights gained by considering Nider's writings on these other issues serve not just to support the conclusions of later chapters but in a sense to justify the very premises of those chapters as well. Of course, continuities still abound, as do the occasional contradictions. Historians labor valiantly to force the past into the Procrustean structures of their arguments. The fit is never perfect. My argument here is that the rise of witchcraft in the early fifteenth century must be understood in the light of other developments in the religious world of that time. It seemed foolish not to let those other developments have some space to speak for themselves.

In situating the rise of witchcraft, particularly the growing clerical concern over this new and terrible crime, among other major aspects of late medieval religious history, I hope to demonstrate that this was not a marginal, fantastical, or historically incomprehensible development. The larger world of the fifteenth century can shed considerable light on the emergence of witchcraft, and the emergence of witchcraft can, if examined carefully, shed some light back on its time. Close to a century ago, Johan Huizinga, in his classic *Autumn of the Middle Ages,* described the fifteenth century as being "more than any other the century of the persecution of witches." In his view, this new horror exemplified the profound decay of late medieval civilization. It was the natural result of typical medieval "credulity and lack of critical thinking," and the final and most horrific embellishment of medieval concerns over heresy and demonic power. The only difficulty lay in explaining how the wondrous new age of Renaissance humanism failed to "immediately reject the cruelties of the witch-hunts."[19] Since Huizinga's time, scholars have progressively abandoned the view that the late Middle Ages were a period of unmitigated decline, as well as modifying the simplistic notion that the Italian Renaissance and Protestant Reformation represented a complete break with earlier medieval traditions and were the birth of all things modern. Yet still the overall dichotomy between the medieval and early modern periods has to a great extent held firm, and in lieu of a sharp boundary the entire fifteenth century has come to be seen as a long transitional period between these two epochs.[20] Events and developments within that century continue to be viewed largely from the perspective of earlier or later eras. While such perspectives can be very informative, they can also obscure certain aspects of the period, and this has certainly been the case with witchcraft. The rise of this new idea in the fifteenth century is still most often seen, from one perspective, as some sort of natural culmination of medieval concerns over heresy and demonic magic, and from the other as a mere preliminary step toward the great witch-hunts that actually did not begin in earnest until the sixteenth century. Without doubt both views are accurate, but they also inevitably overlook many of the unique aspects of the fifteenth century that helped give rise to witchcraft at that specific time.

Having abandoned such simplistic notions as "decay" and "rebirth" to characterize the late Middle Ages, much modern scholarship now tends to leave the impression, doubtless to some extent true, that the fifteenth century was a terribly fragmented age.[21] Especially in regard to religious history, the years from the outbreak of the Great Schism (1378) to Luther's break with Rome (1521) were ones of crisis upon crisis, of such tremendous and rapid transition that contemporaries often failed to see any coherence in their world.[22] Yet certain continuities, if not any single great unity, clearly run through and bind together the religious history of this era, and our understanding of any one aspect of the period will remain incomplete and fragmented until we pay more attention to them. The writings of Johannes Nider, when examined closely, can reveal some of the intricate connections that bound the rise of witchcraft to other developments and ongoing religious concerns in the early fifteenth century. They also may begin to indicate that the phenomenon of witchcraft, far from being marginal or "historically unassimilable," was actually a central characteristic of an age deeply concerned with matters of religious and spiritual reform.

1

THE LIFE OF JOHANNES NIDER

On the twenty-seventh of July 1431 a great procession took place in the city of Basel and a mass was celebrated in the cathedral high over the Rhine. Four days earlier the great ecumenical Council of Basel had officially convened after much delay. Now, on the first Friday after that event, formal ceremonies were being held, and during these celebrations Johannes Nider delivered an opening sermon to the laity who had come to witness the spectacle.[1] Given the importance of the council as a gathering of ecclesiastical leaders from across Western Christendom and the role it was intended to play in the governance of the entire church, as he stood before the assembled crowd Nider may well have felt himself to be standing at the very center of the Christian world.

Throughout the early years of the great synod at Basel, Nider was a leading figure within the council. This is to say that he was a leading figure within the church as a whole at this time. He was also a high-ranking member of the Dominican order, a respected religious reformer, and a skilled theologian. To have risen so high in the church, especially from such humble origins as his (he was the son of a cobbler in a small town in Swabia), marked Nider as a remarkable man, as his contemporaries and near-contemporaries seem to have recognized, for in a world where few people aside from kings and saints could expect to see their lives chronicled, he attracted two early biographers. The Dominican Johannes of Mainz, who served briefly under Nider in Basel, included a long section on his former prior in a history of the Basel Dominicans that he wrote between 1442 and 1444. A generation later, in the 1460s, the Dominican Johannes Meyer discussed Nider in two histories of the reform movement in the Order of Preachers.[2]

Nider himself also seems to have had something of an autobiographical impulse, although, as befitted his severe religious humility, he kept it extremely muted. Nevertheless, much information about his life can be gleaned from his great work, the *Formicarius*. This large treatise takes the form of a dialogue between a theologian and a curious but lazy student, and the theologian is obviously intended to be Nider himself. Questioned by his pupil on a wide array of issues, he always begins his answers, as any good theologian should, by citing earlier authorities—the Bible, the early church fathers, Thomas Aquinas, Bonaventure, Saint Bernard, and so forth. His lazy student, however, always tires of these complex and colorless explanations. He demands contemporary examples that illustrate the points the theologian is trying to make. Thus Nider supplies himself with an excuse to relate edifying stories that he has heard and events that he has witnessed, and many of these accounts present some brief but direct glimpses into his own life. "I learned of the following while I was a student in Cologne," he would write as an entree into one tale, or "While I was in Regensburg with Juan of Palomar I witnessed the following," or "While at the Council of Constance in my youth . . ."

Revealing as these nuggets of information sometimes can be, the reader will understand, of course, that Nider was hardly concerned to present a clear and coherent account of his life. Neither were his two early biographers, Johannes of Mainz and Johannes Meyer. Both men were fervently committed observant Dominicans, members of the reform movement of which Nider had been a leader. Their primary purpose in recounting his life was to praise the noble character and many virtues of one of the heroes of their movement, not to provide a coherent chronology of his life. Still, countless medieval lives have vanished entirely from the historical record, and we are fortunate when we can still see one in any detail at all, even if it is, as it were, through a dark and somewhat fragmented glass.

The primary focus of this book is on Nider as a thinker. My main concern, therefore, has more to do with his ideas and the written works in which he expressed those ideas than with his "lived experience." In fact, many of the events of his life can appear somewhat dull in comparison with the important and often disturbing ideas that occupied his mind. For all his preoccupation with witches, for example, Nider was never a witch-hunter. Indeed, so far as I know, he never personally encountered anyone he regarded as a witch, although he did know at least one necromancer—that is, a learned demonic sorcerer—in Vienna.[3] On only one recorded occasion did he function as an inquisitor of heresy, and even then not in a formal sense.[4] He certainly was active, as a preacher, as a prior, as a professor, and as a member of the Council of Basel, but for the most part, his life revolved around ideas, not acts. Still, ideas are influenced by actions and experiences. Nider's own exposition of ideas in stories drawn from his life in the *Formicarius* provides ample evidence of that. Thus any study that purports to offer an understanding of Nider's thought must first

Jonannes Nider. (Stadtbibliothek Nürnberg, MS Cent II, 8.)

try to come to an understanding of the man, to outline the course of his life, and to examine those events that influenced and shaped him. This story, never before told in any detail in English, is a fascinating and remarkable one.[5] It is the story of a young boy from an out-of-the-way corner of the German empire who rose by dint of skill, intelligence, and devotion until he stood at the center of the religious world in his day. He dealt with emperors, popes, and heretics. He addressed himself to a broad range of ecclesiastical and religious issues. And he helped to formulate some of the darkest ideas that ever sprang from a medieval mind.

NIDER'S EARLY LIFE AND EDUCATION: ISNY TO THE UNIVERSITY OF VIENNA

For all that we know of Nider's life, we can do no more than guess at the year of his birth. Since he entered the Dominican order in 1402 and since early constitutions of the Order of Preachers called for priors not to admit men who were under eighteen years of age, we can estimate that he was born sometime before 1385.[6] He grew up in the small Swabian town of Isny (about sixty miles southwest of Augsburg and some twenty miles inland from the eastern end of Lake Constance), but little is known of his early life or family, only that his father was a poor cobbler who died sometime before his son completed his university education and that his mother never remarried, preferring to live as a chaste widow.[7] The family was almost certainly very pious and encouraged, if not pushed, their son into a religious life. His early schooling most likely took place in the local Benedictine monastery.[8]

While Nider was still in his first years in Isny, three hundred miles to the east, in Vienna, an event occurred that would shape the course of the rest of his life. In 1388 a movement for reform was launched within the Dominican order. Throughout the later fourteenth century, many devout clerics, not just Dominicans but those in other orders as well, were growing concerned with what they perceived to be increasing corruption, lax discipline, and moral decline in religious orders. Several reform movements emerged spontaneously, all calling for a return to strict observance of the original rules and constitutions of the orders as a way to combat this perceived decadence. Thus they came to be known as "observant" movements.[9] Initially the Dominican movement was unorganized. Individual friars sought to adhere to strict observance in convents where the general observance was lax, but this endeavor proved extremely difficult. Then in 1388, at the general chapter meeting of the order in Vienna, Konrad of Prussia, a friar from Cologne, approached his master general, Raymond of Capua, with a simple proposal: each province of the order should establish at least one reformed house, to which friars seeking a strict observance could go. Raymond approved, and by the end of the next year, 1389, the first such house, the Dominican priory in Colmar, was reformed under Konrad's direction.[10]

We do not know when in his youth Johannes Nider first came into contact with the ideas of the Dominican reform movement, but he chose to enter the order at Colmar sometime shortly after April 8, 1402, when this convent was still one of only two reformed Dominican houses, along with the Nuremberg priory, in German lands.[11] Sometime after completing his one-year novitiate, he was sent to Worms for confirmation and ordination. Although Strassburg was the episcopal see nearest to Colmar, the bishop of Worms, Eckhard of Dersch, had a reputation for piety and his office was free from any hint of simony, factors that obviously appealed to the morally strict reformers.[12] It was probably at this point, as a full Dominican friar at Colmar, that Nider met and traveled with another of the early leaders of the Dominican reform in Germany, Johannes Mulberg. Mulberg had been an early disciple of Konrad of Prussia, and by 1400 he was in Basel, just south of Colmar on the Rhine, preaching zealously against corruption in the church and among the laity. In the *Formicarius,* Nider stated that he served for a time as Mulberg's *socius itineris,* his official traveling companion (Dominicans were required to go in pairs whenever they left their convents to travel or to preach), but did not indicate when or for how long the two men were together.[13] In 1404 and 1405, however, Mulberg delivered sermons in Strassburg, and the journey from Basel down the Rhine would have taken him directly past Colmar. Nothing could have been more natural than for Konrad to send his bright new friar to travel as a *socius* of his old friend and companion in reform.

The years after 1405 are a blank in Nider's life, and we have no certain information about him until he appears as a theology student at the University of Cologne sometime before 1413.[14] Typical Dominican practice, however, was for a new friar to undergo two or three more years of training at his home convent after his novitiate. Often this training involved traveling as the *socius* of an experienced older friar, as Nider did with Mulberg. Only then could a Dominican begin his long course of formal studies. Nider had already learned grammar, most likely from the Benedictines in Isny, but he would still have had to complete five years of schooling in the liberal arts at a Dominican *studium* before he could undertake the study of theology. In all, these seven or eight years of training and schooling would account for the period between the end of Nider's novitiate and his appearance in Cologne.[15]

We can easily surmise what sort of training Nider was undergoing during the years before his initial study of theology in Cologne, but we cannot be so sure where this training took place. In his *Formicarius,* Nider seems to indicate that at least some of his preliminary education took place in Vienna, where he would later complete his degree in theology, for he writes at one point of "the time when I first studied arts at the University of Vienna."[16] Since the basic liberal arts education had to precede the study of theology, this statement would indicate that Nider left Colmar and traveled first to distant Austria for several years before returning to the Rhineland to begin his theological education at Cologne. Two strong pieces of evidence, however, suggest that Nider did not begin his studies in Vienna. First, the matriculation records of the university show no sign that Nider studied there at any time before 1422. Second, when Nider did petition for admission to the University of Vienna in 1422, he was required to undergo a public examination, since he was "not well known" to the faculty there, hardly an indication of his having been a student in Vienna only a decade earlier.[17]

The course of Nider's life becomes only slightly more certain after he arrives in Cologne to undertake his training in theology. He mentions on several occasions in the *Formicarius* that he studied in Cologne, but gives no information that could be used to give a firm date to his time there.[18] We do know that when he later studied at Vienna, he almost immediately began to lecture on Scripture and then on the *Sentences* of Peter Lombard. Thus he must already have completed his initial studies in theology, which would have taken at least two or three years. In view of the time necessary for his preliminary education and training in the Dominican order, he may have matriculated in Cologne as early as 1410 and remained there until around 1413.[19] If he had encountered any delays in his early training, however, he might have matriculated a year or even two years later, and thus continued to pursue his studies until 1414 or even 1415, a possibility that might help explain some of the chronology that follows.

After leaving Cologne, Nider was sent to the Council of Constance, which met from 1414 to 1418, and it would be natural enough to assume that he was present from the very beginning of the council.[20] I think it is unlikely, however, that he was in Constance before the second half of 1415. In his *Formicarius*, Nider wrote of the execution of the Hussite heretic Jerome of Prague, burned by the council in the spring of 1416.[21] Nowhere, however, did he give any account of the burning of the principal Hussite figure, Jan Hus, in the summer of the previous year. Arguing from an absence of evidence is always a risky affair, but I find it almost impossible to believe that Nider could have been in Constance in 1415, witnessed the trial and execution of the greatest heretic of the fifteenth century, and yet have made no mention of that fact in all his moralistic writings. However long Nider was at the council, the role he played in this great ecclesiastical gathering must have been slight. He was, after all, a young friar still working toward his degree in theology, and at Constance he would have been surrounded by the greatest theologians of the day, as well as by the leaders of his own order. It was surely hubris, or at least a wistful exaggeration of memory, that would later cause him to write, almost as if he were a participant in the great debates about religious reform that took place at the council, "how I remember how much was discussed concerning reform ... and [how] happy I was then with the things that were said to me ... but we were frustrated in our desire [for reform]."[22]

When the Council of Constance closed in 1418, the course of Nider's personal history again becomes unclear. He did not return to Cologne to complete his education in theology. Most accounts of his life say that he journeyed instead to Italy in order to observe the Dominican reform movement south of the Alps, which had been introduced by Giovanni Dominici in Venice only a year after Konrad of Prussia had reformed Colmar. The evidence for this journey, however, is sparse. We know that Nider was in Italy at some point early in his career, for in the *Formicarius* he related a story that took place in the Dominican priory of Chioggia, near Venice, which he noted he had visited "in my youth."[23] If we assume that Nider was eighteen when he joined the Dominican order in 1402, however, then he would have been thirty-four, and no longer a youth (*junior*), when the Council of Constance ended in 1418. The years after Constance are another blank in the life of Johannes Nider that cannot be filled with any certainty.[24] He may well have journeyed to Italy, perhaps not for the first time, traveling with Italian friars returning from Constance. Or he may have undertaken other tasks for the order. He emerges again into the clear light of record only four years later and some three hundred miles to the east of Constance, in Vienna.

On November 10, 1422, "a certain brother of the Order of Preachers" asked to be admitted to the University of Vienna. The brother was Johannes Nider, and he was duly accepted for study in the winter semester, as the matriculation records of the university confirm. His admission was not without problems, however. "Because he was not well known [to the theological faculty], master Peter of Pulkau was assigned to him, in order to hear him in public in the schools." While awaiting his public examination, Nider was to write to the master general of his order and receive from him the necessary license to study at the university. He had brought with him only the license of the Dominican provincial of Teutonia. On January 24, 1423, apparently after a successful public examination, Nider petitioned the theological faculty again and was admitted as a reader of the Bible. He selected the Dominican reformer Franz of Retz as his master, and was assigned to deliver his first lecture on the book of Jeremiah before February 17, "if he should be able." Following what was the usual course of study, he read the Bible for two years and then, beginning in the winter term of 1424, the *Sentences* of Peter Lombard.[25]

The Dominican order had always stressed scholarship, as good theological training was held to be essential for effective preaching. In Vienna, Nider no doubt received an excellent theological education in general, but he also was exposed to a type of theology particularly attractive to observant Dominicans. In the late fourteenth and early fifteenth centuries, certain intellectual leaders among the clergy, the most famous of whom was Jean Gerson, chancellor of the University of Paris, worked to develop a new form of practical devotional theology (termed *Frömmigkeitstheologie* in German scholarship),[26] which eschewed abstract intellectual debates in favor of addressing actual spiritual problems and pastoral needs. This form of theology found great favor at the University of Vienna, and what has been termed a "Vienna School" arose, including such figures as Heinrich of Langenstein, Nikolaus of Dinkelsbühl, and Nider's own master, Franz of Retz. Nider himself was first a student and later an important member of this group, and throughout his life his intellectual work reflected attention to the practical needs of pastoral duties and the care of souls.[27] Particularly significant for our purposes is the fact that the members of this group frequently showed concern over matters of superstition and sorcery, over the power of demons, the proper interpretation of dreams and visions, and the correct discernment of good from evil spirits.[28] In such areas Nider would become perhaps the leading figure of the Vienna School.

Nider completed his university studies in 1425, being examined in April and formally receiving his degree on June 18 of that year.[29] He then taught in Vienna for one year, but in June 1426 he petitioned to be relieved of his university duties. He left the city sometime thereafter, although perhaps not until a year or more later, in the autumn of 1427.[30] The reason for his departure is unclear. Some scholars argue that he had been appointed vicar over the entire Dominican observant movement in Teutonia in 1426, and this was the reason he left Vienna.[31] There is no support for this argument, however—either that Nider was in fact appointed vicar at this time or that the appointment would have required him to abandon his university post—for the title of vicar in the Dominican order was not held to the exclusion of all other offices. Even if Nider did receive this appointment in 1426, he could have remained on the university faculty, as he did years later when he was again a member of the faculty and yet retained all of his responsibilities within the observant movement. A far more likely reason for his departure was that he had been appointed head of the Dominican priory in Nuremberg, an office he seems to have assumed in 1427.[32]

NIDER AS PRIOR IN NUREMBERG AND BASEL

Nider served as prior in Nuremberg, one of the great centers of the early Dominican observant movement, from 1427 until 1429, when he was transferred to Basel to direct the reform of the priory there. During his few years in

Nuremberg he preached, conducted visitations of other Dominican houses, and produced some of his early treatises. He also helped to reform the female Dominican cloister in Nuremberg, the convent of St. Catherine. This was the first reform that Nider directed, and it brought him into close contact with the master general of his order, Barthélemy Texier. For the rest of his life Nider would be Texier's principal lieutenant for the observant movement in Teutonia.[33]

One attempt to reform St. Catherine's had already been made. Some thirty years before Nider's efforts, his mentor, Konrad of Prussia, had tried and failed to win the nuns over to the strict discipline of the observant movement. According to Nider, when he led the successful reform in 1428, he again faced fierce resistance from the nuns. "With one voice," he wrote, "all the sisters cried out against the reform."[34] When a small group of observant nuns arrived from the convent of Schönensteinbach, near Colmar, they were driven out of St. Catherine's, and only strenuous efforts by Nider and Texier persuaded the obstinate conventual sisters (as nonreformed Dominicans were known) to let the observants back into the nunnery. The conventuals also appealed to their powerful relations in local government, and the entire city became divided over the issue of the convent's reform. Finally, however, Nider and Texier succeeded in convincing the town council of the value of reform, and the fierce struggle ended in victory for the observants.[35] Or so, at least, Nider would have us believe. One study of the reform of St. Catherine's that has examined sources other than those produced by the reform party itself reveals that there was very little resistance to the reform in 1428. True, the observant nuns who came from Schönensteinbach and arrived in Nuremberg on December 6 were not able to enter St. Catherine's until December 13, but the convent chronicle itself reports no struggle between the observant party and the local conventual sisters. What resistance to reform did exist seems to have come independently from the town council, concerned about the effect the economic strictures of the reform might have on the prosperity of the town as a whole.[36]

Dominican houses were usually important property holders and played a significant role in the political and economic life of the communities in which they were situated. Reformers, with their demands for stricter poverty, always threatened to disturb the financial relations of town and convent, arousing the concern of local authorities.[37] In Zurich, for example, the town government, fearful of economic change, played an important role in impeding the reform of the priory there for many years.[38] Female houses had special financial and political importance, as many of the sisters came from wealthy merchant and noble families and brought large dowries with them. When the original attempt at reform failed at St. Catherine's in 1398, a letter from the then master general, Raymond of Capua, guaranteed that the property of the Nuremberg convent would not be alienated against the nuns' wishes, clearly indicating that concerns over the potential economic effects of strict observance factored highly into the overall resistance to the reform.[39] Economic factors were surely also of concern during the second attempt at reform in 1428, but Nider was apparently able to calm the worries of the town leaders (in fact, the introduction of a reform usually had little effect on the overall economic life of a town, since any property or wealth the reformers might dispense with most often was transferred to other local religious houses or even to the town itself). In the end, a relatively peaceful reform would seem to be indicated by the fact that, of thirty-five nuns in St. Catherine's, only eight chose to leave the convent for nonobservant houses when the reform succeeded.[40] Thus we are provided with an important lesson about how far we should believe the accounts of observant friars when they write of the great trials they endured to bring about reform.[41]

Whether the struggle to reform St. Catherine's was really much of a fight or not, it did allow Nider to work closely with the Dominican master general, Barthélemy Texier. In 1428, following the chapter general in Cologne, Texier was conducting a visitation tour through German lands. He came through Nuremberg, and Nider also accompanied him on at least some of his travels.[42] The master general appointed Nider vicar over St. Catherine's, and may have made him vicar general of the entire observant movement in Teutonia shortly thereafter (although some scholars date the event as late as 1430).[43] Clearly by late 1428 and early 1429, Nider was emerging as one of the most important observant leaders in German lands. He would be the master general's choice to lead the next major reform action.

Even as he was engaged in the reform of St. Catherine's in Nuremberg, Barthélemy Texier was already planning the reform of the Dominican houses in Basel. In 1423 the large convent of St. Mary Magdalene an den Steinen had been reformed by Konrad of Prussia.[44] Five years later, however, the two other Dominican houses in the city, the male priory and the wealthy female house of Klingental, just across the Rhine, remained unreformed. Even the earliest sources disagree as to Texier's motives for pressing the reform in Basel in 1428 and 1429. A generation after the events, the Dominican Johannes of Mainz maintained that Texier wanted the priory reformed because of the approaching general council that was to be held in Basel beginning in 1431. Writing one generation later, Johannes Meyer reported that the Basel town council initiated the call for reform. It now seems clear that the town government was actively pressing Texier for a reform, but the pending ecumenical council, a body whose main task was expected to be the reform of the church in head and members, surely also weighed heavily on the master general's mind.[45] Whatever the ultimate cause, Texier began taking steps toward reforming the Basel houses as early as

1427. In 1428 he issued a brief list of points for the reform to follow, basically calling for increased devotion to divine offices, greater observance of poverty, and strict adherence to the rule and constitutions of the order.[46] The master general's steps toward reform immediately raised resistance from the Basel priory and Klingental convent, and outside evidence verifies that in Basel, in contrast to Nuremberg, an actual struggle took place. So strong was the resistance that Texier was forced to turn for help to Pope Martin V, who in November 1428 issued a bull commanding the bishops of Basel, Constance, and Strassburg to aid in the master general's attempts at reform.[47]

The next year, Texier pressed the reform in earnest. On April 30, 1429, Johannes Nider and twelve observant friars from Nuremberg arrived in Basel. As was the typical method of enacting reform, these men took over the key offices of the priory, with Nider himself becoming prior. They then began to enforce a strict observance of the rule and constitutions of the order, a stricter cloistering of friars than was usual among the conventuals, greater emphasis on communal life, and absolute individual poverty along with greater communal poverty.[48] The conventuals within the monastery were given two options: accept the new, much stricter way of life or depart for other, nonreformed houses. To assist Nider and his fellows in their efforts, Texier also issued a second, much longer and more detailed list of directives for the reform in Basel. Again he stressed such general points as increased devotion in the performance of the divine office and strict observance of the rule and constitutions of the order. He also called for an increased cloistering of the friars; they were not to enter those parts of the priory, such as the vineyard, where women worked, they were not to possess keys to various parts of the monastery other than their own cells except in great need, the monastery gates were to remain closed at all times, and a new wall was to be built along the side of the monastery facing the city moat. In addition, no friar was to leave the priory without the permission of the prior and without an appointed *socius,* not even to visit the other Dominican houses of the city, especially the Klingental convent. Moreover, to reduce the chance of "conspiracies" against the reform, the brothers were not even to assemble in groups within the priory without the permission of the prior.[49]

To resist the reform, the nuns of Klingental first turned to their powerful relatives in the city government for help, and then took the radical step of withdrawing their obedience to the Dominican order. Klingental was an old convent, originally under the control of the bishop of Constance (located in so-called Kleinbasel, across the Rhine from the main city, Klingental lay in the diocese of Constance, not Basel), but the sisters had voluntarily placed themselves under Dominican guidance in the early thirteenth century. Now they simply reversed their earlier decision. Complaining to the bishop that they were receiving poor direction from the friars across the river, they asked to be placed back under his supervision.[50] The brothers in the Basel priory did not have this option, but put up a fierce resistance nonetheless. At one point Texier went so far as to offer the conventuals a compromise: they could remain in the Basel priory with the observants without being strictly observant themselves, except for the increased level of cloistering, which was to go into effect for the entire convent. By the summer of 1429, however, it was clear that the reformers, with the support of the master general, the town government, the bishop, and the pope himself, had the upper hand, and most of the conventual brothers chose to depart for nonreformed priories.[51] With the struggle for reform in Basel now over, Nider could begin to prepare himself for the next and most important phase of his career, and for the great church council that would convene in Basel in only two short years.

NIDER AT THE COUNCIL OF BASEL

The Council of Basel was a huge assembly that ultimately spread out across much of the city. Officially, of course, the council was centered in the city's cathedral, and the periodic general sessions, in which all members voted individually on prepared resolutions, were in fact held there. The real work of the council, however, took place in smaller committees. Soon after opening, Basel divided itself into four "deputations" to handle various areas of its business.[52] The deputation on faith dealt with theological matters, mainly the threat of the heretical Hussites in Bohemia. The deputation on peace was to settle disputes among Christians, including the hoped-for reunion of the Greek and Latin churches. The deputation on reform, to which Nider eventually belonged, was to handle reform of the church in head and members.[53] And the deputation on common matters was assigned all business dealing with the council itself. In addition, a sort of "steering committee" of twelve men, three from each deputation, oversaw the whole affair and assigned matters as they arose to the appropriate deputations.

These bodies met in various locations around the city, and the Dominican priory was one of the most important centers of activity. At the outset of the council, the deputation on faith was housed in the Franciscan priory, while the deputation on peace convened in the Augustinian priory. The deputation on common matters met originally in St. Peter's Church, near the Dominican priory, and sometimes in the Dominican priory itself, until 1433, when it transferred itself to the so-called House of the Mosquitoes, just off the cathedral square. The Dominicans also hosted the deputation on reform until 1435, when it transferred itself to the chapter house of the cathedral. Every Thursday the overseeing committee of twelve would meet with the council president in the

Dominican refectory to discuss the week's business, and the general congregation of the entire council met there every Friday until June 1433, when the council's membership grew too large and the congregation had to transfer itself to the
cathedral.[54] In addition, the Dominican priory was the scene of the negotiations
with the Hussite delegation that came to Basel in 1433, and housed the emperor
Sigismund when he came to the city in 1433 and 1434.[55]

As prior of the Dominicans, Nider would automatically have been an important figure at Basel, but he was among the leading members of the council during its early days in any event. Even before other prelates and church dignitaries
began to arrive in Basel, Nider was making arrangements with local officials
to prepare for the opening of the council.[56] Early in 1431, Cardinal Giuliano
Cesarini had been appointed president of the forthcoming ecclesiastical synod,
but he was already occupied with arranging a crusade against the Hussites in
Bohemia and could not immediately come to Basel.[57] Instead he appointed the
Spanish prelate Juan of Palomar and the Dominican Johannes of Ragusa to
act as his representatives at the council. Even these men, however, did not come
to Basel immediately. In mid-March, Ragusa, then in Nuremberg, wrote to
Nider in Basel asking whether the city was "suitable" and "apt" for hosting the
coming activities. Nider responded that Basel was well suited for the council,
and that delegates were in fact already arriving.[58] In May he apparently accompanied Ragusa on a mission to meet with Emperor Sigismund in Nuremberg,
where the opening of the council was discussed.[59] Finally, on July 23, while
Cesarini was still occupied with the crusade against the Hussites, Ragusa and
Palomar officially convened the Council of Basel, and four days later Nider
preached the opening sermon.

In these initial days of the council, before the division into deputations, Nider
was among the small group of clergy who directed the council's affairs.[60] The
first critical issue Basel had to address was the matter of security for the many
clerics and others who would be traveling to and from the city, which could
be provided only by the surrounding secular lords. Although the emperor
Sigismund had personally guaranteed the safety of the council, a conflict
between Duke Friedrich IV of Austria and Duke Philip the Good of Burgundy
was disrupting the area around Basel, and some delegates initially refused to
attend out of fear for their lives.[61] Cesarini, who finally had arrived in Basel in
early September, wrote letters pleading for peace, and in late September he dispatched Johannes Nider, among others, to negotiate with the warring dukes for
a truce. These efforts were successful, and a treaty was signed on October 17.[62]
Basel had its security. Meanwhile, on October 3, Nider had been named by his
master general, Barthélemy Texier, as one of seven official Dominican representatives to the council.[63] On October 6, in order to begin the council's work

toward the reform of the church, Cesarini appointed Nider, along with the Benedictine abbot Alexander of Vézelay and another Dominican, as official conciliar
visitors to all the monastic houses in and around Basel.[64]

In these early days, however, Nider actually performed his most important
service for the council far from the city of Basel. In August 1431, Cardinal
Cesarini had seen the crusading army he had spent so many months raising
crushed in battle by Hussite forces. Shortly thereafter he arrived in Basel, convinced that the church must now prepare to do the unthinkable—negotiate with
heretics. Bringing the Hussites to Basel for these talks, however, would be a
difficult and delicate task. Church councils, after all, had a poor reputation
among the Hussites as faithful negotiators. Memories of the burning of Jan Hus
and Jerome of Prague when they had come before the Council of Constance
were still fresh in Bohemia. The Hussites would have to be convinced of Basel's
good faith. Guarantees of security and safe conduct would also have to be
arranged and accepted by both the Hussites and secular authorities in the German empire, between whom nearly constant war had raged for over a decade,
so that the heretics could travel in peace from Bohemia to Basel. To accomplish
this daunting task, on November 28, 1431, the Council of Basel selected two
men: Johannes of Gelnhausen, abbot of the Cistercian monastery of Maulbronn,
and Johannes Nider. Leaving Basel, these two men traveled to several cities and
courts along the Bohemian frontier before finally arriving in Nuremberg on
December 20, 1431. At each court they visited, the emissaries gave letters from
the council explaining Basel's intent to negotiate and asking for support. Above
all, the council asked that a truce be observed and that no military expeditions
be undertaken against the Hussites that would threaten the chance for negotiations. Finally, from Nuremberg the two ambassadors sent the council's letters
of invitation to the Hussites in Bohemia, and then settled down to wait for a
reply.[65]

At this crucial juncture, a disaster befell Basel. Pope Eugenius IV, although
required to summon the Council of Basel by edict of the earlier Council of Constance, was decidedly anticonciliar in his outlook. In early November, in Rome,
he used reports of Basel's low initial membership and lack of security (which, of
course, Nider had already resolved) to dissolve the council.[66] News of this action
reached Basel only after Nider and the rest of the delegation to the Hussites had
left, and needless to say, it threw their entire mission into uncertainty. Feverish
letters were dispatched back and forth between Prague and Nuremberg and
between Nuremberg and Basel as all parties sought some clarification of the situation. Finally, on February 16, 1432, Johannes of Ragusa wrote to Nider with
a definitive answer: the council had voted to ignore the papal dissolution; negotiations were to continue.[67] Shortly thereafter, on February 27, the Bohemian
council in Prague decided to accept Basel's offer to negotiate, although it proposed

an initial meeting in the Bohemian border town of Cheb (Eger in German) to iron out certain difficult points of security and protocol, and this letter reached Nuremberg on March 12. The face-to-face negotiations at Cheb got under way around April 27 and ended successfully on May 18, and by June 11 Nider was back in Basel reporting on his long mission before the council.[68]

The Bohemian delegation to the council did not come to Basel until January 3, 1433. Then, for the next three months, the entire council focused on the negotiations with the heretics, which took place in the Dominican priory.[69] At this point, however, although Nider must have continued to deal with the Hussites to some degree, since they were staying in his priory, he was no longer centrally involved in negotiations with them. To face the heretics in open debate, the council had instead chosen his fellow Dominicans Johannes of Ragusa and Heinrich Kalteisen, as well as the prelates Juan of Palomar and Aegidius Carlerius.[70] At first glance, Nider's absence from further dealings with the Hussites may seem strange, but a simple answer can be found in the organizational structure of the Council of Basel. On February 22, 1432, while Nider had been away in Nuremberg, the system of deputations had been introduced in Basel. As a theological matter, the dispute with the Hussites fell under the purview of the deputation of faith. While Nider was a theologian, his strong interest in reform would naturally have led him, upon his return to Basel in the summer of 1432, to join the deputation for reform. By the time the Hussites arrived in Basel, we find him active as a member of this deputation, and in November 1433 he was appointed for the second time as a conciliar visitor to oversee the reform of the clergy around Basel.[71]

The following year, 1434, saw a general cooling of relations between the Council of Basel and the Dominican order. The causes were twofold. First, and perhaps more directly, in the summer of 1434 the old conflict between the secular clergy and the mendicant orders of the church broke out anew in Basel.[72] In May a conciliar bull written earlier that year made its way into the hands of Johannes of Ragusa. Some secular clerics in Savoy had complained to the council that certain mendicant friars were preaching errors and drawing the people away from the regular parish clergy through their deceits, and this bull, issued on February 12, commanded the bishops of Asti and Turin to take action against these friars.[73] Although the bull bore the conciliar seal as if it were an official proclamation of the council, clearly it had never been openly debated, and thus could not have been officially ratified, since Ragusa learned of it only many months later. Needless to say, he and all the other mendicant leaders at the council were incensed, both by the attempted subterfuge and by the deep-seated opposition to mendicant activities from which it sprang. They demanded that the bull be debated in all four deputations, which it duly was through the course of that summer, and Basel was rent by the divisive issues that underlay this

immediate matter. Briefly put, the secular clergy objected to the special privileges and the pastoral duties of the mendicants, which they felt impinged on their own prerogatives. The friars, in response, maintained that their privileges had been lawfully granted and their way of religious life had been formally approved by the papacy. Ultimately the bull, so questionable in its origins, was rescinded in August, but the bitter feelings that it had raised would not subside so quickly.[74]

The papacy itself was the second and perhaps more pervasive issue that distanced the mendicants from the Council of Basel. In 1431 and 1432, Basel had weathered Eugenius IV's attempted dissolution well. Prelates and secular authorities around Europe recognized that the pope's actions were self-serving and not in the best interests of the church, and they widely supported the council. By July 1432, only six of twenty-one cardinals remained in Rome with the pope; the rest had turned to Basel.[75] Finally, in 1433, Eugenius submitted to the council: he withdrew his dissolution and declared that Basel had been a fully legitimate synod since its inception. The capitulation seemed complete. Having formally recognized the council, however, the pope then dispatched two emissaries to act as his representatives there, appointing them co-presidents along with Cesarini, and immediately problems arose. In early 1434, debate raged at Basel regarding these new presidents. The council, having fought so hard to win its independence, now feared that the pope was scheming to subvert it from within. Eugenius, however, having recognized the council in the most generous terms, had removed almost all possible objections the council fathers could raise to his authority. It was in this presidency debate that the full flower of Basel conciliarism became evident; that is, the argument that the council's authority should be supreme and fully independent of even a legitimate pope untainted by any charge of heresy, schism, or malfeasance in office.[76] Some council members, however, felt that this position was too extreme. They may have remained suspicious of Eugenius, but they no longer saw any grounds for disobeying the pope or ignoring his established right to appoint the council's leadership.[77]

As the majority at Basel made increasingly clear its belief in its own superiority over the pope under all circumstances, many Dominicans in particular grew concerned. The mendicant orders had always existed under special papal protection, and any threat to papal power was also a threat to their privileges. This circumstance, combined with the clear hostility of many of the secular clergy at Basel toward members of the mendicant orders, drove most of the Dominicans at the council firmly into the papal camp. Friars such as Juan of Torquemada, Heinrich Kalteisen, and Johannes of Montenegro would become staunch papalists and would be among the pope's strongest defenders in his future struggles against the council.[78] Nider himself never went so far over to the papal side, but he cannot have been unaffected by the general chill in relations between Basel and his order.[79] Some observers have seen the decision of the Dominican leadership to hold their general chapter for 1434 in Colmar rather than in Basel as an indication that the entire order was distancing itself from the council.[80]

On May 16, 1434, this general chapter appointed Nider to the post of Dominican lecturer on the *Sentences* at the University of Vienna.[81] Whether this was a deliberate step by the order to remove one of its principal members from the council or whether the decision was made independently of such concerns is unknown. Upon leaving the university in 1426, Nider had, after all, expressed his desire to return someday if the opportunity arose. Now, in the summer of 1434, he left Basel for Vienna, but only temporarily to reform the Dominican priory there, and not yet (it would seem) to take up his university post.[82] He was still active at the council when, in the fall, he was dispatched as part of a delegation to attend a conference between the Bohemians and the emperor Sigismund in Regensburg. In November he was back in Basel reporting to the council.[83] Sometime shortly after that, however, Nider did depart Basel permanently for Vienna. University records indicate that on April 22, 1435, he was assigned to take over the Assumption Day sermon from a certain Master Rudolf of the faculty of medicine, and a year later, on April 14, 1436, he was elected dean of the university's theological faculty.[84] He appears to have returned to Basel only once after this point, stopping there briefly around Pentecost in 1438 and preaching in the city and surrounding areas.[85]

Nider spent the final years of his life in Vienna. He was dean of the theological faculty for both the spring and winter terms of 1436.[86] Also in 1436 he reformed the Dominican priory of Tulln, near Vienna. In 1438 he journeyed to the Rhineland, stopping briefly in Basel before reforming the Dominican convent of St. Catherine in Colmar in early summer. It was while returning from Colmar to Vienna that he died in Nuremberg on August 13, 1438. His supposed last words, as recorded over thirty years later by the Dominican historian Johannes Meyer, were in response to the brother who came to administer the last rites. Presented with the Eucharist and asked, "Do you believe this is Christ, who saves the world?" Nider answered simply, "I believe it," and then spoke no more.[87] He was buried in the Nuremberg priory in a place of honor next to the former master general of the order, Raymond of Capua.

Nider spent only about six years in Basel, yet this was the longest period during his peripatetic adult life in which he remained settled in one place. Even then, his diplomatic missions and other duties for the council often took him away from the city for long periods of time. Nevertheless, these years and the few he spent in Vienna immediately afterward were the most important and productive of his life. Almost all of his major treatises can be dated to this busy period. We may wonder where he found the time to be so productive but we should not be surprised that he found so much to write about.[88] At the Council of Basel, Nider had stood for a time at what for churchmen of his day was the center of the world. He had met and dealt with many of the great religious figures of his time. He had heard and participated in the great debates: the reform of the church in head and members, questions about lay poverty and the status of beghards and beguines, and the struggle against heretics. And he had heard stories, filtering down from the Alpine valleys in the lands to the south of Basel, of what to the medieval mind was surely the most chilling heresy of all, the total apostasy of diabolical witches, who, in exchange for maleficent power, completely forsook Christ and worshiped Satan.

Scholars have long recognized that the Council of Basel must have served as an important center for the early formulation and diffusion of the stereotype of witchcraft.[89] Certainly the council brought together a large number of clerics, especially theologians, from around Europe very near to those regions where ideas of witchcraft were beginning to emerge, and at the exact time when those ideas first appeared. But the matter of witchcraft figures not at all among the official debates of the council. Whatever interest or concern over witchcraft there was at the great synod must have been unofficial, in the form of informal discussions and stories exchanged between council members, many of which doubtless took place in the corridors and courtyards of the Dominican priory.

Nider, of course, provides the most extended and important example of the fruits such interchanges might bear. Although he wrote his principal work on witchcraft, the *Formicarius,* in 1437 and 1438, while he was in Vienna, he clearly became interested in witches and began collecting accounts of them in Basel. His primary examples of witchcraft come from the diocese of Lausanne, and especially from the Simme valley, in the territory of Bern. He learned of the witches there from a secular judge named Peter of Bern, with whom he claimed to have discussed such matters "extensively and profoundly,"[90] and the only obvious occasion for Nider to have done so was while he was in Basel. At another point in the *Formicarius,* Nider told of learning of the "witch" Joan of Arc from an official of the University of Paris who was a delegate to the council.[91]

In the early years of the fifteenth century, the idea of diabolic witchcraft first began to take shape in Europe. In Johannes Nider, collecting stories at the Council of Basel and formulating disparate notions into a more ordered understanding, we are as close as we are likely to come to an eyewitness to and participant in the birth of this new concept. His accounts of witchcraft provide some particularly important insights into how this idea took shape in learned clerical minds, even as his life provides some of the larger context needed to explain how and why he understood this idea as he did.

2

WITCHCRAFT IN THE WRITINGS OF JOHANNES NIDER

T he subject of witchcraft is vast and complex. One cannot get past even the term "witch" before the complications begin, for this one word can have a variety of meanings.[1] In the early fifteenth century, the Latin word that Johannes Nider and other clerical authorities most commonly used to mean "witch" was *maleficus* (or *malefica* in the feminine). This word literally meant a person who performed harmful sorcery, *maleficium*, against others. Typical acts of *maleficium* included committing crimes such as theft or murder by magical means, causing pestilence or disease, withering crops or afflicting livestock, and conjuring lightning and hail. Of course, the use of magic in many forms was widespread in the premodern world, and its real efficacy was broadly accepted. Persons believed to perform harmful sorcery have faced condemnation and persecution from both secular and religious authorities in almost every human society that has ever existed. In the West before the rise of Christianity, however, such authorities most often directed their censure against the negative effects of sorcery rather than against the act of sorcery itself. In other words, certain uses of magic were prohibited as being harmful, but neither the magical act (a ritual, a spoken invocation, a written charm, whatever) nor the magician who performed it was condemned per se.[2] In contrast, in Europe during the late Middle Ages and on into the period of the great witch-hunts, it was very much the person of the witch that came to embody the darkest crimes and the most terrible corruption imaginable, and it was she herself, as a moral and social evil, rather than her supposedly harmful actions, that both ecclesiastical and secular authorities sought to eradicate.

Beginning around 1400 and for centuries thereafter, a very specific image of the witch held force in Europe, and the practice of witchcraft entailed far more than just the use of harmful sorcery to attain one's goals and to afflict one's neighbors. Certainly a witch was still a person, usually a woman, who performed harmful sorcery against others, but the fully developed stereotype of witchcraft involved crimes far worse than simple *maleficium*. Witches were commonly assumed to work their magic through demonic agency, and hence came to be accused of idolatry, since clerical authorities were convinced that such magic always involved the supplication and worship of demons. Typically witches also stood accused of apostasy—that is, of completely rejecting their faith, forswearing Christ and his church, and surrendering their very souls to Satan or his minions. As demon worshipers and servants of the devil, witches were thought to be members of a vast conspiratorial cult headed by the Prince of Darkness and standing in opposition to God's church on earth.[3] These cults gathered in secret at regular nocturnal conventicles that would eventually come to be known as sabbaths. Here groups of witches would assemble in the presence of their demonic master, who usually attended in the form of a black cat, goat, or other animal. Before him they would desecrate the cross and stolen Eucharists, as well as forswear Christ, the Virgin Mary, and all the saints. They were expected to worship the demon and to offer him homage, usually symbolized by the *osculum infame,* the obscene kiss on the devil's posterior. They would also kill and devour babies that they had brought with them, both their own and those of other unfortunate people, and they would engage in abominable sexual orgies with one another, with attendant demons, and with Satan himself.[4]

Although clearly rooted in long-standing Christian conceptions of sorcery and diabolism, this fully developed notion of diabolical, conspiratorial witchcraft emerged only in the fifteenth century. Before 1400, while concern over harmful and potentially demonic sorcery was common, the witch in this narrow and precise sense simply did not exist. By 1487, however, the infamous witch-hunting manual *Malleus maleficarum* provided a description of witchcraft focusing on idolatry and apostasy, as well as simple *maleficium*. While this characterization was never universally accepted and often contested, Kramer's manual helped to establish a basic image of witchcraft that endured for the next several centuries. Yet the *Malleus* itself contained little that was new (nor, it must be said, did it contain every aspect of the full witch stereotype). The earliest true witch trials in Europe were held in the first decades of the fifteenth century, mainly in the lands of western Switzerland, Savoy, Dauphiné, and northern Italy, and the first learned treatises and written accounts of witchcraft, containing essentially the stereotype later popularized by the *Malleus maleficarum,* began to appear in the 1430s.[5] Of these early tracts and treatises, the writings of Johannes Nider were the most extensive and influential.

Through Nider we have access to the idea of witchcraft at almost the very moment it first appeared, and his writings provide important insights into the origins of this new phenomenon. Specifically, he offers the perspective of a member of the university-educated, reform-minded clerical elite. As such, he will not reveal much about the origins of the "reality" of witchcraft; that is, the actual practices that underlay the accusations and condemnations taking shape in the courts and the social, cultural, legal, and economic factors that drove the actual trials. Only comprehensive local histories and in-depth archival research can supply these details.[6] Nevertheless, for understanding how learned authorities, both ecclesiastical and secular, constructed a unified and coherent concept out of the various elements of the new crime that was emerging in these trials, Nider is a most useful source. Beyond simply clarifying how such authorities might have conceived of witchcraft, moreover, he can offer some understanding of why these men would so readily accept, develop, and promulgate such terrible ideas.

Among the key questions concerning the early development of the idea of witchcraft are why this concept finally emerged only in the early fifteenth century and why it was accepted so widely and so readily by elites who had the intellectual, legal, and social authority to ensure its survival for centuries even as they worked for its eradication. The roots of the various elements of witchcraft are not difficult to trace. They lie in earlier medieval conceptions of sorcery, demonology, heresy, and related issues. Secular authorities had always been concerned about the potentially harmful social effects and possible criminal uses of sorcery, while clerical authorities, in theory at least, had long been concerned about the moral dangers inherent in magical activity.[7] From the time of the early church fathers, religious thinkers were convinced that most magic, whatever its ultimate aims or purposes, relied on the agency of demons. Given that in the Christian worldview, such creatures were inherently evil and any traffic with them was prohibited, all potentially demonic magic automatically fell under grave suspicion.[8] Yet for centuries many theologians, canon lawyers, and other clerical authorities treated even supposedly demonic sorcery more with contempt than with fear. The offense was typically regarded as a matter for penance and gentle correction rather than for harsh condemnation, active persecution, and complete eradication. Only in the later Middle Ages did such authorities really begin to press the connection between the performance of harmful sorcery, *maleficium*, and entanglement with demonic forces, a stance that led ultimately to the notions of idolatry and apostasy that underlay the crime of witchcraft. Yet even then many individuals, churchmen among them, refused to accept the existence of a vast conspiratorial sect of diabolic sorcerers. Papal injunctions urging inquisitors to take action against witches despite opposition from various quarters are numerous, and famously, the *Malleus maleficarum* itself began with the question "whether the belief that there are such beings as witches is so essential a part of the Catholic faith that obstinately to maintain the opposite manifestly savors of heresy?"[9]

That Nider and other such educated and intelligent men, engaged by the major religious issues of their day, should have been so concerned about the existence of witches—indeed, that they should have accepted this idea at all—must not be taken as a foregone conclusion. Rather we must ask why they were drawn to this idea and why it troubled them so deeply. We must ask, in short, how witchcraft fitted into the larger world of their thought and concerns. As a first step, I will here outline exactly what the clerical concept of witchcraft entailed and situate Nider's writings within the tradition of steadily increasing clerical concern over demonic sorcery that characterized the later Middle Ages.[10] Within this tradition he was a key transitional figure, representing the culmination of growing anxiety over sorcery and diabolism, on the one hand, and on the other the beginning of a new phase of clerical thought that would ultimately help feed into the great witch-hunts of the sixteenth and seventeenth centuries. He provides a particularly clear view of how the figure of the witch emerged from earlier ideas about the practice and the practitioners of demonic sorcery, and also of how witchcraft quickly transcended those earlier conceptions of mere sorcery as the image of the witches' sabbath began to crystallize and the specific elements of the witch stereotype began to take shape in the minds of learned authorities.

THE ORIGINS OF WITCHCRAFT IN CLERICAL THOUGHT

When Johannes Nider turned his attention to the subject of witchcraft, he was able to draw on a long tradition of religious thought, if not on witchcraft itself, since that was only a recent construction, then on the various elements that had merged into this new crime. For witchcraft was a multifaceted concept, mixing ideas drawn from numerous traditions. While individual cases could, of course, produce any number of interesting variations, all of the major elements of the witch stereotype beginning to take shape in Nider's time may be grouped into four categories: (1) harmful sorcery, or *maleficium* proper—killing or causing disease, raising storms or destroying crops, or any number of other maleficent acts done through magic; (2) diabolism, or the belief that such sorcery involved the supplication of demons, pacts made with them, and ultimately the worship of demons or the devil—the crimes of idolatry and apostasy; (3) heretical stereotypes—notions of conspiratorial cults, secret nocturnal gatherings, and cultic activity such as orgies, desecration of sacred objects, infanticide, and cannibalism; and finally (4) folkloric elements such as the night flight of witches to a sabbath, witches' transformation into animals, and so forth.

Arguments have been put forward favoring each of these categories as the key to understanding the true origin of the idea of witchcraft, but no consensus has yet been reached.[11] Indeed, it seems clear that no single factor, idea, or event brought about the appearance of the witch in late medieval Europe or served as the sole cause of the witch-hunts that were to come. My intent here, certainly, is not to provide a single complete explanation for why witchcraft appeared. Rather I intend only to trace briefly the route by which certain clerical authorities came to be concerned about the practice of demonic sorcery and convinced of the existence of sects of diabolic sorcerers that gathered secretly, worshiped the devil, and performed maleficent magic directed against the Christian faithful. At the end of this process stands Johannes Nider, and his descriptions of witches and of witchcraft provide particularly clear insight into how these notions may have developed, at least in the minds of the clerical elites of Europe.

The limit here to clerical concerns and conceptions of witchcraft is, of course, dictated by my ultimate focus on Nider. Some would argue (and have done so) that to concentrate on such elite concerns is to ignore the significance of more commonly held beliefs and the effects of popular concerns.[12] I disagree. I hope that in what follows the importance of common magical practices and nonelite conceptions of sorcery in the development of witchcraft will be clearly evident. Nevertheless, I am also convinced that understanding elite perceptions of these matters is critical to any overall understanding of how and why the witch stereotype first appeared. For, as much as common beliefs and folklore contributed to the idea of the witch, ultimately it was a small elite of ecclesiastical and secular authorities who accepted this new concept, shaped it into a coherent system, and propagated it across Europe to such dire effect. In short, if the end result of the idea of witchcraft is burned flesh, I see elite authorities standing closest to the flames.[13]

How, then, did this destructive idea take shape in the minds of authorities, particularly clerical ones, in the Middle Ages? At the root of most later witch trials lay charges of *maleficium*—harmful sorcery. Yet *maleficium* alone was not the most important element of witchcraft for most witch-hunting authorities, certainly not for ecclesiastical ones. Indeed, throughout the early Middle Ages many church authorities saw *maleficium* as more of a secular than a religious crime, and when canon lawyers began to renew ecclesiastical sanctions against such sorcery in the twelfth and thirteenth centuries, they typically ignored earlier medieval legislation and based their pronouncements on late antique and patristic sources.[14] In these sources, *maleficium*, along with many other forms of magic, was condemned insofar as it was perceived to rely on the agency of demons and to entail pacts made with these creatures.[15] Yet even deeply rooted Christian concerns over diabolism and the demonic nature of much, if not all, sorcery did not lead immediately or directly to the terrible figure of the human witch. Instead, early Christian authorities tended to see the demon as the true

agent behind evil magic, and thus the true foe to be combated; the human sorcerer involved was regarded as far less significant and threatening.[16] Demons,
moreover, although powerful agents in Christian cosmology, were limited by the
greater power of God. Their main function was to trick and to tempt. Thus well
into the Middle Ages, disdain rather than deep concern typified clerical reaction
toward much supposed demonic activity. The famous tenth-century canon *Episcopi*, for example, while condemning various magical practices, described one
particular belief at great length:

> Also it must not be omitted that some wicked women, turned away
> after Satan and seduced by the illusions and phantasms of demons,
> believe and profess that, in the hours of the night, they ride upon certain
> beasts with Diana, the goddess of the pagans, and an innumerable mul-
> titude of women, and in the silence of the dead of night traverse great
> spaces of earth, and they obey her commands as of their mistress, and
> are summoned to her service on certain nights.[17]

Centuries later, such beliefs would be transformed into the concept of the
night flight of witches to a sabbath. Initially, however, these women were thought
simply to have been deceived by "the illusions and phantasms of demons."
They were deserving of pity and proper religious instruction rather than fierce
persecution.[18]

Although the diabolism perceived to underlie much magical activity would
seem clearly to have marked the practice of sorcery as heretical, the connection
between the persecution of heresy and the rise of witchcraft is also far from
straightforward. Just as there was relatively little concern over demonic activity,
there was little organized repression of heresy until the eleventh and twelfth centuries, when Europe suddenly appears to have become a "persecuting society."[19]
Charges of secret conventicles, nude and orgiastic rites, cannibalism, and devil
worship were all standard elements in medieval antiheretical polemic and
clearly helped to shape the later stereotype of witchcraft. The very first heretics
to be burned in the medieval West, for example, a group of clerics at Orléans in
1022, were accused of participating in a diabolic ritual that centuries later
would find a strong echo in the witches' sabbath:

> They [the heretics] gathered, indeed, on certain nights in a designated
> house, everyone carrying a light in his hands, and like merrymakers they
> chanted the names of demons until suddenly they saw descend among
> them a demon in the likeness of some sort of little beast. As soon as
> the apparition was visible to everyone, all the lights were forthwith

extinguished and each, with the least possible delay, seized the woman who first came to hand, to abuse her, without thought of sin.... When a child was born of this most filthy union, on the eighth day thereafter a great fire was lighted and the child was purified by fire in the manner of the old pagans, and so was cremated. Its ashes were collected and preserved ... being given to the sick as a viaticum at the moment of their departing this world.[20]

Despite the fact that many elements of the witches' sabbath clearly stemmed from earlier accounts such as this, the transference of such allegations from heretics to practitioners of *maleficium* was by no means immediate.

The history of the hereticization of sorcery, briefly, runs thus. In the 1230s Pope Gregory IX began to commission inquisitors to pursue heretics, primarily in southern France and the Rhineland, and not surprisingly some of the more zealous among them began to uncover sects practicing horrific diabolical rites similar to those described above.[21] Yet cults of witches—that is, of demon-worshiping heretics practicing *maleficium*—did not appear. In fact, in 1258 Pope Alexander IV issued the bull *Quod super nonnullis,* in which he specifically drew a distinction between heresy and "divination and sorcery," ordering all papal inquisitors to avoid investigating charges of the latter unless they also "clearly savored of manifest heresy."[22] Only in the fourteenth century did the ecclesiastical condemnation of sorcery as demonic and therefore heretical begin to advance more steadily, particularly during the papacy of John XXII (1316–34).[23] In 1320 he ordered the inquisitors of Toulouse and Carcassonne to proceed against all sorcerers (*maleficos*) who "make sacrifices to demons or adore them, or do homage to them by giving them as a sign a written pact or other token, or who make binding pacts with them."[24] Six years later he issued the bull *Super illius specula,* which formally proclaimed all those who trafficked with demons for magical purposes to be outside the church:

> Grievingly we observe that there are many who are Christians in name only, who ... enter an alliance with death and make a pact with hell, for they sacrifice to demons, adore them, make or have made images, or a ring, mirror, or phial, or some other thing in order to bind demons magically therein. They ask things of them and receive responses from them, and demand their aid in achieving their depraved desires. They exhibit shameful servitude for the most shameful things.... Upon all and singular who, against our most charitable warnings and commands, presume to engage in such things, we promulgate the sentence of excommunication.[25]

A century later Nider cited John XXII's edict in his handbook for confessors as the ipso facto grounds for the excommunication of all those who invoked demons or sought their aid.[26]

Yet John XXII's ruling did not lead to the rise of witchcraft, at least not directly and far from immediately. The sorcerers here, although excommunicated and condemned as heretics and demon worshipers, were not described as members of any large satanic cult. Nor did papal inquisitors begin to uncover such cults in the early fourteenth century. When the Dominican Bernard Gui, inquisitor in Toulouse from 1307 until 1324 and thus one of the recipients of Pope John's decrees, compiled his extensive inquisitorial handbook, the *Practica inquisitionis heretice pravitatis,* in his final years in that office, he included a section on sorcerers and diviners, but he made no mention of anything like witchcraft.[27] Likewise half a century later the Catalan Dominican Nicolau Eymeric, who wrote another highly influential inquisitorial manual in 1376, discussed the invocation of demons at length. Here he argued that such invocation necessarily entailed worshiping demons or honoring them in ways due only to God, and thus had to be considered idolatry. But he too made no mention of conspiratorial sects, sabbaths, or other standard elements of witchcraft.[28] In fact, throughout the fourteenth century, whenever ecclesiastical authorities expressed concern over the invocation of demons, they seem clearly to have associated such practices most often not with common *maleficium* but with a decidedly learned form of demonic magic known as necromancy.[29]

As ecclesiastical authorities conceived it, necromancy was very much an elite art involving complex rituals and invocations. Knowledge of these rites was contained and transmitted in books written in Latin, and the ceremonies themselves were often quasi-sacerdotal in nature, so that this was clearly a primarily clerical form of magic. Indeed, one modern scholar has aptly identified a "clerical underworld" of necromancy.[30] Throughout the later Middle Ages there existed a canon of texts dealing with learned demonic magic. Such famous tomes as *Picatrix, Key of Solomon,* and the *Sworn Book of Honorius* were well known both to the necromancers and to the authorities who prosecuted them. The inquisitor Nicolau Eymeric mentioned in his writings that he had seized and burned copies of both the *Key of Solomon* and the *Sworn Book of Honorius* from necromancers whom he had tried, and the Zurich canon lawyer Felix Hemmerlin, who wrote on magic and witchcraft in the mid-1400s, was also familiar with such texts.[31] Nider too had at least a secondary acquaintance with them. In Vienna he had befriended a Benedictine monk who before taking monastic vows had been a famous necromancer in possession of several "books of demons."[32]

Only at the very end of the fourteenth century and in the early years of the fifteenth did authorities really begin to broaden their concern over demonic magic from elite necromancy to include more common forms of harmful sorcery. For reasons that are not yet entirely clear, the number of trials for sorcery rose sharply during these years, especially in lands surrounding the western Alps, and increasingly the courts added charges of demonic activity and diabolism onto initial accusations of *maleficium*.[33] A heightened level of concern is also evident in other sources. Consider the difference between two papal bulls written a century apart. In 1326, John XXII had condemned as heretical the invocation of demons by means of crafted images, rings, mirrors, and phials. Here the pope was clearly thinking of complicated ritual magic of the type well known to learned authorities in the papal curia and other courts at this time.[34] Moreover, while the practices John condemned were certainly demonic and those who performed them supposedly "bound themselves to demons" and "made a pact with hell," there is no indication that they belonged to any large diabolic cult. In 1437, however, the very year Nider wrote his *Formicarius*, Pope Eugenius IV described invocation of demons in a very different form. In a letter to all papal inquisitors he wrote:

> News has reached us, not without great bitterness of spirit, that the prince of darkness has bewitched [*infascinavit*] by his cunning many bought by the blood of Christ, so that he might make them participants in his own damnation and fall. These ones, eagerly adhering to the persuasions and illusions of the devil and his servants with noxious blindness, sacrifice to demons, adore them, seek and accept responses from them, do homage to them, and as a sign of this give them a written contract or some other sign, binding themselves to demons, so that by a single word, touch, or sign, they may inflict or remove whatever evil sorcery [*maleficia*] they wish. They cure diseases, provoke bad weather, and make pacts concerning other evil things.[35]

Here the pope clearly implied the notion of an organized conspiratorial cult headed by Satan himself. The members of this group were accused of eagerly adhering to or following the false teachings of the devil (the Latin word is *sectantes*), and they worshiped, adored, and gave homage to demons in exchange for the ability to perform various acts of sorcery, not through complex ritual invocations but merely by simple signs and gestures.

In labeling common *maleficium* as demonic, authorities were trying to understand traditional magical practices in terms of the major system of magic that they knew, learned necromancy.[36] Demonic ritual magic and common sorcery were, however, worlds apart. A necromancer acted through complex rites and ritual invocations designed to compel an essentially unwilling and dangerous agent, a demon, to come and serve him.[37] Eugenius IV, however, feared men and women, clearly uneducated, who could perform terrible demonic sorcery "by a single word, touch, or sign." Likewise, at one point in his writings on witchcraft, Johannes Nider maintained that the agency behind giving someone the evil eye might be demonic.[38] Thus a witch was supposed to be able to command a demon's obedience with a mere glance of her eyes.

To learned minds intent on explaining typical *maleficium* as demonic, common sorcerers must have appeared as tremendously malevolent figures surrounded at all times by attendant demons eagerly awaiting their least sign to go and perform terrible magical acts. How could simple people gain such complete and easy mastery over demons when learned necromancers and even clerical exorcists had to engage in long and complex rites and still often failed to compel demons to obey their commands?[39] The answer, of course, was that these people had entered into pacts with the devil to gain their power. Worse, they had surrendered their very souls to Satan, had become members of a cult or sect under his direction, and were thus completely his servants. In short, they had become witches.

Johannes Nider wrote his extensive accounts of witches and their activities at almost the exact moment when the idea of witchcraft emerged as a clear and distinct concept on the intellectual landscape of Europe. Indeed, his theologically informed discussion of witchcraft did much to help shape this idea into a coherent form. Yet buried within his accounts we can see, more clearly than in any other learned source, indications of the actual magical practices and common beliefs about sorcery that underlay the idea of the witch. By paying attention to how he reworked and reconceived these practices, we can see the process by which clerical authorities unhesitatingly applied their own notions of necromantic magic to much simpler common sorcery, and how as a result this common sorcery became the terrible crime of diabolic witchcraft and the simple peasant sorcerer became the monstrously evil and all-threatening witch.

NIDER'S ACCOUNTS OF SORCERY AND WITCHCRAFT: TWO TRADITIONS MERGE

Nider's stories of witches and his descriptions of witchcraft, standing at the end of over a century of steadily increasing clerical concern over sorcery, invocation of demons, and diabolism, still reveal a sharp dichotomy between elite and common magical practices. But his writings also show that he, like other learned authorities, did not recognize that any such distinction existed. He easily conflated aspects of elite and common practices into the new conception of diabolic witchcraft. As an educated cleric and theologian, Nider was of course familiar with the tradition of learned necromancy as it existed in the later Middle Ages. Indeed, this highly complex, ritualistic, and often quasi-liturgical method of invoking demons was primarily the province of the clerical elites, and in his *Formicarius* he presented two tales of specifically clerical magic. The first brief account concerned the local priest of a certain rural village in the diocese of Constance near Isny, a man of "light morals" and "religious in name only." This man, according to Nider, was suspected of being a wizard and of practicing harmful sorcery. Using his power, he had tried to force a young virgin of the village to fall in love with him, inspiring lustful fantasies in her. She, however, appealed to the Virgin Mary for aid. The Virgin inspired her to marry, as marriage would apparently put her out of the reach of the lecherous cleric, but to remain chaste in her marriage.[40] Nider's emphasis here fell more on the value of chastity than on the powers of the corrupt cleric, and in fact the cleric himself seems to have been more like a common sorcerer, albeit a priest, than a learned necromancer.

In the fifth book of the *Formicarius,* however, Nider offered a more detailed account of specifically necromantic sorcery involving an individual with whom he was personally acquainted, a monk named Benedict, living in Vienna. When Nider knew him, Benedict was leading a worthy and entirely respectable religious life, but earlier, before he took up his monastic vows and still lived in the secular world, "he was a very famous necromancer, for he had books of demons concerning necromancy, and following these he lived rather miserably and dissolutely for a long time." In Vienna he often conferred with Nider on matters of sorcery and witchcraft, drawing on his past expertise as a necromancer.[41] From him, if from no other source, Nider would have learned exactly how such demonic magic supposedly operated. Central to necromancy, and indeed to most forms of magic in clerical minds, was the ubiquitous (or near-ubiquitous) agency of demons and the necessity of a pact between summoned spirit and summoning magician. Such notions, however, while by no means entirely foreign to the common understanding of magic in the Middle Ages, were not the primary concern to most people. Records of sorcery and witch trials from the late Middle Ages clearly reveal that most of the initial charges brought by people against their neighbors in the courts centered on simple *maleficium,* and only in the course of proceedings were authorities able to introduce charges of diabolical agency lying behind acts of sorcery.[42] Thus it seems clear that when common people thought of magical power, they generally thought first of concrete results, of the harm or good such power could cause in their lives and the lives of their neighbors. Only as a secondary matter, if at all, did they then ponder the theological explanations and diabolical implications of the operation of magic. Moreover, while learned necromancy explicitly functioned through complex ritual invocations of demons, common sorcery was usually performed through relatively brief verbal charms and symbolic gestures or actions that gave no overt indication of demonic involvement.

Nider, however, and other authorities in the early fifteenth century drew no distinction between demonic magic as they understood it and more popular notions of sorcery as practiced by many sorts of people across Europe. Nider articulated this perceived unity of all magical practice explicitly in the *Formicarius*. At one point in this dialogue between a student and a theologian, the younger man asked whether necromancy differed at all from more common forms of *maleficium*, or witchcraft. "Because you made mention of necromancers," the pupil stated, "I ask whether there is any difference between them and witches? And if so, what is it that they do?" The theologian responded that in common usage the two groups were essentially similar:

> They are properly called necromancers who claim that, by means of superstitious rites, they are able to raise the dead from the earth in order to speak on occult matters. . . . Nevertheless, in common usage they are called necromancers, who, through a pact with demons [and] through faith in ceremonies, predict future events, or manifest certain hidden things by the revelation of demons, or who harm those around them by evil sorcery [*maleficiis*], and who are often harmed themselves by demons.[43]

Just like learned necromancers, Nider was convinced, witches performed their evil magic through the agency of demons with whom they had entered into pacts. He had already made this point clear in the *Formicarius* by the time he declared explicitly that witches and necromancers were basically identical. In an earlier chapter he had detailed how witches could do nothing by their own power, "but they are said to harm through words, rites, or deeds as if through pacts initiated with demons."[44] Likewise in another work dealing in part with sorcery and witchcraft, his *Preceptorium divine legis,* written shortly after the *Formicarius,* he explained that witches could work magic only through the cooperation of demons by means of a pact made with them "at the beginning of the world." Here he went on to show how such pact magic was supposed to function. When a witch wished to cause rain, for example, she might simply dip a broom handle in water. This action, however, had no efficacy in itself, and was only a sign given to a demon, who, bound by a preexisting pact and apparently hovering in wait nearby, would then hasten to cause the actual storm.[45]

In linking the performance of harmful sorcery, *maleficium,* to pacts with demonic powers, Nider was in one sense simply following a line of theological argument that stretched back to such authorities as Thomas Aquinas and ultimately to Saint Augustine.[46] But in the later Middle Ages, as a result of developing notions of necromancy, increased clerical concern over demonic power, and arguments that invocation of demons automatically entailed heresy and idolatry, clerical authorities were coming to see this linkage as carrying even more sinister implications. Convinced that simple *maleficium* was essentially identical to necromancy, authorities freely overlaid their own concerns about diabolism onto common sorcery, ultimately transforming such practices into satanic witchcraft. As a witness to this process, Nider is a particularly useful source, for in his accounts he actually presented two rather different pictures of "witchcraft," although he himself did not distinguish between them, just as he drew no distinction between learned necromancy and more common sorcery in general. These differing pictures represent earlier and later stages in the development of the idea of witchcraft, the first closer to actual traditional magical practices, the second a far more fantastic and horrific creation already infused with the clerical fear of demons.

Aside from the former necromancer Benedict, Nider had two main sources for his tales concerning witches, as he revealed in the *Formicarius.* These were contemporary accounts he had heard from a Dominican inquisitor of Autun who had often dealt with matters of witchcraft, and the stories of the secular judge Peter of Bern, who as bailiff of the Simme valley in the Bernese Oberland (a mountainous region to the south of the city of Bern) had conducted numerous witch trials several decades earlier, in the very early 1400s.[47] Thus Nider's accounts of witchcraft in the *Formicarius* would seem to represent two stages in the development of that idea, separated by as much as thirty years. Andreas Blauert, however, has suggested that Nider's accounts of witchcraft in the Simme valley were not accurate descriptions of events as they had occurred several decades earlier, but actually represented the witch stereotype as it stood in the late 1430s. Either Peter of Bern had misremembered events that happened many years previously or Nider reinterpreted Peter's accounts in the light of current ideas as he wrote.[48] This argument is compelling, and certainly I do not think Nider perceived any difference between "witchcraft" in the very early 1400s and that existing around 1437. As we shall see, he very freely conflated descriptions from these two periods. Nevertheless, in spite of Nider's own conflation, a close reading of the *Formicarius* still allows us to separate two distinct versions of witchcraft and provides insight into how and why clerical authorities shaped that idea as they did.

Certainly the most graphic tales of witchcraft in the *Formicarius* involve detailed descriptions of witches' sabbaths. Two of these tales were drawn from the testimony of Peter of Bern, the first concerning specifically how and why witches would devour babies. Nider wrote:

> It was, moreover, generally known, the aforesaid judge Peter told me, that in the territory of Bern thirteen infants had been devoured within a short period of time by witches, wherefore public justice was indeed inflamed harshly against such murderers. When, moreover, Peter had questioned a certain captured witch as to the means by which the infants were devoured, she responded, "The method is thus: With infants not yet baptized, or even baptized ones, especially if they are not protected by the sign of the cross and by prayers, these ones, through our ceremonies, we kill in their cradles or lying at their parents' sides, who afterwards are thought to have been crushed or to have died in some other way. We secretly remove them from the graves. We boil them in a cauldron until, with the bones having been torn out, almost all the flesh is made into a liquid draft. From the more solid matter we make an unguent suitable for our desires, and arts, and transmutations. With the more liquid fluid, we fill up a flask or a leather bottle, [and] he who drinks from this, with a few ceremonies added, immediately is made a member and a master of our sect."[49]

Here we see a clear picture of witches organized into a malevolent and threatening cult. Focusing only on the murder and cannibalism of children, this account does not describe any of the other stereotypes of the sabbath, but Nider immediately presented a second account, also drawn from Peter of Bern, which does offer a fuller picture:

> Moreover, this same method was more clearly described by another young witch who had been captured and burned, although in the end (so I believe) he was truly penitent.... For the aforesaid young man, brought to trial in Bern with his wife and placed in a separate tower from her, said, "If I can obtain forgiveness for my sins, I will freely disclose all that I know about witchcraft.... The order," he said, "in which I was seduced is this. First, on the Lord's Day, before the holy water is consecrated, the future disciple, along with the masters, must enter directly into the church, and there before them deny Christ, his faith, baptism, and the universal church. Then he must do homage to the *magisterulus*, that is, to the little master. For thus and not otherwise they call the demon. Finally he drinks from the bottle mentioned above

[that is, in the quote above], by which act instantly he feels himself to have received within himself images of our arts, and to retain the principal rites of this sect. In this way I was seduced."[50]

In this fuller description we see the developed idea of witches operating as an organized sect directed by a demon and focusing on apostasy and devil worship in exchange for magical powers.

Both of these accounts of sabbaths were related to him, Nider claimed, by Peter of Bern. Do they really represent testimony given to that judge in the first decades of the 1400s, however? Evidence suggests not. For one thing, trial records from the period (unfortunately, the records of Peter's trials in the Simme valley have been lost) make no mention of the idea of the sabbath.[51] This concept seems to have fully developed only in the 1430s. Moreover, Nider himself presented a third example of a contemporary sabbath that closely resembles his other two accounts. Consider:

> Finally, this year I learned from the aforesaid inquisitor [of Autun] that in the duchy [sic] of Lausanne certain witches cooked their own newly born babies, and ate them. Moreover, the means of learning such art was, so he said, that the witches came together in a certain convocation, and through their efforts, they saw a demon visibly in an assumed human form, to whom the disciple had to pledge that he would deny Christianity, would never adore the Eucharist, and would secretly trample on the cross whenever he could.[52]

Here we see again the portrait of a diabolically organized sect of witches based on apostasy and with the added horror of infant cannibalism, and this image of the sabbath is explicitly dated to 1437 or early 1438, when the *Formicarius* was written. Nider presented these various descriptions of the sabbath together and drew no distinction between them. The evidence, therefore, strongly suggests that what Nider claimed were Peter of Bern's descriptions of sabbaths that occurred in the early 1400s were in fact later revisions of the actual trial testimonies, updated, so to speak, either by Peter or by Nider himself in the light of the new idea of a cult of witches that achieved full form only in the 1430s.

What, then, was going on in the Simme valley in the early 1400s that served as the basis for these later, more terrible charges? The answer must be, as in other trials of the period, common *maleficium* practiced by individuals, not organized cults of witches; and even if such sorcery was demonic, it certainly did not involve apostasy or Satanism.[53] This was the common tradition of sorcery that had not yet been transformed by learned authorities into the terror of witchcraft, and despite Nider's heavy-handed conflation of all forms of sorcery with witch-craft, such simpler practices can yet be seen recounted in the *Formicarius*. Aside from dazzling and horrific descriptions of sabbaths, Peter of Bern related to Nider more tempered tales of witchcraft (although in these cases the term *maleficium* might continue to be better rendered as "harmful sorcery"), mostly centering on the figure of a single "great witch" (*grandis maleficus*) named Staedelin. Nider's, or rather Peter's, Staedelin stories have the sort of details that convince, not the least of which being that they center on an individual who is actually named.

Nider introduced Staedelin in the context of examples focusing on witches' practice of murdering children. In comparison with the accounts of witches' dragging murdered children's corpses from their graves, boiling them down in cauldrons, and eagerly slurping up the resulting brew, Staedelin's account was rather tame. Certainly he still killed children, but in a more mundane fashion. Arrested and brought before Peter's court, he confessed that he had murdered seven babies in the womb of a certain woman, magically inducing her to abort every child she conceived over several years. He also afflicted the fertility of all the animals belonging to this woman and her husband. His method was sim-ple, he confessed. He had buried a lizard under the threshold stone of their house. When authorities removed the lizard, or rather the dust into which it had crumbled in the course of years, the fertility of both humans and beasts was immediately restored.[54] This activity amounted to nothing more than typical *maleficium,* which often aimed to destroy the fertility of humans, livestock, and crops. There was no hint of infant cannibalism, even though that was expressly Nider's topic when he introduced the story. Moreover, no demonic agency seems to have been involved, although Nider would doubtless have rationalized that the lizard served merely to signal to the demons which household they should afflict. Barring such typically clerical predilections, however, the use of the lizard seems more simply an element of symbolic or perhaps even natural magic, and this may well be how Staedelin thought of his sorcery as operating.

In another account, Staedelin did reveal an explicitly demonic element in his magic. Peter of Bern demanded that he confess how he conjured hailstorms to destroy crops, and Staedelin complied: "First, in a field we implore the prince of all demons with certain words that he should send some [demon] of his, who would strike the place designated by us. Then, with a certain demon arriving, we immolate a young black fowl at some crossroads, throwing it high into the air. The demon takes this up, obeys [us], and immediately rouses the air ... by cast-ing hail and lightning."[55] Here, clearly, was demonic sorcery, although one must wonder whether these were Staedelin's own words or those of a confession forced from him by the judge. In any event, even if Staedelin and his fellows were invoking demons, with the sacrifice of the black fowl symbolizing some sort of offering from sorcerer to demon, there is no indication here of any more elaborate or permanent demonic pact, apostasy, or other terrible aspects of later witchcraft.

Nor, despite Staedelin's use of the plural "we," is there any reason to suspect that he was a member of a large sect of witches. In fact, Nider indicated specifically that Staedelin had learned his black arts not from the devil in the context of a sabbath but from a known lineage of individual human teachers. Approximately sixty years earlier, Nider wrote, or around 1375, a man called Scavius (literally, the scabby man) lived in the Simme valley and was the first great "witch" there. Among his many powers, he was supposed to have been able to transform himself into a mouse and thus escape capture. He had a disciple named Hoppo, and it was he who made Staedelin into a "master of witches."[56] These two men, Staedelin and Hoppo, clearly practiced magic together for some time. Nider wrote:

> These two knew how to carry over a third part of the dung, hay, or grain, or whatever sort of thing, when it pleased them, from their neighbor's field to their own field, with no one seeing them, how to raise enormous hailstorms and destructive winds with lightning, how to hurl children walking near water, in the sight of their parents, into that [water] with no one seeing them, how to bring about sterility in people and animals, [and] how to harm those near them both bodily and in goods.[57]

Again, all such harmful actions were elements of traditional *maleficium*, without any overt indication of demonic involvement.[58] In the stories concerning Staedelin we have a description of common sorcery much as it probably was being practiced by many rustics and others in the late 1300s and early 1400s, without the addition of such fantastic elements of the sabbath as appeared only in the 1430s. Staedelin worked his magic, which he may or may not have actually thought of as demonic, in order to harm his neighbors. He worked either alone or with one accomplice, seemingly motivated only by his own greed or malice. We certainly find no overt indication that he worshiped Satan or was a member of a vast diabolical cult.[59]

Nider, however, seems to have recognized none of these distinctions. He facilely conflated the type of sorcery Staedelin was performing with notions of witchcraft developed much later, even as he had read the contemporary notion of the witches' sabbath back into Peter of Bern's accounts. Nider simply would not or could not accept traditional magical practices for what they were; he assumed that they must be what he thought them to be—rough equivalents of the explicit invocations of demons by which learned necromancy was known to function. The firmness of his conviction and his failure of understanding go far to explain how common sorcery appeared in the minds of learned clerical authorities as a demonic conspiracy, and why they transformed traditional magical practices into the far darker operations of witchcraft.

INVENTING THE SABBATH

As the idea of a satanic cult of witches became established and accepted, authorities naturally began to attribute elements of standard antiheretical polemic to the emerging figure of the witch. Notions of secret conventicles, perverse and often demonic orgies, infanticide, cannibalism, and other horrific elements quickly came together to form the full stereotype of the witches' sabbath. Several of Nider's most detailed accounts of witchcraft focused on these dark assemblies. The similarities between the witches' sabbath and earlier heretical conventicles are immediately apparent, although minor changes were effected in the polemical tradition so that it would bear more directly on magical practices in the sabbath. For example, the very first heretics to be burned in the medieval West, at Orléans in 1022, had been accused of participating in rites similar to those of later witches' sabbaths. Among other atrocities, they supposedly murdered and cremated children in order to use their ashes to make a potion that, when drunk, prevented members of the sect from ever returning to the true faith. In one of Nider's descriptions of the sabbath, witches made a similar potion from the "liquid parts" of the bodies of children. From the "more solid parts" they concocted magical potions and powders with which to carry out their "desires, and arts, and transmutations." In yet another description of the sabbath, witches drank this potion in order to gain an instant understanding of how to perform their maleficent arts.[60]

Much scholarship has focused on elements of witchcraft that originated in European folklore. Ideas such as the magical transformation of witches into animals and the night flight to the sabbath were rooted in what appear to be the remnants of archaic shamanistic practices widespread in European (and indeed Eurasian) culture. Authorities simply uncovered these beliefs and practices among the peasantry and, misunderstanding them, twisted them into witchcraft.[61] Yet, while such elements would eventually figure prominently in the witch stereotype, in the earliest phase of that idea's formation they appear only marginally, if at all. In none of Nider's several descriptions of sabbaths, for example, did night flight figure in any way. Indeed, the only gathering of witches for which he specifically provided a location supposedly occurred in a parish church, not in some dark cavern or on a night-shrouded mountain peak.

While entirely absent from Nider's accounts, night flight did appear to varying degrees in other sources from the 1430s.[62] The one that presented what would later become the most typical image of flight, witches mounted on brooms flying to a satanic conventicle, was a brief anonymous tract titled *Errores Gazariorum*.[63] This source was long thought to date from around 1450, whereas Nider, drawing on the reports of Peter of Bern, was thought to represent an idea of witchcraft as it existed near the beginning of the 1400s. Thus the accounts in the *Formicarius* were seen as depicting an early and undeveloped concept of the sabbath without night flight, while the *Errores* was considered to represent the developed stereotype. As we have seen, however, Nider's descriptions of sabbaths in the *Formicarius* actually present a contemporary account of the idea as it existed in the late 1430s. Also, the *Errores* has been redated more accurately to the mid-1430s. Thus the two accounts are contemporary and, rather than showing a development in the notion of the sabbath, they reveal that in the decade when that idea originated, night flight was not yet an established part of the stereotype, but could be included or omitted as a particular author preferred.[64]

Interestingly, Nider did include a long account of night flight in his *Formicarius*, but he placed the story in the second book of that work, on false dreams and visions, rather than in the fifth book, on witches and their deceptions. Here he recounted a story about a woman who claimed that she flew at night with a large company led by the goddess Diana. A Dominican friar, hearing the story, asked to be allowed to observe her during her supposed flight, and she consented. That night, as was her custom, she placed a small cauldron on top of a stool and set herself inside it. Covering herself with unguents and muttering magic words, she then fell asleep. Dreaming that she was in flight with the goddess, she rocked so violently that the cauldron fell from the stool. Physically, however, she never left the room, and when she awoke, the friar was able to convince her that her visions were merely illusions caused by demons.[65] Nider then offered a similar story drawn from the legend of Saint Germanus of Auxerre, concerning a family in a certain village who would set out food as offerings for the "good women of the night"—witches whom they believed to be their neighbors. Staying awake to observe one night, Germanus realized that the creatures in question were demons disguised as women, and that the actual neighbors were all asleep in their beds.[66] This legend perhaps echoes the ancient Roman belief in the *strix*—a birdlike vampiric creature, often believed to be an old woman magically transformed—or other archaic beliefs in night-flying beings that had to be pacified with offerings of food. Such beliefs, remnants of ancient myths and folk practices, often did become included in the developing stereotype of witchcraft.[67] Again, however, Nider placed this story among accounts of false dreams and visions, not with his stories of witchcraft.

The only time Nider actually mentioned flight in direct relation to witchcraft was to say that the "witch" Staedelin and his master Hoppo were able "to go from place to place through the air," and even here he was careful to add the qualifying phrase, "so they thought."[68] Whether their flight was to be seen as real or only as a delusion, Nider presented it simply as one of the magical powers that Staedelin and Hoppo possessed, bearing no relation to the idea of night flight to a sabbath. The only other example of flight in the fifth book of the *Formicarius* involved a knight who, riding out late one night, encountered an army of the dead in a forest clearing. Offered a place in their company, he rode with them to Jerusalem and back in the course of a single night. Witches did not figure in the story at all.[69]

Nider recognized the power of demons to transport people through the air (even if he generally maintained that it was most often only an illusion).[70] He also accepted the reality of cults of witches gathering at periodic sabbaths. He did not, however, link these two ideas in any significant way. Thus he reveals that ideas of night flight or spiritual transportation to a nocturnal gathering, which may well have been relatively widespread especially among the European peasantry as a vestige of some archaic form of shamanism, nevertheless were not yet firmly linked to the emerging idea of witchcraft in the 1430s, when all the other important elements of that concept were being assembled. Rather, the idea of the sabbath, a gathering of witches based mainly in earlier clerical polemic against heretics, arose directly from the notion of witches' idolatry and particularly their apostasy. Having sold their souls to the devil and become his servants, they then gathered periodically to worship him and to receive from him instruction in the magical powers with which they could then attack the Christian faithful. The need to explain common magical practices in this way arose from the collision and conflation, in the minds of learned authorities such as Nider, of two quite different systems of elite and common magic. Other elements of the stereotype of witchcraft and the witches' sabbath, while important, were secondary to these central concerns.

WOMEN AS WITCHES

Perhaps the most immediately apparent aspect of the witch stereotype is its strongly gendered character. During the great hunts of the sixteenth and seventeenth centuries, the persons sent to the stake for practicing the black arts were overwhelmingly female, typically between 75 and 90 percent, depending on location and time.[71] Like other aspects of the idea of witchcraft in the early modern period, this fatal prejudice originated in the fifteenth century, where it found its most famous expression in the profoundly misogynist witch-hunting manual *Malleus maleficarum,* written by the Dominican Heinrich Kramer in 1486.[72] Yet the idea of witchcraft as an especially female crime predated the *Malleus* by at least fifty years. Johannes Nider, in his *Formicarius,* was the first clerical authority to argue explicitly that more women than men were inclined toward witchcraft. Indeed, Nider's discussion of women as witches provided a model that Kramer would copy, at times almost verbatim, into his *Malleus,* and on which he would then elaborate.[73]

The specific association of the crime of witchcraft with women has received a great deal of scholarly attention, so much that Stuart Clark has rightly cautioned that medieval and early modern sources actually discussed witchcraft as a woman's crime, and indeed conceived it as such, far less often than modern scholars do. Thus we run the risk of introducing an anachronism if we attempt to understand witchcraft only as evidence of medieval misogyny.[74] Nevertheless, to modern scholars the issue of witchcraft as a primarily female crime is clearly and rightly critical, and it has never been adequately or entirely explained. Or perhaps one should say that it has been explained too often, as several distinct arguments have been advanced to explain why witches came to be thought of as predominantly female. The classic explanation provided by such "founding fathers" of witchcraft studies as Jules Michelet, Henry Charles Lea, and Joseph Hansen in the nineteenth and early twentieth centuries was that the association of witchcraft with women derived solely from the misogyny inherent in the medieval church, which saw women as weaker in faith and more carnal in nature than men, and thus far more open to the seductions of the devil. More recent studies have considered numerous other factors—social and economic, psychological, and cultural.[75] An important but contentious point remains the degree to which certain magical practices, particularly healing and harming through sorcery, really were more typically practiced by women than by men in premodern Europe. The oft-repeated argument that many witches were actually midwives and that accusations served male authorities as a means to drive women from a socially powerful and respected profession has now been thoroughly debunked; nevertheless, healing in general was probably more a female than a male occupation in most premodern societies, and many aspects of such informal folk healing could carry dangerous associations with sorcery.[76] Certainly we cannot escape the fact that the majority of persons tried for witchcraft were women, and this clearly seems to reflect the widespread opinion that women were more likely than men to be performing such acts.[77] Ultimately, as with all complex historical phenomena, each of these factors, and perhaps others as yet undiscovered, doubtless contributed to the preponderance of women who were sent to the stake for the supposed crime of witchcraft.[78]

The contribution of clerical misogyny to the particular association of women with witchcraft was not negligible but it was far from absolute, nor was it really an active force in the construction of the stereotype of the witch. Rather, it seems to have been a familiar bastion to which ecclesiastical authorities fled when they were confronted by the rather shocking notion of women wielding incredibly powerful demonic magic. Surviving trial records from the first half of the fourteenth century, a hundred years before Nider wrote his *Formicarius,* indicate that over 70 percent of the persons accused of sorcery were men. In the second half of that century, however, the proportion of men accused fell to 42 percent, and by the first half of the fifteenth century, women accounted for roughly 60 to 70 percent of the accused.[79] This surge probably reflects the general increase in the number of trials for sorcery at this time, and seems to confirm the idea that women may have been more commonly associated than men with magical practices. Although this view may have been widespread within the general culture of late medieval Europe, however, to educated clerics such as Nider the prevalence of women involved in maleficent and, to them at least, necessarily demonic sorcery must have been shocking.

Of course, women had often been accused of sorcery in the past, and medieval Christianity's dim view of female morality was usually a factor in such accusations.[80] Nevertheless, especially to clerics familiar with elite necromantic practices, demonic magic must have seemed to be a fundamentally male activity. Necromancy proper was limited almost entirely to men. At a minimum, literacy in Latin and often at least some sacerdotal training was required to be able to perform such magic. In any case, the act of summoning a demon up from hell, on which clerical authorities believed almost all magic was based, was very much a masculine act, requiring intelligence, strength of will, and even a kind of courage. Medieval Christianity typically attributed none of these qualities to women. Nider seems to have been alluding to such attitudes when he briefly but pointedly had the lazy student in the *Formicarius* express surprise that so many women were involved in activities associated with witchcraft.

The occasion for his shock was the discussion of the recent trial and execution of Joan of Arc, burned at the stake in 1431. After her sudden and startling rise as a military commander for the French in the later stages of the Hundred Years' War, Joan was captured by the Burgundians and handed over to the English. Thus her trial was primarily political and her conviction was a foregone conclusion. She was charged with a variety of crimes, some involving sorcery and diabolism, although these charges actually did not figure in her final condemnation.[81] Nevertheless, Nider clearly considered her to be guilty at least of the crime of demonic sorcery, for she had admitted to having a "familiar angel," which authorities determined to have been a demonic spirit, and this spirit had "made her a sorceress." He reported similar cases of three other women, one from around Cologne and two from Paris, all of whom were judged to be "sorceresses or witches."[82] These women behaved much like Joan. They were rebellious figures who overstepped the lines of proper female decorum and were condemned for their unorthodox behavior. At this point in the dialogue, the lazy pupil interrupted his master to exclaim, "I cannot wonder enough how the fragile sex should dare to rush into such presumptions." The theologian wryly answered, "Among simple ones like yourself these things are wonders, but in the eyes of prudent men they are not rare."[83]

My suspicion, however, is that even "prudent men" of Nider's day were still shocked by the thought of women engaging in such activities and wielding such powers. In the dialogue that makes up the *Formicarius,* Nider repeatedly employed the device of placing widely held but in his view incorrect opinions in the mouth of the lazy pupil, thereby allowing the theologian to refute them. This is precisely what he has done here. Responding to his student's statement of surprise, the theologian launched into a long account of female inferiority and iniquity. While women certainly had the potential for good, if they failed to realize this potential, they risked falling into the depths of evil. "There are three things in nature which, if they exceed the limits of their conditions, either in diminution or in excess, attain the pinnacle of either good or evil, namely, the tongue, the cleric, and the woman. These, if they are ruled by a good spirit, are usually the best of all things, but if guided by an evil spirit they are usually the worst."[84] He then went on to ponder the depths to which women could fall. Citing the Bible, he noted that "there is no head worse than the head of a serpent, and there is no anger above the anger of a woman. It will be more pleasing to abide with a lion and a dragon than to dwell with a wicked woman" (Ecclesiasticus 25:22–23). Drawing on Saint John Chrysostom's commentaries on the Gospel of Matthew, he described women as "the enemy of friendship" and a "necessary evil." From Cicero he quoted the adage that "individual desires drive men to each evil act, a single desire leads women to all evils." From what he termed the proverbs of Seneca, he derided female duplicity: "A woman either loves or hates, there is no third.... Two sorts of tears there are in the eyes of women; one is of true sadness, the other is of treachery. When a woman thinks alone, she thinks of evil things."[85] In his *Preceptorium divine legis* he addressed the question "why it appears that women often are found [involved] in superstition and witchcraft in a greater number than men." Here he presented his readers with three arguments based on women's moral, physical, and mental inferiority. First, women were weak in faith and therefore more open to the deceits and seductions of demons. Second, their weaker physical nature made them more susceptible than men to visions and delusions. Third, they were far more loquacious than men, and thus quickly spread the evil arts among themselves.[86]

If women could and often did attain the "pinnacle of evil," however, they could also attain the heights of good. Immediately after discussing female depravity and susceptibility to witchcraft, Nider recounted the great deeds of which good women might be capable. "Concerning good women," he noted, "there is such praise that it is even written that they sanctified men and saved peoples, lands, and cities." He presented as examples such powerful women from the Old Testament as Deborah, Judith, and Esther. Throughout the New Testament, also, women could be seen to be among the most important means of "drawing unbelievers into the Christian nation," and even after biblical times women continued to play an important role in converting men and nations to Christianity. Nider noted that King Stephen of Hungary was converted, along with his entire kingdom, by his wife, Gillian, daughter of the Roman emperor, and that the Franks were converted when their king, Clovis, became a Christian under the influence of his wife, Clothild. Well might the Bible tell, Nider concluded, of how "the unbelieving man is sanctified by the faithful woman" (1 Corinthians 7:13–14), and how "happy is the husband of a good woman, for his years are double" (Ecclesiasticus 1:1).[87]

Thus Nider's view of women, even when he argued that they were more likely than men to become witches, was not exclusively misogynist. Women's propensity to fall into such depths of sin as witchcraft was counterbalanced by their capacity to attain the heights of sanctity. This portrayal of women was hardly more realistic than were the slanders on which the stereotype of the female witch was founded, but at least it was not a wholly negative portrayal. Nider's arguments about women and witchcraft represent a dichotomous view of the female sex that was fairly typical of medieval clerics.[88] That he would fall back on standard arguments of feminine weakness when confronted with what was already emerging as a predominantly female evil is by no means surprising. That he should have been able to do so, however, reveals a subtle but important aspect of witchcraft. Earlier views of demonic magic and maleficent sorcery in the thirteenth and fourteenth centuries tended to highlight the power and authority of the human magician. Learned necromancers were highly skilled and educated men, if still condemnable, and even common sorcerers were often seen as wielding impressive demonic power. As the full stereotype of witchcraft began to develop, however, authorities no longer placed so much stress on the power and authority of human sorcerers. Now the emphasis fell on susceptibility to temptation and submission to demonic forces, with the ability to perform powerful sorcery obtained only at the cost of complete subservience. Thus authorities were able to accept the notion that most witches were women, a "reality" already present in the accusations and trials, because they conceived of witchcraft, quite unlike earlier forms of demonic sorcery, as essentially a female crime.[89]

As one of the earliest theorists of witchcraft to write about this new phenomenon, Nider provides many insights into the initial formation of the witch stereotype among ecclesiastical authorities and the secular officials who followed their
lead.[90] Particularly in his discussions of common *maleficium* and elite necromancy, which he saw as essentially identical, and in his presentation of two
different forms of witchcraft—one more closely reflecting actual common magical practices, the other more fully developed and replete with learned diabolical
concerns—he reveals the conditions behind the early formation of the idea of
witchcraft and demonstrates how and why that concept took root in the minds
of learned clerics. His descriptions of witches' sabbaths help to clarify what elements were truly central to that emerging concept. And his treatment of women
illustrates some of the forces that actually drove the increasingly gendered character of the crime of witchcraft.

But why was Nider so concerned with witches? Why did he devote so much
attention to them? Why was he so concerned to understand and explain their
activity? Why did he even believe they existed? Although clerical authorities
played a major role in developing the idea of witchcraft, it was hardly a foregone
conclusion that all such authorities would accept this idea. Initially many did
not, and skepticism persisted even throughout the centuries of the great witch-
hunts. Moreover, all the components from which the stereotype of witchcraft
was constructed, maleficent sorcery and demonic sects and all the rest, existed
long before the figure of the witch ever appeared. So the question remains: Why
did Nider, busily engaged with maters of heresy and religious reform at the
Council of Basel and immediately afterward, become so preoccupied with
witches? The answer lies in how witchcraft related (or did not relate) to his other
occupations, considerations, and concerns. Thus to fully understand Nider's involvement in the problem of witchcraft, we must consider other related aspects
of his thought, particularly his concern (or lack thereof) over heresy and his
desire for ecclesiastical and spiritual reform in the broadest sense. Only then will
we be able to return to witchcraft per se and situate it more clearly as but one
issue among many in the troubled religious world of the early fifteenth century.

3

THE THREAT OF HERESY

HUSSITES, FREE SPIRITS, AND BEGUINES

The connection between witchcraft and heresy in the late Middle Ages seems obvious. Insofar as witches summoned and worshiped demons, they were guilty of idolatry and thus were excommunicated as heretics; and insofar as they gathered at secret conventicles, engaged in abominable and unholy rites, and became apostates by forswearing the Christian faith, they behaved like a heretical sect.[1] Moreover, there are compelling arguments that the earliest true witch trials, which occurred in western Switzerland, Savoy, and Dauphiné in the first half of the fifteenth century, emerged out of trials for heresy in those lands, and the suggestion has been made that papal inquisitors in particular often turned to the investigation and prosecution of sorcery and witchcraft when easier heretical targets were lacking.[2] Thus we might well suppose that a profound concern over witchcraft such as Nider exhibited would be paralleled by and perhaps even rooted in an equally profound concern over heresy and zealousness in the matter of condemning and persecuting heretics. Nider, however, confounds all such expectations. While at the Council of Basel, during the very time in which he was collecting accounts of witchcraft, he also dealt extensively with matters of heresy. Yet here he appears calm, rational, and even restrained in the face of what many other clerics regarded as truly profound heretical threats.

In general, it must be said that in the fourteenth and fifteenth centuries, especially in German lands, concern over heresy was not particularly intense, at least by medieval standards, nor were heretics typically regarded as a constant and overwhelming problem.[3] Certainly no heretical movement of the later Middle Ages ever achieved such spectacular success as the Cathar heresy did in southern France and northern Italy in the twelfth and thirteenth centuries.[4] Intense waves of persecution were still possible, however, and many churchmen, especially inquisitors and theologians, were deeply concerned about what they perceived to be serious threats of heresy. Precisely during the years when Nider was active, the 1420s and 1430s, the Hussite heresy was posing a tremendous, if somewhat localized, challenge to religious and secular authorities in the German empire. Named after one of its early leaders, the Czech preacher and religious reformer Jan Hus, who had been declared a heretic and executed at the Council of Constance in 1415, the Hussite movement quickly became as much a political as a religious force. In 1420 the Hussites seized control of Bohemia from the emperor Sigismund and the German nobility. They retained power in that region for most of the next two decades, while their ideas spread throughout the German empire, reaching as far as the Rhineland.[5] Supposedly even more pervasive and enduring was the heresy of the Free Spirit, whose adherents held that through spiritual and mystical exercises they became one with God and as a result were above all human religious authority, above all moral law, and indeed above even the possibility of committing sin. Thus they could perform whatever immoral acts they wished. In fact, no such organized heretical movement ever existed. What actual Free Spirits there were seem to have been individuals, or at best small groups, engaged in extreme forms of otherwise fairly orthodox late medieval mystical spirituality concerned with the search for God. But many clerical authors, readily accepting and perpetuating one another's ill-founded assertions, were convinced of the existence of a vast network of clandestine sects spread across much of Germany.[6] Nider was such an author. At one point in his *Formicarius,* he based his description of widespread Free Spirit heresy in the Swabian Ries on a mid-thirteenth-century account by the great Dominican theologian Albertus Magnus.[7]

Often associated with the heresy of the Free Spirit, particularly by religious authorities, were beghards and beguines. These were lay people who sought to lead lives of intense religious devotion without taking monastic vows or entering religious orders. The female beguines tended to live communally in special houses established in many towns and cities, and supported themselves through work or by receiving alms. Their less numerous male counterparts, the beghards, tended to be itinerant and to support themselves by begging.[8] Both groups came to occupy an ill-defined middle ground between the regular laity and the religious orders; they can perhaps best be described by Nider's term "lay religious" (*secularium religiones*). Many bishops, theologians, and other religious authorities (to say nothing of secular officials) looked on these men and women with suspicion at best and frequently targeted them as heretics. Beginning in the fourteenth century, indeed, many ecclesiastical sources often used the word "beguine" as virtually a synonym for the heresy of the Free Spirit.[9] Beguines also faced persecution simply for their way of life. Many clerics questioned the legitimacy of any attempt by lay people to lead a vigorous *vita apostolica* through communal life, poverty, mendicancy, and chastity, and beginning in the early fourteenth century efforts were made to ban the entire beguine status outright.[10]

As with so many of the crises and concerns that religious leaders faced in the early fifteenth century, all of these issues, particularly the Hussite threat and the questionable status of the beguines, were discussed and debated at the Council of Basel. Nider became deeply involved in these matters, and he provides an important but neglected perspective on both the council's activities and the issues that lay behind them.[11] His approach to the problem of heresy and his degree of concern over the Hussite threat especially may appear somewhat surprising, especially for a man who is too often known only for his clamorous alarm over witchcraft. Although he was of course opposed to any and all groups that had been officially branded as heretical, he showed surprisingly little interest in matters of heresy. As for the questionable status of the lay religious, here he rose to become one of the most thorough defenders the beguines were to find in the late Middle Ages, and in his consideration of these women and their moral status he presented a rather different view of female spirituality than that revealed in his writings on witchcraft. Ultimately Nider was driven not by any great fear of the spread of heretical corruption but by his desire for positive moral and spiritual reform among the Christian faithful. In such matters, the supposed threat of heresy played little or no role.

NIDER AND THE HUSSITES

The Hussites represented perhaps the most threatening and dangerous heresy to arise in the later Middle Ages, and certainly in German lands during the early fifteenth century they dominated the concerns of religious authorities.[12] Moreover, as one scholar has written, the Hussite movement was not just a heresy, it was "both a reformation and a revolution, in fact *the* revolution of the late Middle Ages, the history of which period cannot be properly understood if the Hussites are left out."[13]

Beginning in the mid–fourteenth century under the emperor Charles IV, a movement for religious reform developed in Bohemia. In the course of the late fourteenth and early fifteenth centuries, the desire for reform spread among both the clergy and the laity, and, becoming infused with certain ideas of the radical theologian John Wyclif of England, eventually developed into a true popular movement.[14] Even taking the Wyclifite influence into account, many modern scholars maintain that at least the moderate wing of this movement, represented by Hus himself, actually remained essentially orthodox. Nevertheless, Hus was condemned as a heretic at the Council of Constance, and the movement he represented was declared heretical.[15] Against the perceived spiritual and political threat that the Hussites represented, prelates of the church and the secular lords of the German empire worked together to raise several crusading armies that were sent against the Bohemian heretics. That these armies all met with defeat heightened both religious and secular alarm in the lands bordering Bohemia. At Vienna and Nuremberg in the late 1420s, Nider would have found himself very much on the front lines of this conflict. At some point during these years he helped to preach a crusade against the Hussites, most likely while he was in Nuremberg.[16] His most intense involvement with the Bohemian heretics came, however, while he was in Basel.

Nider composed his major work on the Hussites, *Contra heresim Hussitarum* or "Against the heresy of the Hussites," in Basel, although probably before the opening of the council there.[17] His purpose in writing the treatise remains unclear, but even before the council convened, he would have known that the heresy in Bohemia would be one of the most important issues the fathers at Basel would have to face, and perhaps he simply wanted to provide the council with his theological opinion on the matter. *Contra heresim Hussitarum* was to have been a general treatment of all aspects of the Hussite movement. The first part of the treatise set forth the errors of the Hussites, proved them to be heretics, and argued that they should be opposed both through theological debate and with the sword. The second part was to discuss the four major points of the Hussite program, the so-called Four Articles of Prague. These articles covered reception of the Eucharist in both kinds—that is, both bread and wine—by the laity, as well as freedom of preaching, curtailment of clerical wealth, and the punishment of sin.[18] Part three was then going to respond to the Hussites' arguments supporting their positions as set forth in previous debates and in the many propaganda pamphlets that they had issued, some of which had spread throughout the German empire and even into other lands.[19]

Such a treatise, had Nider in fact completed it, would have provided the Council of Basel with a complete handbook for dealing with the Hussites. The work survives in only two known manuscript copies, however, and both break off at the beginning of the second part, in the middle of the question of utraquism, or reception of Communion in both kinds.[20] Even so, the treatise was still probably of use to the council. Nider's contemporaries would doubtless have found helpful his collection and summary of various arguments against the Hussites.[21] For the modern reader, however, *Contra heresim Hussitarum* must stand as the least original and interesting of Nider's treatises to be considered here. Nider fully accepted that Hus and his followers had been justly condemned. He therefore addressed them in harsh yet ultimately standard anti-heretical terms. At the very outset of *Contra heresim Hussitarum* he referred to the heretics, in the words of Saint Matthew, as "false prophets who come … in the clothing of sheep, but inwardly they are ravening wolves" (Matthew 7:15), and he used this image of the Hussites as wolves among the flock of the Lord as a sort of leitmotiv throughout his treatise. Wreaking havoc on the church and throughout the whole of Christian society, they "flatter the worldly, condescend to the carnal, disparage the monastic life, and fight with material swords."[22]

Nider then listed twenty-three errors and heretical beliefs of which the Hussites were guilty, "some more, some less," for he was aware that the Bohemian heretics were not entirely unified. "Not all of them think alike," he wrote, "nor do they call themselves by one name, because some are Taborites, some Orphans, some from the New Town, others from the Old," referring here to the two great military brotherhoods of the Hussite movement, bearing the biblical names of Tabor and Oreb, and to the citizens of two of the contiguous but legally separate and distinct towns that comprised the city of Prague in the late Middle Ages.[23] Nevertheless, all the Hussites were guilty of some heretical beliefs and acts, including errors concerning the Eucharist and other sacraments, destruction of church buildings and images (even statues of Christ and the saints), denial of purgatory and the efficacy of indulgences, denial of the intercession of the saints and the destruction of relics, denial of the authority of canon law, of the pope, and of other church prelates, and opposition to the monastic life. This last issue particularly seems to have angered Nider. He specifically mentioned that the Hussites had destroyed many monasteries in Bohemia, and that they believed "that the rules of the holy fathers Augustine, Basil, Francis, Benedict, and others are evil."[24] In his *Formicarius*, written more than half a decade after *Contra heresim Hussitarum*, he again had occasion to describe the heresy of the Hussites, and again he noted that they destroyed monasteries, killed monks, and "would allow neither Carthusians, nor reformed [monks], nor unreformed ones to live in their kingdom."[25]

Such opposition to God's church, Nider felt, warranted the most severe response. Having preached a crusade against the Hussites himself earlier in his career, he now exhorted all the prelates of the church to urge "just war" against the heretics.[26] Indeed, he devoted several chapters to the benefits gained by those who fought for the faith. Drawing on Aquinas, he outlined the notion of just war in defense of the *res publica*, and he cited such biblical injunctions as "present your bodies as a living sacrifice" (Romans 12:1) and "he that does not take up his cross and follow me is not worthy of me" (Matthew 10:38). Those who lost their lives in the struggle against heresy, he declared, would be martyrs and would not have to face purgatory, for to have died defending the faith was like a second baptism, a "baptism of blood," which washed away all sin.[27]

For all of Nider's harsh rhetoric against the Hussites, however, he seems to have been strangely indifferent to them and particularly to the doctrinal challenge they presented. His response to the Bohemian heresy, despite its severity, was largely mechanical and reflexive. It amounted to little more than standard antiheretical diatribe and took the form of simple negation rather than any creative argument. Insofar as the Hussite heresy was actually a movement for religious reform, it called for a major restructuring of the ecclesiastical hierarchy and even a basic reconceptualization of what the "church" was; the Hussites sought to curtail the powers of the pope and his bishops and to allow the laity more active participation in religious matters.[28] In response, many treatises written at Basel addressing the Hussite positions centered on issues of ecclesiology, reform of the papacy and Roman curia, and so forth. Such prominent council members as Juan of Segovia and Nider's friend and fellow Dominican Johannes of Ragusa developed their own ecclesiological and conciliar positions in direct response to the Hussite threat.[29] Yet Nider seems never to have been inspired to respond to the Hussites in this way. Moreover, despite his fierce denunciation of the Bohemians as heretics and his stark support for war against them, he was not as extreme or as rigid in his opposition to them as might be expected. Ultimately he was calm, rational, and pragmatic in his approach to the Hussite problem, and he was willing to accommodate a moderate solution if one presented itself. Before the Council of Basel entered into open negotiations with the heretics, clerical authorities had already debated with the Hussites on several occasions, and Nider was quick to defend the value of these exchanges. Since the heretics were "wolves in sheep's clothing," every opportunity had to be seized to expose them for what they truly were. He briefly noted the biblical injunction "Do not contend in words, for it is of no use" (2 Timothy 2:14), but concluded, "Nevertheless it is not denied that in many situations it is licit and useful to dispute with heretics."[30] A danger certainly existed that the laity might be swayed into error by hearing heretics speak, and Nider warned that no lay people should ever be allowed to hear heretical doctrines explained or defended. He pointed out, however, that disputes over points of faith were precisely what theologians were trained to handle.[31]

Of course, theological debate had its limits. "It is not sufficient," Nider wrote, "and it is rare and difficult and at all times uncertain" to convert stubborn heretics back to the true faith. Since they "devour and kill" the soul, often they have to "be altogether exterminated" by military force.[32] However, he also concluded that it could be licit to enter into a truce with heretics, provided one maintained a crucial distinction between a truce, which was a "security" for people in times of discord, and true peace, which was an end to discord. A "mutual truce" (*treuga mutua*) might indeed be contracted licitly with heretics, but "peace in itself" (*pax proprie*) was for Nider unthinkable. Peace was the end of discord, "but such concord of heart can never be with heretics."[33]

In advocating, however tentatively, truce and negotiation as tools for ultimately eradicating heresy, Nider, writing before the opening of the Council of Basel, presaged the exact strategy that the council would eventually employ against the Hussites. It was Cardinal Giuliano Cesarini, the council president, who seems to have been primarily responsible for persuading his fellow council members that negotiations with the Bohemian heretics were necessary. Having witnessed the crushing defeat of the final military crusade against the Hussites at Domažlice in August 1431, he arrived in Basel in September convinced that the council must deal with the heretics under whatever terms they required.[34] The magnitude of this defeat also helped others to accept the cardinal's strategy, for when news of the crusade's failure reached Basel, even that city, far as it was from Bohemia, was gripped by fear of an imminent Hussite attack, and the council fathers worried that any number of German cities might soon succumb to the heretical menace.[35] On September 28 the council decided to invite the Hussites to negotiate, and it chose Johannes Nider, along with Johannes of Gelnhausen, abbot of the Cistercian monastery at Maulbronn (and thus often referred to simply as Johannes of Maulbronn) to head the preliminary delegation to the Bohemians.[36] While in Nuremberg awaiting the Hussites' response to the council's letters of invitation, Nider corresponded frequently with Johannes of Ragusa, the senior Dominican in Basel and the man in overall charge of the negotiations.[37] Aside from official business, Nider also reported some less straightforward matters to his fellow Dominican. He wrote that he had learned from the Bohemian nuncio that "there are people in Prague, especially in the Old Town . . . who are at heart faithful." According to the nuncio, their religious services were entirely Catholic, except for the fact that they took Communion in both kinds, both the bread and the chalice. This belief in utraquism, however, was the only questionable doctrine they held in common with the more radical Hussites.[38]

Given the eventual outcome of the Council of Basel's negotiations with the Bohemian heretics, one can only wonder what circumstances might have surrounded the writing of this letter. After years of negotiation and delicate maneuvering, both in Basel and in Prague, the council eventually succeeded in splitting the Hussite movement and turning the more moderate factions in Prague against the radical militant brotherhoods of Tabor and Oreb. With the moderates the council was able to conclude an agreement that in its essence allowed for Communion in both kinds so long as the Bohemians otherwise conformed to regular religious practice and doctrine. The basic terms of this compromise were established in the Compactata of Basel, signed in Prague in November 1433. This agreement then served as the basis for the ultimate Peace of Jihlava in 1436, through which most of the Hussites were reconciled to the church.[39] Thus in his letter of early 1432, almost two full years before the final agreement took shape, Nider had already indicated his attention to exactly those details that would figure centrally in that agreement, namely, the existence of a large moderate faction among the Hussites and their unity with the radicals only on the issue of the lay chalice. Had Ragusa or Cesarini instructed Nider to probe for such weaknesses among the Hussites? Or had he independently determined that this information was important, and in doing so perhaps first indicated to the council fathers the course they should pursue against the heretics? We do not know. We do know that Ragusa read out Nider's letter before the entire council, but its effect on that body is not recorded.[40]

The Bohemians accepted the Council of Basel's proposal of open negotiations, but before actually undertaking to send a mission to Basel, they requested an initial meeting in the town of Cheb (Eger), located on the Bohemian border directly between Prague and Nuremberg. Here delegates from both sides would meet face to face to work out the specific conditions for the later formal debates in Basel. The council quickly dispatched four additional delegates, with instructions on what conditions might be offered. They dealt mainly with matters of security, both military and spiritual. For example, the Bohemian delegation to the council was to be kept as small as possible, and was to come peacefully and "without conspicuous weaponry" (*sine notabilibus armis bellicis*). Most important, while at the council the heretics were in no way to preach or attempt to spread their doctrine, nor were they to distribute books or any sort of writing.[41] Despite these few explicit instructions and the expansion of the delegation, however, Nider and Maulbronn seem to have remained in overall charge of the negotiations, since all correspondence back to the council continued to come solely from them, and the delegation continued to have wide discretion to negotiate. Thus the agreement at Cheb, which brought the Hussites to Basel the following year, must be seen largely as the accomplishment of these two men. Amazingly, despite their staunch opposition to heresy (we can assume that Maulbronn was no more favorably disposed toward heretics than Nider was), they were willing to concede almost every point that the Hussites demanded, causing most scholars of the Hussite movement to see the negotiations at Cheb as the greatest victory that any heretical group ever achieved in the Middle Ages.[42]

Aside from the necessary preliminary matter of conditions for the Hussites' journey to Basel, the discussions at Cheb centered mainly on how the later debates at the council were to be structured. Naturally, the Hussites demanded that they be received as equals in an open debate, and not as prejudged heretics who were to be examined by authorities. Also, for the talks to be meaningful, the ultimate authorities on which matters of dispute could be settled had to be limited to those that the Hussites accepted. Thus they excluded all canon law, papal decrees, and decisions of earlier councils, especially those of the Council of Constance, which had burned Jan Hus and condemned Hussite doctrine. Argument and settlement of disputes were to be based only on the Bible, the examples of Christ and the Apostles, and the practices of the early church. On all these points Nider and Maulbronn conceded fully to the Hussites' demands.[43] The talks at Cheb lasted only a few weeks. By the middle of May 1432 they were over, and by June the conciliar delegation had returned to Basel. Half a year later, in January 1433, the main Hussite delegation followed, and negotiations began in the Dominican priory, but by this time Nider was no longer formally involved in the council's dealings with the heretics. He participated directly in Hussite affairs on only one later occasion, when he joined a conciliar delegation that met with the Bohemian heretics and the emperor Sigismund in Regensburg in 1434.

Nider's approach to the Hussite threat is difficult to categorize. While other theologians at Basel viewed the movement in Bohemia as presenting a serious intellectual challenge on matters of ecclesiology and religious doctrine, and they to some extent formulated their own reform ideas in response to Hussite arguments, Nider regarded the Bohemians purely as heretics, and he saw nothing of value in their doctrines or in their program. Despite this clear opposition to their cause, however, he displayed a pragmatic moderation in his approach to dealings with the Hussites, both in his writings and in direct negotiations with them. In his treatise he argued that truces with heretics were allowable, and that negotiations with them could often prove profitable, even if an outright peace was never to be allowed. In direct dealings he put these principles into action, granting the Hussites every condition they demanded in order to bring them to the table at Basel, while at the same time remaining alert for signs of weakness, such as internal divisions between moderates and radicals, which could be used against them.

Perhaps the most remarkable aspect of Nider's involvement with the Hussites is his apparent lack of interest in them. The threat of heresy seems simply not to have been among his main concerns. His treatise against the Hussites is extensive, but it is unclear whether he ever completed it. Moreover, this treatise, aside from the brief section on negotiations and truces with heretics, is probably the least original and least interesting of his major works covered here. Even more telling is the fact that in his magnum opus, the *Formicarius,* Nider afforded the Hussites only brief mention, and when he did mention them, his accounts tended to focus much more on the miracles and wonders that occurred in the course of the long struggle against the Bohemian heretics than on Hussite errors and doctrines per se.[44] When he did treat matters of heresy directly in his great work, the focus was not on the Hussites but on the Free Spirit. Consider that he related two stories of heretical beghards and beguines whom he encountered in Regensburg in 1434 but never once even mentioned the meeting with the Hussites for which he had traveled to that city.[45]

When we turn to the topic of the beguines, we shall see that here too Nider was far less concerned with the potential threat of heresy, even the terrible heresy of the Free Spirit of which beguines so often stood accused, than he was with the positive aspects of the lay religious way of life. He was an opponent of the Free Spirit because as a loyal son of the church he had to be, but in regard to beguines themselves, so often seen by late medieval clerical authorities as an equally dangerous and perhaps even more pervasive threat than Free Spirit heretics, he was an ardent supporter and defended them in the most absolute terms when they came under attack at the Council of Basel.

FREE SPIRITS, BEGUINES, AND THE PROBLEM OF THE "SECULAR RELIGIOUS"

Since their appearance early in the thirteenth century, the beguines, lay women who sought the *vita apostolica* through communal life, poverty, and devotion yet remained outside the approved religious orders, along with their less numerous male counterparts, the beghards, had presented a problem for medieval clerical authorities. Condemnations arose almost as soon as the beguines appeared, but they reached a new level in the early fourteenth century with the Council of Vienne (1311–12). This council, as one scholar has rightly noted, marked the beginning of a new chapter in the history of the beguines, while another scholar has described the century from the Council of Vienne to that of Constance as a "hundred years' war against beghards and beguines" carried on particularly by the church in Germany.[46] From Vienne emerged two key documents issued, after a rather extended delay, by Pope John XXII in 1317. These were the bulls *Ad nostrum* and *Cum de quibusdam mulieribus.* We must begin here with these decrees, for they established the basic issues of debate over Free Spirits and beguines down to Nider's time, and would prove fundamental in his consideration of these issues.[47]

Ad nostrum described beguines and beghards as an organized heresy, an "abominable sect of certain wicked men, who are commonly called beghards, and certain faithless women, who are called beguines." The decree went on to describe the errors of which such people were supposedly guilty, centering on the belief that a person could become so perfect in spirit as to be freed from all human law and morality—in other words, the antinomian heresy of the Free Spirit.[48] Before this decree, beguines had rarely faced charges of antinomianism.

Afterward their name became synonymous with the Free Spirit.[49] Profound as *Ad nostrum*'s condemnation of beguines was, however, *Cum de quibusdam mulieribus* was perhaps even more devastating. This bull also accused the beguines of errors, here more to do with their actions than with their beliefs, but went beyond charges of specific heresy and condemned the beguine form of life per se. It described "certain women, commonly called beguines" (here there is no mention of male beghards), who "debate and preach about the highest Trinity and the divine essence, and assert opinions contrary to the Catholic faith concerning articles of faith and ecclesiastical sacraments." Seeing the beguines as such a profound threat both to themselves and to the souls of others, *Cum de quibusdam* then continued, "the status of these [women] must be perpetually forbidden . . . and completely abolished from God's church."[50]

Such a sweeping condemnation would, at first glance, seem to have resolved the question of beguine status there and then, leaving little for future generations of clerical authorities to debate. *Cum de quibusdam* concluded, however, with an "escape clause" that reads: "However, if there might be some faithful women, promised to chastity or not, living honestly in their dwellings, who should wish to practice penitence and to be devoted to the virtue of the Lord in humility of spirit, by no means through the aforesaid do we intend to prohibit that this should be licit for them, for the Lord shall have inspired them."[51] Some scholars have seen this final clause as a blatant and confusing contradiction of the bull's main intent. I would argue, however, that *Cum de quibusdam* was not, in fact, originally intended as a condemnation of all beguines, but only of those who were guilty of the specific errors the decree mentioned.[52] Nider, as we shall see, clearly felt this to be the case, and he was able to cite many other authorities to this effect. Thus the extent of the pope's condemnation of beguines still remained very much a debated point over a century after the original decrees were issued.

Despite the possible nuances of the Vienne decrees, however, *Cum de quibusdam* and *Ad nostrum* generated a wave of persecutions, beginning in Strassburg in 1317 and then spreading to many other Rhineland cities, including Basel.[53] To make matters worse, in December 1317 Pope John XXII issued the bull *Sancta romana*, which seemed to include the beguines in its condemnation of the *fraticelli*, a heretical faction of the Franciscan order, and their lay followers the beguins in southern France and Italy.[54] Opponents of the lay religious in northern Europe now used *Sancta romana* and *Cum de quibusdam* jointly as grounds to move against beguines who were actually lay "tertiaries," that is, members of the Franciscan third order.[55] The next year Pope John tried to clarify the situation regarding licit and illicit lay religious, issuing the bull *Ratio recta* on August 13, 1318. Here he attempted to explain *Cum de quibusdam*'s

condemnation of beguines more clearly, and he expanded on the escape clause
in that bull, pointing out that many women "commonly called beguines" were
nevertheless not guilty of heresy, lived honestly, attended church, and obeyed
their parochial clergy. "We declare and wish," John commanded, "that beguines
of this sort, guiltless, as set out above, and not suspect, not be included in the
aforesaid prohibition and abolition." Bishops were instructed that they should
in no way "molest" members of such legitimate lay religious groups.[56] Yet accusations against beguines did not stop with John XXII's decree. For the next
century, beguines in Germany suffered wave after wave of persecutions and
repressions by zealous religious and secular authorities, some simply ignoring
the pope's approval of certain forms of beguine life, some focusing on other perceived errors not covered by the papal decrees, and some doubtless honestly con-
fused over what constituted a "good" as opposed to a "bad" beguine.[57] One of
the most severe and most successful of these persecutions took place in Basel at
the beginning of the fifteenth century, instigated primarily by Nider's former
socius and mentor in the Dominican reform, Johannes Mulberg.[58] In the face
of such constant and long-standing suspicion and repression, Johannes Nider
did well to remark, "It is clear how perilous the status of beghards and beguines
is seen to be."[59]

Large-scale persecution of beguines began to drop off precipitously in the
early fifteenth century, mainly after the Council of Constance.[60] By this time,
however, the damage had been done, and in many parts of Germany virtually no
independent beguines survived, having either given up their way of life entirely
or having adopted the (somewhat) safer habit of the Franciscan third order.[61]
Despite the reduced levels of repression after the Council of Constance, however, the status of the beguines remained suspect, and debate over their way
of life raged again at the Council of Basel. Here, it must be said, charges of heresy played only a small role. Indeed, throughout the late fourteenth and early
fifteenth centuries, even during the terrible persecutions in Basel itself, opposition to the beguines generally focused on the permissibility of lay poverty and
mendicancy rather than on supposed heretical beliefs.[62] Yet we must not think
that beguines were no longer commonly suspected of grave heresy.

In his *Formicarius* Johannes Nider presented a veritable catalog of the errors
of the lay religious, from the merely sinful to the truly heretical, and he once participated in a trial involving a case of the heresy of the Free Spirit. A woman,
apparently a vagrant who wandered from town to town spreading error, had
been imprisoned in Regensburg in 1434. Nider and the Spanish prelate Juan of
Palomar, who were representing the Council of Basel at negotiations between
the emperor Sigismund and the Hussite heretics, were asked by local authorities
to examine her, and she admitted to them that she believed she had divine

visions, that she did not need to obey the pope, and that she could not sin. Nider attempted to demonstrate her error to her through "most persuasive words," but she remained obstinate and declared herself willing to go to the flames for her beliefs. It was then that Juan of Palomar suggested torture, and, drawing Nider aside, told him that he should appear to object, so as to gain the woman's trust. The following day, after the woman had been tortured, Nider came to her, and she immediately began to tell him about the agony through which she had been put. He comforted her, but clearly held out the threat of further torture, and then told her how many people, even the wise, had been deceived by false visions, whereupon the woman recanted her errors and was saved.[63]

Nider told of other Free Spirits as well. The heretic Nikolaus of Basel, for example, who enjoyed a small sect of followers in the late fourteenth century, preached that Christ was in him and he was in Christ. Another story involved a "beghard or lollard" who was accustomed to gain entry to beguinages (Nider wrote of "houses of devout women") by adopting the appearance of a member of the *fraticelli* (*sub specie devoti fraticelli*). There he would select several women and corrupt them by telling them that chastity was unnecessary for perfection. Ultimately he would hold orgies with them. Nider was also convinced of the existence of a large sect of Free Spirits in the Swabian Ries, in southern Germany, consisting of people of both sexes, clerics as well as lay people. Members of this sect supposedly held, among other heretical beliefs, that they were not bound by any oath, and that they did not need to adhere to any normal human morality. They could, for example, freely murder anyone, "even their father or mother," without sin. They never fasted, they did not observe Lent, and whenever they could they secretly worked on religious holidays. They also refused to obey the pope or other ecclesiastical authorities.[64]

Nider also related several tales of beghards and beguines who were guilty of lesser errors and deceptions. Again in Regensburg, for example, he encountered a beghard who practiced false mendicancy. The man was actually quite rich, but he was so greedy that he pretended to be a pauper to get even more money from alms. One day this man encountered Nider and Juan of Palomar in the streets. Palomar, thinking him truly poor, gave him some money, but Nider knew the man and told Palomar of his deception, at which point the man fled. Nider also knew of a "*fraticellus* and semibeghard" in the city of Bern, about whom he learned from the Dominican inquisitor Nikolaus of Landau. This man had managed to convince people that he received divine visions, and that he could (for a price, of course) converse with the spirits of the deceased. Sometimes beguines and beghards themselves were deceived and led into error. At the time of the Council of Pisa, in 1409, Nider related, a beghard named Burgin in the diocese of Constance, convinced that he was receiving divine visions, began to gather followers, and even wrote a rule for them to follow. Sadly, his visions were only the deceptions of a "malign spirit" disguised as an "angel of light." Nider also recounted a story he heard from a pious woman who had entered a beguinage. A certain priest, she told him, a "truly corrupt man," often visited the beguines, and began to teach some of them "special doctrines." Telling them, among other things, that Christ had hung naked on the cross, he persuaded several beguines, including the woman who later confessed to Nider, to engage with him in nude rites that involved taking a false Eucharist. He does not appear to have deceived these women into actual sexual intercourse, however, for Nider still referred to the woman who confessed to him as a virgin.[65]

Yet for all this error and potential for grave heresy, Nider remained convinced that many of the lay religious led very positive lives. He wrote of a female recluse in the area of Basel whom even clerics sought out for advice, and whose counsel was "Catholic enough" (*consilia in dubiis satis catholica*). There was also an abbess of a house of secular canons in the diocese of Strassburg who worked to reform her house. In this effort, she once confessed to Nider, she was often sustained and strengthened directly by God, who granted her visions of a chalice containing the Eucharist. Beyond these individual accounts, Nider related at two points in the *Formicarius* that in the lands around Basel and Constance there were so many good and pious women seeking to lead devout religious lives that not enough convents existed to hold them all, and there were even too few beguinages to accommodate the numbers who sought entry.[66] Moreover, the entire *Formicarius* is full of positive examples of individual pious laywomen, most of whom Nider described as virgins. While he did not explicitly term any of these women "beguines," surely many of them must have been.[67]

In addition to the various tales involving beguines in the *Formicarius,* Nider wrote two important treatises on the questionable status of the lay religious and on the issue of lay poverty and mendicancy, *De secularium religionibus* (On the lay religious) and *De paupertate perfecta secularium* (On perfect poverty for the laity). These works, which exist only in manuscript copies, have received scant scholarly attention. Both were written, in all likelihood, in the mid-1430s at the Council of Basel, in the context of the debates over the status of beguines.[68] As noted in Chapter 1, a major dispute between the secular and mendicant clergy in Basel arose in the late spring of 1434, and in such conflicts beguines, who frequently had close associations with the mendicant orders, often served as easy targets. As early as the mid-thirteenth century, William of St. Amour, the leader of the secular clerics at the University of Paris, had attacked beguines as a part of his overall opposition to the mendicant orders, and this pattern continued throughout the fourteenth century as well.[69] The severe wave of persecutions directed against beguines in Basel in the early fifteenth century grew partly out of tensions between the secular and mendicant clergy in the city, and only a few years later, Franciscan tertiaries came under attack at the Council of Constance as part of a more general effort to limit the privileges and rights of the mendicant orders.[70] At the Council of Basel, beguines came under fire particularly in respect to their right to live in voluntary religious poverty, which was regarded as an issue of ecclesiastical reform. An anonymous tract on reform issued in early 1433 included among its points a call for "lollards and beguines" to stop receiving alms and to support themselves through their own labor, and in 1435 the Spanish cleric Andreas of Escobar called for a ban on beguines altogether. Again in 1439 the anonymous *Reformation of Kaiser Sigismund* demanded that beguines stop begging and work to support themselves. In addition, the treatise *Contra validos mendicantes* (Against healthy [lay] mendicants), written in 1438 by the well-known opponent of beguines Felix Hemmerlin, circulated widely in Basel during the council.[71]

Many religious reformers tended to look upon beguines with suspicion at best, not only for their (perceived) frequent connection to heresy but even more for their practice of voluntary poverty. Lay poverty and especially lay mendicancy seemed dangerous innovations that clearly challenged such biblical injunctions as Genesis 3:19, "In the sweat of your face you shall eat bread." Nider's former mentor, the Dominican reformer Johannes Mulberg, who led the persecution of beguines in Basel in the early 1400s, based his opposition to the lay religious life almost entirely on his conviction that only members of the approved mendicant orders were allowed to beg, because they had specific papal dispensation to do so.[72] Thus Nider faced an interesting dilemma when he confronted the issue of the lay religious. Would he, as a mendicant, support them in the face of attacks coming mainly from the secular clergy, or would he, as a dedicated reformer, follow the lead of Mulberg and others by condemning them as a threatening deformation in the church? Ultimately Nider did allow himself to be guided by his reformist convictions, but they led him to a conclusion that was diametrically opposed to Mulberg's. For Nider not only defended the beguines, he championed them, and his support was based not on the calculated interests of his order but on his own profound conviction of the value of voluntary poverty among the laity and of the lay religious way of life in general.

In the earlier of his two treatises on the lay religious, *De paupertate perfecta secularium,* Nider directly addressed the issues of lay poverty and mendicancy that so often lay at the heart of attacks on beguines in the later Middle Ages. True poverty, for him, meant evangelical poverty—the voluntary privation of temporal goods out of the desire to follow Christ's injunction "If you wish to be perfect, go sell what you have, and give to the poor" (Matthew 19:21).[73] Whether this type of poverty was appropriate for the laity, however, was much debated in the Middle Ages. Many authorities, both ecclesiastical and secular, disapproved of lay people's attempting to live a quasi-religious life, not because they objected to voluntary poverty taken up for Christ but because they feared these people would lead idle lives without engaging in productive work.[74] Nider was determined to overturn this line of condemnation. His first step was to prove that manual labor was not morally necessary for a good life. Here he drew a distinction, typical among the medieval religious orders, between physical labor and other forms of work, primarily the spiritual labors of prayer, contemplation, and so forth. Citing such authorities as Augustine and Aquinas, he argued that if physical labor impeded more useful activities, "it is better to abstain from manual work." While avoiding manual labor out of laziness was clearly a sin and remained impermissible, the laity was as entitled as those in religious orders to abstain from labor in order to contemplate and pray.[75] He then turned to the question whether mendicancy was permitted to the laity to support a life of contemplation and religious devotion. That is, could lay people not only live from charity and alms freely given but actively beg for them just as the mendicant orders did? Here he relied again on the greatest authority his order had produced, Thomas Aquinas, to argue that "mendicancy assumed for the sake of Christ not only must not be reproached, but should be greatly praised."[76]

Yet Nider was not content to end the matter there. He pressed the further question whether lay mendicancy was in fact superior to a life of poverty spent in manual labor. The issue here became extremely difficult, and ultimately, while Nider clearly sought to privilege mendicancy as much as possible, he did not want to argue completely against manual labor, which so many authorities had praised. His position, therefore, became both highly convoluted and highly qualified, wending through a thicket of seemingly contradictory earlier authorities either defending mendicancy or praising the value of labor.[77] To the modern mind, such argumentation can appear stultifying (and thus I refrain from expounding upon it at length), but in fact this was the very heart of the medieval scholastic enterprise. Convinced of the existence of a single definite truth on which all authorities must ultimately agree, Nider was certain that if he could harmonize apparently contradictory positions, he would arrive at this truth. That his arguments were so convoluted merely revealed the complexity of the issues involved. That he pressed himself to clarify the value of lay mendicancy when he could simply have ended his defense by proving its permissibility shows how deeply committed to the matter he was.

The conclusion Nider reached was a nuanced one in three parts. First, in most cases, to live at least partly through alms was more virtuous than to live entirely by labor, since doing so allowed time for other religious pursuits. Yet if the poor were able to support themselves sufficiently by relatively brief periods of honest labor, then it was better to do so than to live entirely by mendicancy and never labor at all. Yet a third conclusion was that if it was possible to acquire some but not all necessary sustenance from a few hours of labor, then it was better to live partially from labor and partially from mendicancy.[78] These conclusions, although somewhat convoluted, have several merits. By praising mendicancy while still valuing labor, Nider had crafted a compromise solution designed to appeal to as many people as possible. In a setting like the Council of Basel, where every member had an equal vote and compromise usually carried the day, such a moderate argument would doubtless have found a great deal of support. We can also see, however, how he managed to extend not just his defense but indeed his support to almost every type of lay religious—both those who labored and those who begged.[79] Finally, by resolving, at least to his own satisfaction, seemingly discordant earlier opinions, Nider would have been convinced that he had uncovered the truth.

Having worked out a way not only to protect but also to praise virtually all forms of lay poverty, Nider went on in his treatise dealing with the lay religious, the more general and more widely circulated *De secularium religionibus,* to address the question of the oft-condemned beguine status per se. He was fully aware of the long history of condemnation that the beguines had suffered, and he accepted that these condemnations were often justified and that beguines often did fall into error. He began his treatise, therefore, by outlining many of the key documents in that history, listing the eight charges of Free Spirit heresy directed against the beguines in the papal bull *Ad nostrum* and then noting that "the sect of the so-called beguines is specially condemned in its own right by *Cum de quibusdam.*"[80] He also cited John XXII's bull *Ratio recta,* which referred to the general condemnation in *Cum de quibusdam* and to the decision of an episcopal synod in Mainz in 1318 that used the newly issued *Cum de quibusdam* to ban all beguines from the diocese. He was also able to cite the condemnation of beguines by Bishop Johannes of Strassburg in 1317.[81]

Despite his familiarity with the many condemnations leveled against the beguines, or perhaps because of it, Nider was determined to defend the status of the lay religious as completely as he had defended them on the issue of poverty. He first considered the case of the Franciscan tertiaries, clearly the most easily defensible of all the lay religious. Such people, he was certain, were in no way affected by papal legislation against beguines, even if they lived exactly as the beguines did, since they were members of an approved order adhering to a papally sanctioned rule.[82] Although this position was by no means universally accepted in the late Middle Ages, he was able to draw on many standard legal authorities for support. Commentators on canon law such as Johannes Andreae, author of the ordinary gloss on the Clementines, as well as Paul of Liazariis and William of Monlezun and "almost all contemporary authorities," agreed that *Cum de quibusdam* did not apply to tertiaries.[83] Having exonerated those beguines who were members of the Franciscan third order from condemnation, he then broadened his defense to other lay religious not formally incorporated into an approved religious order. His argument here was that the legislation stemming from the Council of Vienne, over one hundred years earlier, on which many attacks against beguines were still based, had used the terms "beghard" and "beguine" very narrowly to refer only to lay people who were guilty of certain specified errors. In common usage, however, "beghard" and "beguine" could and did apply to anyone who followed a lay religious form of life, and thus for more than a century confusion had reigned over the extent of the papal condemnation. He noted, for example, the so-called escape clause in *Cum de quibusdam,* added directly after its seemingly total condemnation of the beguine status, which explicitly excluded from persecution "faithful women" who led honest and devout lives.[84] He also cited John XXII's bulls *Ratio recta* and *Cum de mulieribus,* in which the pope attempted to clarify the Vienne decrees and specified that beguines who lived free of error should not be molested by ecclesiastical authorities.[85]

Nider's argument seems clear and straightforward, and his interpretation of the Vienne decrees is actually in agreement with the most recent modern scholarly investigations of those documents.[86] But in the fifteenth century, with much clerical opinion running against beguines for a variety of reasons, few authorities saw fit to advance such a broad defense of the lay religious. We need only look back a few decades to the wave of persecutions directed against the beguines in Basel in the early 1400s. Here, as so often happened, attacks quickly spread from "independent" beguines, those unaffiliated or only informally affiliated with the mendicant orders, to the Franciscan third order itself. Numerous champions arose, mostly among the Franciscans, to defend the tertiaries, but no one attempted to protect the other beguines. In fact, almost every document drew a distinction, in some variation of phrasing, between the licit tertiaries and the other "beghards, lollards or *beghocs,* and female beguines or *swestriones* ... condemned under the law."[87] Doubtless this was a sound strategy, as officially recognized tertiaries were far easier to defend than other beguines, and thus the Franciscan order could at least save its own. Nider, however, refused to make such a compromise and vigorously supported all the lay religious, provided they did not fall into specific and identifiable error. The reason, it would appear, was that he regarded these people as an important and positive example of religious reform.

As a devout member of a religious order himself and as one committed to the reform of both his order and the Christian world at large, Nider could think of no better model for the laity than that provided by the religious orders. In his defense of lay poverty, he stated explicitly that any member of the laity able to observe one or all of the monastic vows of poverty, chastity, and obedience would benefit greatly by doing so, and he also advocated a monastic ideal for the laity in many of his sermons and other vernacular works.[88] The esteem in which he held those whom he termed the lay religious is evident throughout his writings, most notably in his *Formicarius*. There he recounted numerous examples of great piety among lay people, mainly women, many of whom were probably beguines. We shall have occasion to consider these examples more closely in Chapter 5, which explores Nider's great work at length. Here I simply note the contrast between his clear admiration for the piety of female beguines and his revulsion at the female iniquity that he believed underlay much of the horror of witchcraft.

Many clerical authorities in the later Middle Ages saw in the beguines and especially in the heresy of the Free Spirit, with which these women were often associated, a danger and a depravity only slightly less terrible than that represented by witchcraft. Moreover, beguines, at least, seem to have presented a far more immediate threat than witches, since they lived openly in numerous communities across much of northern Europe.[89] Where others feared potential abuse and error and even the looming threat of heresy, however, Johannes Nider was far more optimistic. In fact, as is evident particularly in regard to the Hussites, he seems to have been relatively unconcerned about the threat of heresy to the Christian faithful in his day. Although deeply involved in Hussite affairs for a brief period and strongly opposed to the Bohemian heretics, he adopted a pragmatic approach to them, and in the larger field of his thought they hardly seem to dominate. Likewise he was convinced that the heresy of the Free Spirit was fairly widespread, yet his accounts of its adherents, while often colorful, were relatively few. Clearly he was far more taken up with what he saw as the extremely positive aspects of lay religiosity, which were to be defended and encouraged, not attacked and eradicated. Thus the apparently easy connection between heresy and witchcraft, the quick slip from concern over one to anxiety over the other, does not hold. Nider, at least, was far less preoccupied by the threat of heresy than by the horrors of witchcraft. In reality, many witch trials certainly did develop out of the ongoing persecution of heresy in the early fifteenth century, and among inquisitors and secular judges in the field (so to speak) the search for heretics certainly did often shift into a hunt for witches. Many cases exist to support this assessment.[90] Yet on a theoretical level, the idea of witchcraft was quite distinct from the idea of heresy. Although the two had many similar characteristics, interest in and concern over one by no means depended on or entailed concern over the other.[91]

Nevertheless, a consideration of Nider's ideas on heresy and the lay religious does shed some light on where witchcraft might connect to other areas of his thought. The issue of reform has emerged as a central concern here. Most notably, Nider formulated his arguments in support of lay poverty and the lay religious way of life within the context of the larger debates on reform at the Council of Basel. Basel was, of course, also where he became interested in witchcraft, and, as we shall see, his ideas on this subject too were formulated and deployed very much within the context of reform. In order to understand the connection between witchcraft and reform in Nider's thought, however, we need first to understand exactly what reform meant for him and exactly what type of reformer he was.

4

REFORM OF THE ORDERS, REFORM OF THE RELIGIOUS SPIRIT

In modern scholarship Nider's prominence as an authority on witchcraft overshadows all else, but in his own age he would have been best known as a reformer. For at least the last decade of his life he was the principal leader of the observant movement in the Dominican province of Teutonia, which encompassed the entire southern half of the German-speaking world and was the scene of some of the most vibrant reform activity of the late Middle Ages. He personally introduced strict observance to at least five Dominican houses, and probably participated in the reform of many more.[1] In addition, through his involvement in the Council of Basel, his reputation and influence would have spread well beyond his own order. At the council, Nider's authority came from his position as a theologian, and it was during his time at Basel that he produced both of his major theological works on reform. Each of these treatises focused particularly on issues of reform and strict observance within the religious orders, but Nider's concerns were actually much broader. Like other prominent religious reformers of the fifteenth century, he simply tended to approach the idea of general rejuvenation and reinvigoration of the entire faith through the narrower issue of the reform of the orders.[2] Indeed, all of his other theological and pastoral works were deeply influenced by his reformist concerns, and thus an understanding of his approach to reform, and indeed his concept of reform, is essential to an understanding of all other areas of his thought.

Matters of religious reform appear at least tangentially in many of Nider's written works, and he addressed this issue directly in two major treatises. The first was the long work *De reformatione status cenobitici* (On the reform of the cenobitic status), written in mid to late 1431, as the Council of Basel was just beginning. It proved to be one of Nider's most popular works, circulating widely in manuscript form in the fifteenth century and going through three printed editions over the next two hundred years.[3] It probably served, as one expert thinks,

as a standard handbook for the Dominican observant movement, something
that no previous observant leader had yet produced.[4] Nider's other treatise, *De
abstinencia esus carnium* (On abstinence from eating meat), was written a few
years later in the latter half of 1434, also in Basel. Here he ostensibly dealt only
with abstinence among Benedictine monks, which was a subject of serious
debate at the council, but in fact he took the opportunity to address some much
broader reformist concerns as well.[5]

In these two treatises Nider revealed his ideas about reform more clearly than
in any other of his writings, yet even here he never really discussed such issues
directly. Such a wide variety of reform programs existed in the late Middle Ages
that only a careful analysis will reveal the variety of reform Nider advocated,
how he actually conceived of it, and what he saw as its ultimate goal and purpose. Too hasty a reading would distort the true nature of his reformist impulses
and render impossible a proper understanding of how reformist concerns inter-
acted with and informed the other areas of his thought and activity. He was not
an advocate of the type of reform most commonly associated with the early
fifteenth century, the movement for a general reform of the entire church in head
and members (*reformatio in capite et membris*). This variety of reform, which
actually focused mainly on issues of papal power and perceived abuses in the
Roman curia and other elements of the ecclesiastical hierarchy, dominated the
major late medieval councils of Constance and Basel. Nider, however, supported
a more limited sort of reform, focusing entirely on the "members" of the church,
primarily the religious orders. While in this sense his approach to reform was certainly more narrow than the general efforts of the great councils, it was in fact
neither simple nor direct. Although reformist activity within religious orders
typically centered on returning to a strict observance of the original rules
of those orders, his conception of this process and his understanding of its ultimate goals were far from straightforwardly conservative (as some scholars have
accused all late medieval religious reform programs of being).[6] He also allowed
for a progressive aspect of reform as a movement forward, a form of "novelty"
that would result in an improvement over earlier states. In fact, these two
conceptions of reform interwove in complex ways in his thought, so that ultimately the reestablishment of a previous state was seen as a progressive movement forward. This concept applied to religious orders and even (it would seem)
to the entire church, but to a greater degree it centered on moral and spiritual
regeneration within the individual faithful.

Promoting this spiritual reform was for Nider the most important type of
reformist activity, and all the institutional reforms he championed were aimed at
achieving a spiritual result. The real purpose of strict observance of the orders'
rules was to support spiritual regeneration among all the individual members

of the religious clergy. Yet his ultimate goals were broader still. For Nider, life within a religious order represented the clearest and most perfect example of the internal spiritual ascent toward God that was the true basis of all Christian life. He argued for strict observance because he felt that it promoted this internal striving for the divine. This is a critical point, for such spiritual reform, while obviously grounded in a monastic ideal, could apply to the laity as well. It was reform in this broadest sense that Nider hinted at when he advocated an essentially monastic ideal for the laity and held up the lay religious as an example of a beneficial and laudable form of Christian life. More generally, it was this conception of reform that he sought to address in his greatest work, the *Formicarius*, and that ultimately helped to shape his concerns about witchcraft.

VARIETIES OF REFORM IN THE EARLY FIFTEENTH CENTURY

Perhaps more than any other concept, the idea of reform dominated and in many ways defined the later fourteenth and especially the fifteenth century (as well as, almost needless to say, the sixteenth and early seventeenth centuries). Or, more accurately, many ideas of reform dominated this period, for a wide variety of movements—religious, social, political, and cultural—all categorized themselves as forms of *reformatio*, and what that concept might entail was understood in a wide variety of ways.[7] Even when the word "reform" was limited to its religious and ecclesiastical variants, it could contain a multitude of meanings. Unfortunately, rather than paying attention to the nuanced (and sometimes not so nuanced) differences in authorship, argument, and audience that marked late medieval reformist writings, too often historians have tried to comprehend all aspects of reform within the debates about the proper structure of the ecclesiastical hierarchy that dominated the great councils of Constance and Basel, and that thus also dominate the most readily available records of reformist activity from this period.[8] Such an approach would seriously distort Nider's efforts at reform and obscure the goals he hoped to attain. Worse still, it would obscure, if not obliterate, the connections between his reformist concerns and other areas of his thought. Thus we must be careful to distinguish exactly what his approach to reform really entailed and what his conception of reform really was.

In the early fifteenth century, issues of religious reform were often closely tied to issues of conciliarism, and the progress of reform was often seen by contemporaries (as it is by many modern scholars) as being linked to the success or failure of the great ecumenical councils of that period. Among the goals at which these councils, especially those of Constance and Basel, aimed was a general reform of the entire church in head and members. In practice, however, the councils focused most of their official energies on reforming the papacy and the Roman curia.[9] Leading theologians such as Jean Gerson, chancellor of the University of Paris and a prominent member of the Council of Constance, conceived of a general reform as necessarily rooted in the proper restructuring of the ecclesiastical hierarchy. Pierre d'Ailly, Gerson's teacher and another leading figure at Constance, also believed in the necessity of regular general councils to oversee an essentially top-down process of reform, and this view was fairly general among the other council fathers.[10] It was in the struggle of the councils to force change on intransigent popes that the doctrine of conciliarism, the idea that the rulings of a general council of the church superseded even papal authority, came into full force.[11]

Although conciliarism did represent one particular program of reform, however, it by no means encompassed all varieties of late medieval reform, nor were conciliarist and more general reformist concerns always identical.[12] Not all reformers, even those who generally supported the work of the councils, were necessarily conciliarists. Nor were all reformers convinced that a hierarchical approach, beginning with the head of the church and moving down, was the best method for achieving real and needed change. Johannes Nider, for one, despite his active support of the Council of Basel, at least in its early years, remained entirely unconvinced of the value of large general assemblies for advancing meaningful reform. In fact, he considered those who vested all their hopes for reform in the council to be "simple-minded." "I do not doubt," he wrote in his major treatise on reform, *De reformatione status cenobitici,* "that the general council can do much good, but it cannot reform everything at one time."[13] Rather than expecting any great success to emerge from Basel, he actually expressed grave concern that opponents of reform would simply use the council as an excuse to shirk other reform efforts, by declaring that the general council would soon reform the entire church and that in the meantime no other action should be taken. Nider scoffed at this argument, seeing it merely as a strategy to postpone more limited but ultimately more realistic and effective efforts at reform indefinitely. "To wish to be reformed only when all other things are reformed," he wrote, "is to wish never to be reformed except in the valley of Jehosaphat at the time of the Last Judgment."[14]

Such dour predictions cannot have won Nider much admiration from the more optimistic council members during Basel's early days, when excitement over the new synod's possibilities was running high. Still, his opinion was hardly unjustified. Nearly two decades earlier he had witnessed the failure of the Council of Constance to enact any meaningful general reform. In his *Formicarius* he described how high the hopes of the reformers at Constance had been, and how they had been frustrated in achieving their goals.[15] And though he had not attended the aborted council of Pavia-Siena in 1423–24, he surely would have been aware of its complete failure to enact any real reform.[16] Nor did he have cause to change his opinion after witnessing the course of the Council of Basel for six years. Writing in his *Formicarius* in 1437, he still expounded the same opinion of the possibility of a general reform of the entire church that he had earlier set forth in *De reformatione status cenobitici.* In the later work, however, he expressed his reservations even more clearly and vehemently. Through the character of a lazy student in dialogue with a learned theologian, Nider pointed out that six years of discussion and debate at Basel had produced few real reforms. He then had the student wonder whether the great council was of any worth at all. To this provocative statement he replied, in the voice of the theologian, that neither of the recent general councils, meaning Constance and Basel, had been held "entirely in vain." The first, after all, had healed the Great Schism, which had rent the papacy and all of Western Europe from 1378 until 1417, while the second had ended the threat of the Hussite heresy and restored Bohemia to the true faith. He wrote quite explicitly, however, that as far as a complete and general reform of the entire church was concerned, either immediately or in the near future, "I have within me no hope." There was too little support for such a reform among the rank-and-file clergy, there was too little leadership from the prelates of the church and the ecclesiastical hierarchy in Rome, and those within the church who truly desired real change were too much beset by the "persecutions of evil men" and could not concentrate fully on the work of reform.[17]

Given his bleak view of the ability of the Council of Basel to enact any meaningful general reform, we might well ask whether Nider hoped for any positive reformist action to come out of the council. As an obedient member of his order, he of course had no real choice in being assigned to the priory in Basel or in participating in the council once it convened there. Yet given the zeal with which he performed his tasks and the responsibility the council placed upon him, it seems clear that he was an enthusiastic member of the assembly. He told in his *Formicarius* how excited he had been by the reformist debates at Constance, and there seems little reason to doubt that he was any less excited about the possibilities at Basel.[18] The discussions he would have wanted to hear, however, would not have been deliberations about reforming the papacy, the curia, and the rest of the ecclesiastical hierarchy. Rather he would have anticipated with much optimism the more narrowly focused work for the reform of the religious orders that took place in Basel under the auspices of the council, but for the most part not officially by the council itself.[19] For, as he wrote in his *Formicarius,* if a general reform of the entire church was beyond reach, still a more limited rejuvenation within religious orders, and ultimately within individual religious houses, remained possible.[20]

The Council of Basel gathered together hundreds of abbots, priors, and their representatives, as well as theologians and thinkers from every religious order and from all across Europe. The council thus served as a center of communication and a forum for the spread and exchange of ideas.[21] There seems to have been a great deal of excitement in some orders over the opportunity to discuss and resolve at Basel matters of purely internal reform. Meetings were arranged and tracts and treatises were composed and read to influence opinions in the discussions both within and among religious orders.[22] In fact, the very first recorded discussion of reform associated with the Council of Basel took place between two like-minded clerics clothed in different habits. In February 1431, months before the official opening of the council, the Benedictine abbot Alexander of Vézelay was one of the first foreign prelates to arrive in the city. He "immediately sought out the prior of the Order of Preachers," Johannes Nider, and the two men began discussing the subject of reform.[23]

Beginning, perhaps, with this conversation, and certainly during the rest of his time at Basel, Nider worked diligently to promote and support the reform of the orders. Both of his reformist treatises, the general *De reformatione status cenobitici,* written shortly after the council opened, and the more focused *De abstinencia esus carnium,* which must have been written in late 1434, only shortly before Nider's departure for the University of Vienna, deal specifically with this subject. Certainly he was not averse to using the council as a means toward such limited reform. Consider the context in which he wrote *De abstinencia esus carnium.* Abstinence from meat was a reform issue in many religious orders, but particularly among Benedictine monks. In this work Nider argued strongly that all Benedictines should observe strict abstinence, in accordance with the Rule of Saint Benedict. The major obstacle to his argument was the fact that since 1336 the Benedictines had enjoyed an official and fairly explicit papal dispensation to eat meat, at least on certain days of the week. He tried valiantly to rationalize this ruling away, but in the end he simply stated that in this case the pope, Benedict XII, had been wrong, and his authority "must simply be denied."[24] Although Nider made no explicit reference to the power of a general church council to overturn papal rulings, the implications of such a treatise written at the Council of Basel would have been fairly obvious, especially in 1434, when the second major crisis between Pope Eugenius IV and the council was just beginning to brew and some members of the council were beginning to develop fairly radical doctrines of conciliar authority. Yet if Nider was no supporter of arbitrary papal power, neither was he really a conciliarist. Rather, he was a reformer, and if he seemed to support the council over the pope, he did so only because, like the members of observant movements in many orders, he felt that the cause of religious reform could be advanced more effectively through the

Council of Basel, whatever its limitations in enacting truly universal reforms, than by the obstructionist Pope Eugenius IV.[25]

Given the overall situation at Basel, in which observants from many orders were brought together and were able to confer on issues of common interest, it is perhaps not surprising that Nider's reformist concerns, while limited in the sense that they did not entail much support for a general reform of the entire church, were nevertheless hardly restricted to his own order. In his programmatic writings on reform, he clearly saw himself as a member of the religious clergy generally, not just as an observant Dominican. When in 1431 the Dominican master general, Barthélemy Texier, asked him to write a treatise specifically on the reform of the Dominican order, Nider responded with the far more general *De reformatione status cenobitici,* covering all clergy following a cenobitic way of life. In *De abstinencia esus carnium,* in contrast, he dealt with a single religious order, that of the Benedictine monks rather than the Dominican friars, but with an issue, abstinence from meat, that was important to observant movements in many orders.[26] In each of these treatises he was careful to include examples and arguments drawn from numerous religious orders, clearly attempting to make his work relevant and appealing to as many of his cenobitic brethren as possible. Especially to the Franciscans, longtime rivals of their fellow mendicants the Dominicans, he seems to have held out his hand, perhaps never more pointedly than in *De abstinencia esus carnium,* where he countered the greatest authority of his own order, Thomas Aquinas, with arguments of the Franciscan theologian Alexander of Hales. Whereas Aquinas held that for monks to eat meat was not a mortal sin, "Alexander of Hales says that [those] monks sinned very gravely who first introduced the abuse of eating meat, and even today those who knowingly continue this abuse out of desire and lust for pleasure sin very gravely."[27] The fact that a Dominican author would cite a Franciscan authority in a treatise ostensibly addressed only to Benedictine monks shows just how widely reformist concerns were spread among the religious orders in the early fifteenth century.

That Nider should have demonstrated a concern for inclusion and a desire to appeal broadly to all the religious orders is not surprising. In the wake of the terrible papal schism, which had divided all of Western Europe for nearly forty years and which had been healed only at the Council of Constance not even two decades earlier, unity and solidarity were important watchwords at the Council of Basel (notwithstanding the fact that within a few years the council itself would choose schism rather than submit to Pope Eugenius IV's command that it disband). In fact, one of the major goals set for the council was to achieve a union between Rome and the Orthodox Church in Constantinople, thus drawing the Greek East into Western Christendom and ending a schism that dated back long before the great rupture of the fourteenth century.[28] One of the most powerful arguments that critics of reform raised at Basel was that reformers, through their demands for strict observance and their refusal to compromise, were causing a great deal of strife and division within religious orders, and Nider was forced to counter this attack in *De reformatione status cenobitici*.[29] Beyond any concern to avoid unnecessary and damaging dissension in the ranks of the religious clergy, however, his inclusiveness was founded on his very conception of reform. Had he viewed reform only in the purely conservative sense of undoing certain specific corruptions that had crept into religious observance, he might well have found little common ground with the members of other orders, each with its own ordinances. But Nider saw a higher and more general purpose to reform, a progressive aspect of religious renewal that ultimately united all the orders and made their work central to the perpetual development of the faith.

RELIGIOUS REFORM AS SPIRITUAL REFORM

Nider's conception of religious reform was guided by his deeply held conviction that the cenobitic status, when properly observed, provided the most perfect model of life available to humanity on earth. Indeed, the religious orders, when they were true to their own ideals, offered a much-needed example for the rest of the Christian world to follow, or at least to which the lesser Christian faithful might aspire.[30] If we hold this view in mind, his reform treatises, which at first appear to be narrowly focused on self-regulation within the religious orders, can upon closer inspection reveal broader vistas of thought. For Nider, reform was as much a progressive force as it was a conservative one, and ultimately his concept of reform had less to do with institutional change than with individual spiritual regeneration and personal reunion with God.[31]

In the most basic sense, to an observant friar as indeed to any observant member of a religious order in the late Middle Ages, reform meant to remake, to return to an earlier, superior state that had been lost.[32] For the religious orders reform entailed a return to and strict observance of their original rules and early constitutions. Nider clearly addressed this notion of reform at the very outset of *De reformatione status cenobitici*. He dedicated this work to the master general of his order, Barthélemy Texier, who, so Nider wrote, worked diligently for the reform of his "collapsed order." At Texier's request, Nider had written this work in the hope that his master's "form of religious life, once so beautiful but now, alas, lost to many, can more easily be reintroduced."[33] Later in his treatise he wrote even more explicitly that the religious status—that is, the proper form of cenobitic life—was defined above all else by the rules and statutes of the orders.

Where these rules were no longer observed, reform was the "introduction anew" of this lost form of life.[34] *De abstinencia esus carnium* also clearly addressed this concept of reform, since the entire treatise focused on encouraging the strict interpretation of two chapters about abstinence in the Rule of Saint Benedict.[35]

By the early fifteenth century, conditions in many religious orders had changed drastically since those orders had been in their infancy. Over the years, the original rules and statutes established by the founding figures of the orders had been interpreted and even altered to accommodate changing conditions, until actual practice and observance sometimes bore little relation to the original regulations. For reformers like Nider, the liberal granting of dispensations—that is, exceptions and modifications to the original rule—stood as one of the chief causes of the orders' collapse into decadence. "Every dispensation asked of a prelate," he cautioned, "ought to be granted [only] to the honor of Christ, in whose person he dispenses, or to the utility of the church, which is the body of Christ."[36] Practices at variance with the rule that had grown up over time, he argued, should be seen not as "customs" but as "corruptions" of the order, and any dispensation that violated a point on which the original rule was clear and absolute was "not a dispensation but a dissipation."[37] To bolster his arguments, he provided some visceral examples of the harm wrought by deviation from religious ordinances. Drawing on an account from his own order, for example, he related the story of a Dominican prior who had granted a dispensation to eat meat to two friars without proper cause. That night the prior awoke with a start to find that a demon had entered his chamber. Terrified, he asked the creature why it was there, and it replied, "I came to visit those brothers who had eaten meat."[38] Seen in this light, an illicit dispensation might well appear, as Nider rather wryly noted, to be merely an official license for a monk or friar to enter into hell.[39]

Thus far, Nider as a reformer appears to have been entirely conservative. His concept of proper religious life was contained entirely in the rules and constitutions of the religious orders, and he was suspicious of any development that might have been at variance with those early statutes. He conceived of religious reform as the return of the orders to strict observance of their rules. This does not mean, however, that late medieval religious reform, even when rooted in such cenobitic ideals, was entirely conservative, or that reformers were fixated totally on the past even as a new age was about to break on Western Europe. Rather a certain duality was inherent in the Christian conception of reform. In their ideals reformers were firmly rooted in the past, but in their return to the past they also saw a progression into the future. This notion of progressive reformation, or "creative imitation," as one scholar has put it, can be difficult to grasp, for our own notion of progress is now considerably different than that

common in the Middle Ages.[40] Nider, however, represents this dichotomy perfectly, both confirming and complicating our notions of the conservative nature
of late medieval religious reform. For even in his reformist works he was not
entirely opposed to novelty and progress. Indeed, he thought of reform as being
crucial to the progress of the faith.

This dichotomy begins to become clear when we examine Nider's handling of
the issue of "novelty" (*novitas*) in *De reformatione status cenobitici*. Certain
opponents of reform, he noted, argued that reform was itself a novelty, a new
development that aimed to change long-standing practice, and therefore should
be opposed. This was a common objection to reform in the late Middle Ages,
essentially an attempt by opponents to hoist the strict observants on their own
conservative petard. The response to this objection should have been obvious—
that reform was in no way a new development, but was in fact a return to the
past. Nider, however, did not choose to make this argument. Rather, he launched
into a long defense of the very concept of *novitas*.

Novelty, he wrote, could be of two sorts. Certainly there was wicked novelty,
but there was also a positive sort of new development. He reminded his readers
of the words of Saint Paul, "We should serve in newness of spirit, and not in the
oldness of the letter" (Romans 7:6), a somewhat surprising reference from the
leader of a reform movement dedicated to the strict observance of the written
rule of his order. He went on to cite five forms of "good novelty" found in Scripture. First there was the newness of heart with which one repented of one's former life. Then there was the new voice with which to speak the words of Christ,
and, in the words of the Psalms, to "sing a new song unto the Lord." One would
also find new relationships with others when one entered true belief. One gained
a new reputation and "new name" by repenting and turning to God. Finally,
and most important, there was new life in the Lord and a new way to salvation
through the blood of Christ.[41] Clearly, none of these forms of novelty or newness
really entailed progress in the modern sense. Rather, at the heart of each lay a
going back, a return to the Lord, a repentance of sin, a renewal of faith. Even if
acquiring the faith was a new development for the individual, this development
was based on a return to the age-old principles of that faith, not on some new
idea or innovation. Far from employing these examples as part of an argument
against innovation, however, Nider was demonstrating that reform was an innovation of a positive sort, a good new thing, *bona novitas*. In these examples,
then, he must have seen progress and innovation. To him they represented, like
reform itself, the only possible form of good progress—a progress that was
not just rooted in the past but in fact was moving toward the past.

One aspect of this type of progressive reform was certainly institutional, most
clearly exemplified by the founding of new religious orders. The Cluniac order,

Nider noted, originated in a reform of earlier Benedictine monasticism. The Cistercian order, too, was founded in a reform of the Benedictines, and represented a return to a stricter interpretation of the Rule of Saint Benedict. He also held up the origins of the Premonstratensians and the Dominicans as examples of such reform.[42] He regarded these orders, apparently, as new, progressive developments, but also as regressions of a sort toward some original, perfect form of religious life. In fact, he clearly considered the foundation of every religious order to be, in this sense, a reform. He explicitly referred to Saint Benedict, Saint Augustine, Saint Basil, and even Saint Anthony, the founder of monasticism, as reformers, and shortly thereafter he added Saint Dominic and Saint Francis to the list.[43] But Nider's greatest example of innovative reform, and his most intriguing, was his clear implication that Christ himself, in founding the church on earth, was acting as a religious reformer, the first and greatest of the great tradition that would then stretch down through all the monastic fathers.[44] This continual line of reform would apparently break only at the end of time, when the church, now fully reformed back to its original perfection, would appear as the New Jerusalem of Revelation descending out of heaven.[45]

The book of Revelation, however, obviously has more to do with the final coming of God's kingdom and the ultimate salvation of the faithful than with any institutional renewal, and for Nider the inherent good of reform, the progress and the "good novelty" it entailed, was not primarily institutional. Rather true religious reform resulted in a spiritual sort of progress within the reformed monks and friars, a rejuvenation of faith and a closer union with Christ. He indicated to some extent this true purpose of reform in his selection of biblical examples of "good novelty," all of which dealt with internal spiritual renewal, but he developed this point much more extensively, although still not very directly, in his discussion of the results reform was supposed to achieve and the benefits it would bring. Here he made clear that institutional reforms, to which he actually gave rather scant attention, merely facilitated personal spiritual repentance and renewal. The real goal of reform was, in short, not simply the improvement of religious observance within the orders but the resurrection of true religious life.

THE RESULTS OF REFORM

The scope of Nider's reformist concerns and the broad impact he expected from even limited reform within the religious orders is evident throughout his major treatise on the subject, *De reformatione status cenobitici*. Rather than a narrow handbook specifying steps that the religious clergy needed to take in order to eliminate specific abuses in their orders, he produced an extensive theological defense of the very idea of reform, and inasmuch as he was addressing members of all orders, he was necessarily expansive in his descriptions and arguments. There is no need here for a detailed examination of all the individual points raised in this treatise, but a brief overview of its structure will help flesh out Nider's view of religious reform and reveal how, in a way, its very breadth was critical to its ultimate point. Divided into three books, *De reformatione* treats in turn the various lapses that existed among the contemporary religious, the means to reform, and finally the benefits reform would bring. In the first book, Nider set forth fifteen general arguments commonly used to justify the current nonobservant way of life in many monasteries and convents, such as that official dispensations had sanctioned current practices and that reform movements caused harmful dissension within the orders.[46] He then proceeded to debunk each of these arguments in turn. As for how lapsed orders could be reformed, he felt no need to set out any detailed program, since he believed that the authentic religious status was based simply on strict observance of the original rules and constitutions of the orders. In the treatise's second book he did list various specific causes of decay within the orders, such as wicked prelates, illicit dispensations, and lack of religious study, but his solution to all such problems was simply to avoid them in the first place.[47] The problem of wicked prelates, for example, could be solved simply enough by not promoting unworthy men to such offices.[48] Otherwise he listed only a few common-sense points as to what was needed to conduct reform successfully, such as that capable men must be available to carry out the reform and that all officials involved must be united in their commitment to reformist goals.[49]

In the third book of *De reformatione status cenobitici*, Nider turned to the manifold "fruits of reform," which he divided into three broad categories: the purely temporal, those that benefited both body and spirit, and the purely spiritual.[50] Whatever category they fell into, these benefits were all of an extremely general moral nature, and ranged from the mundane (not needing to enter into marriage) to the sublime (the assurance that one would be leading a life in conformity with the life and passion of Christ).[51] None is very surprising to hear from a medieval religious cleric. What is interesting is that these "fruits of reform" are so general that they would seem to apply to all the religious clergy, not specifically the observant members of the various orders, and except for the opening rubric of the book Nider did indeed refer to these results throughout as the *fructus religionis*, not the *fructus reformationis*. Here we have arrived at the very heart of his conception of religious reform and the largest, although never clearly stated, point of his reformist treatises. Within the orders, strict observance represented not just a superior form of religious life but the only true form of religious life.

Throughout his reforming treatises Nider adopted a moderate tone, stressing understanding, compromise, and unity in the enactment of reform. That reform should not take place at all, however, was unacceptable and unimaginable. Those who stubbornly opposed reform were to him the most evil of men, and, abandoning his usual restraint, he railed at the "astute and perverse men" who sought at every turn to block pious reform with "very sly objections and arguments."[52] Such corrupt clerics—not those who simply had difficulty living up to all the requirements of strict observance but those who reveled in their decadence and sought in every way to maintain their corrupt way of life—he compared to the Israelites who fled Egypt and fell into idolatry in the desert.[53] Those who did not accept reform were not just inferior religious, they were not religious at all. Responding to the argument that reformers were dividing the orders, Nider's reply was simple, straightforward, and brutal. Reform did not divide an order, but rather revived it, while among the nonreformed (or the "deformed," as he would have it) "no order remains, but eternal horror dwells."[54] Taken in isolation, this statement might be dismissed simply as forceful rhetoric. Seen in the light of the treatise's conclusions, however, this brief explosion of anger seems to reveal the core of Nider's entire reform program.

According to Nider, the reform of the religious orders for which he worked so diligently throughout his time at the Council of Basel would benefit the church "in many ways."[55] The greatest single benefit, never stated explicitly but clearly intimated, was that reform allowed for true religious life. Only then could all the other specific benefits enumerated in the third book of his long treatise, which he more accurately termed the fruits of religious life itself rather than the fruits of reform, begin to accrue to those who followed a strict religious observance. As a devout friar himself, Nider was fully convinced that the religious orders represented the highest and most perfect form of life possible on earth, and this view was generally held by most people, lay and clerical, throughout the Middle Ages. By turning their backs on all things worldly, the monks and friars freed themselves to concentrate solely on spiritual matters. Obviously, at least to Nider and other reformers who shared his views, if earthly concerns for wealth, property, or pleasure crept into monasteries and convents and were allowed to remain there, this focus on the divine would be shattered. Nonreformed members of religious orders, of course, had rather different opinions on these matters. They were not all corrupt and decadent, and many truly believed their way of life was appropriate.[56] Nider, however, found them contemptible and brushed aside all their arguments.

The greatest of the "fruits of reform," the overall goal toward which Nider directed his efforts and arguments, was simply the reestablishment of true religious life within the orders. And the ultimate purpose of the cenobitic life was to support and sustain the personal striving toward the divine in which all religious were supposed to engage. The external aspects of reform, then, were really critical only insofar as they supported the spiritual regeneration that Saint Paul had deemed essential to the Christian faith so long before.[57] When religious reform is understood in this sense, its broad importance for Nider becomes evident, and clarifies many aspects of his reform program on which we have already touched. Promoting strict observance within religious orders was a matter not simply of correcting some specific abuse or corruption but rather of advancing the personal spiritual reform that was one of the most basic elements of Christianity. Thus such reform might be seen as essential to the progress of the faith as a whole toward its appointed biblical end. Very clearly, this sort of reform was the necessary first step toward a real general reform of the entire church, which the Council of Basel was erroneously trying to achieve immediately and directly by structural change.

In this understanding of religious reform as an essentially spiritual process lies also the connection between Nider's deep commitment to strict observance and his other activities. For his concern with reform did not stop at cloister walls but extended to all of Christian society, and he regarded the reform of the religious orders as merely a first step toward an ultimate, if distant, general spiritual reformation throughout the entire body of the church. Clearly the ideals of repentance of sin, renewal of faith, and increased reception of divine love were not limited solely to the religious orders of Western Europe. All believing Christians were, or at least should have been, deeply concerned with such matters. The religious clergy, leading lives more intensely spiritual than those of either the laity or even the secular clergy, simply provided the best example of these virtues. Having turned their backs on this world even while living in it, they stood somewhere between earth and heaven, and it was they who were expected to lead the way into God's kingdom.[58] One of the specific benefits of reform within the orders to which Nider pointed was that observant monks and friars would serve as examples to others, both clerics and laity; they would win conversions, and by their example they might prevent many of the faithful from lapsing into sin.[59] For him the reform of the orders was only a single, albeit crucial, aspect of larger spiritual renewal within the faith.

Nider was not interested in the sort of structural reforms of the ecclesiastical hierarchy most often associated with the late medieval councils of Constance and Basel. Indeed, he thought such reform efforts were hopeless and might do more harm than good. The reform he promoted was more limited, focusing on the religious orders. Yet even here his conception of reform was not simply conservative and reactive, nor was it really institutional. He located true religious progress in personal spiritual reform, which the cenobitic life, when free of corruption, most perfectly exemplified. But even such spiritual reform within the orders he saw as only the first step in a larger process that would eventually encompass all the Christian faithful. He based his support for beguines and other lay religious on his conviction that lay people would benefit greatly from adopting religious vows and leading a quasi-religious life. Yet he also understood how rigorous the monastic life was, and that anything like a literal imitation of it was beyond the capacity of most of the laity.[60] Since to make a vow and then to fail to uphold it was a serious sin, he concluded that in the end, most people might be better advised simply to practice poverty (or chastity or other forms of monastic devotion) diligently without swearing to it, rather than making a hasty vow and risking a lapse.[61]

As a reformer, Nider was deeply interested in the moral struggles and the spiritual advancement of all the laity, however strong their faith. Some were so devout that they could match monks or friars in their spiritual exercises and in the rigor of their lives. Most, however, could look to the reformed orders only for inspiration rather than in the hope of real imitation. Yet these people too could experience some level of moral and spiritual rejuvenation. Indeed, the closer they stood to sin, the more desperately they needed this sort of personal reform. As a theologian and a member of the Council of Basel, Nider developed and expounded ideas of reform that focused on cenobitic ideals and centered on religious orders. As a Dominican, a member of an order specially charged with preaching and with the pastoral care of souls, he sought to spread the message of personal reform as widely and as forcefully as possible to all of Christian society.[62] In this reform effort, his magnum opus, the *Formicarius*, stands as his most significant work (although, needless to say, he included in it no complex theological arguments on reform, which would have been lost on most of the people he sought to reach). Here Nider's reformist desires and concerns, as well as his obvious and understandable monastic inclinations, shaped his perceptions of lay spirituality and of the moral state of the entire world around him. These factors also contributed to the intense concern over demonic power and activity in the world that would ultimately give rise to his preoccupation with witchcraft.

5

THE REFORM OF THE CHRISTIAN WORLD

JOHANNES NIDER'S *FORMICARIUS*

"Go to the ant, O sluggard, and consider its ways and learn wisdom."[1] With this injunction from Proverbs 6:6, Johannes Nider began his great but diffuse collection of morally edifying stories, the *Formicarius,* and he continued to use ants, their forms and qualities, as a loose structuring motif throughout—hence the title of the work, which translates as "The anthill." The *Formicarius* was by far the most important of all his writings. That statement was doubtless as true for Nider himself as it is in regard to the later influence of this lengthy and varied treatise. Nider clearly invested more of himself in the *Formicarius* than in any other work. As we have seen, it featured the character of a Dominican theologian who instructed and enlightened a lazy but curious student of his order, the "sluggard" of the proverb.[2] Although unnamed, the theologian clearly represented Nider himself, and in this guise he related stories he had heard and events he had witnessed throughout his life, from his earliest youth down to his time in Basel and Vienna. Thus the *Formicarius* served as a kind of personal *summa* collecting a lifetime of religious experience and observation. None of Nider's other works was to achieve the same level of baleful influence attained by his accounts of witchcraft in the fifth book of the *Formicarius,* especially when they came to be broadly quoted in the infamous *Malleus maleficarum,* written some fifty years later. Indeed, the entire fifth book was later included in several early printings of the *Malleus,* and thus helped to shape European thought on witchcraft for centuries to come.[3]

Given the importance of the *Formicarius,* especially the significant influence it exerted on later literature dealing with witchcraft, it is not surprising that in modern scholarship this work is by far the best known of Nider's writings. Nevertheless, as recently as 1991 Carlo Ginzburg was still able to refer to this magnum opus as "more quoted than analyzed."[4] Some more recent studies of late medieval witchcraft have begun to read the *Formicarius* more closely and to apply more careful analysis to it, most notably the partial edition of the work along with extensive commentary by Catherine Chène in the collection *L'imaginaire du sabbat,* and the excellent study by Werner Tschacher, *Der Formicarius des Johannes Nider.* With these few notable exceptions, however, the *Formicarius* remains largely unexplored. In particular, relatively little effort has been made to understand the work as anything other than a treatise on witchcraft.[5]

To some extent, this remarkable ignorance about such an important source for late medieval religious and cultural history can be blamed on the *Formicarius* itself. The work is essentially a long collection of loosely related stories, instructional or illustrative of certain moral points, told by the theologian to his young pupil. Clearly these are exempla, brief edifying tales intended for excerption and use in sermons.[6] Thus the *Formicarius* naturally lends itself to being quoted. At the same time, it stubbornly resists analysis. While the work has its precedents in earlier religious literature, it is very much sui generis, not quite fitting into any of the easy categories that encompass most of Nider's other writings.[7] All of his other works discussed here have been more or less straightforward theological treatises, each advancing a coherent position or argument and each more or less clearly situated within an ongoing debate in late medieval religious culture. The *Formicarius* is a far more literary work that can be read in many ways and for many purposes. For this reason, it is an extremely important source for the study of religious life in the early fifteenth century generally, allowing access and insight into numerous aspects of the late medieval religious world. In earlier chapters I have considered this work insofar as it contains material touching on issues of witchcraft, heresy, and reform. But for my ultimate purpose, such a piecemeal approach will not suffice. The larger meaning of the *Formicarius* and the full meaning of the accounts of witchcraft it contains can be grasped only when the treatise is considered as a whole.

Overall, the *Formicarius* is best seen as a work of reform. Here, however, Nider was not arguing for a return to strict observance and practice within a single ecclesiastical institution or religious order, nor was he debating with other theologians and reformers about the acceptability of a certain narrow status or mode of life. Rather, he aimed at a reform of the most basic and most important sort—a moral and spiritual regeneration among the faithful at all levels of Christian society. Given that his great work was essentially a collection of preaching exempla, Nider would have intended this material to reach a wide segment of Christian society through the medium of popular sermons. As R. N. Swanson has written about late medieval popular preaching generally, such sermons would have been intended to "define sin, castigate, urge penance and a return to something like pristine innocence by the rejection of sin, and offer hope of salvation by acceptance and enactment of the requirements of the Christian life."[8]

FORMICARIVM
IOANNIS NYDER,
S. THEOLOGIAE
DOCTORIS, ET ECCLE-
SIASTÆ PRÆSTANTISSIMI,
IN QVINQVE LIBROS
D·I·V·I·S·V·M·

Quibus Christianus quilibet, tũ admirabili Formicarum exem-
plo, tum historijs pro re accommodatis, & ad parandam
sibi sapientiam, & ad vitam honestè piéq; insti-
tuendam, efficacissimè eruditur.

Opus singulare, miraculis & exemplis refertissimum,

Ad complura vetera exemplaria collatum, ab innumeris
mendis expurgatum, & breuibus notis illustratum.

Opera & studio GEORGII COLVENERII Alosten-
sis, S. Theol. Licent. & Profess. & librorum
in Academia Duacena Visitatoris,

DVACI,

Ex Officina BALTAZARIS BELLERI, Typo-
graphi iurati, Sub Circino aureo.
ANNO M. DCII.

Title page of *Formicarius*, Douai 1602 edition. (Courtesy, the Newberry Library.)

331

Liber Quintus.

DE MALEFICIS ET EORVM
DECEPTIONIBVS.

Colores diuersi quid in sacra scriptura significant.
Quòd tribus modis deluduntur hominū men-
tes, & de nocturnis exercitibus & equitibus,
quid in bono, vel in malo significent.

CAPITVLVM I.

 LTIMO loco per libellum quintum
sub formicarum proprietatibus de maleficis & eorum deceptionibus conclu-
dere restat. *Sunt autem formica in coloribus*
varia, quia quædam nigra, alia rufa, aut pallida. Per
colores autem talium varia conditio vitiorum potest intelligi; quamuis ipsa animalia de se bona sint,
sicuti omnes Dei creaturæ. Sicut enim per albedi-
nem, & cādorem vestium secundum beatum Gre-
gorium, virtutum puritas, & munditia, ita per colores declinantes ab albedine secundum maius &
minus vitiorum fæculentia, sacro testante eloquio,
consueuit accipi. Hinc est quòd beatus Ioannes vidit in Apocalypsi vj. sub quatuor coloribus equo-
rum vnum nigrum. Nam primus albus, secundus
rufus, tertius niger, & quartus pallidus fuisse de-
scribitur: vbi per album Christi caro purissima: per
rufum,

1 Tim. 4.
Greg. ho-
mil. 21.
& 29. in
euang. di-
cit gaudiū
& sólēni-
tatē mētis
designare.
a. b. m.
fætulētia.

Incipit of the fifth book of *Formicarius*, Douai 1602 edition. (Courtesy,
the Newberry Library.)

This is precisely the purpose that the stories in the *Formicarius* were designed to achieve. It was through these essential preaching functions familiar to any member of the Dominican order—the definition of sin, castigation, and exhortation to penance and right behavior—that Nider hoped to effect a reform in the broadest sense across Christian society.

Like the *Formicarius* itself, the analysis here will be somewhat diffuse, but an overriding purpose will prevail. The overall structure and larger literary context of the treatise, as well as the forms, antecedents, and traditions on which it drew, provide the necessary background for understanding Nider's great work. Whatever its roots in earlier theological and didactic traditions, however, the *Formicarius* was very much a work of its own time. The various stories of miracles, wonders, and sin that Nider collected present a rich picture of the moral and spiritual landscape of Europe in the early fifteenth century. Writing as a reformer, he pointed out many religious failings and shortcomings of faith, as well as much sin and corruption, but he also readily praised what was laudable in the religious world of his day, and he continually rehearsed the ways in which men and women could grow stronger in the faith. Although he intended his message for a general lay audience, his perceptions of the world and his concerns were deeply influenced by his own situation as a member of a religious order. This is perhaps nowhere clearer than in his preoccupation with chastity and virginity. Yet here, as elsewhere, his ideas were neither simple nor entirely straightforward. Although such matters occupy only a portion of Nider's attention in the *Formicarius,* exploring his thought in these areas clarifies his perceptions of female spirituality and ultimately, of course, his perception of women as especially susceptible to the seductions of the devil and the crimes of witchcraft. Yet Nider's concern over witchcraft was not rooted primarily in any fear of the sinful nature of women. Throughout the *Formicarius* he recounted a wide range of spiritual dangers that he perceived as threats to Christian society. He focused time and again on tales of visionary and demonic experiences. Indeed, it would not be unfair to say that such experiences were the principal subject of his great work. His preoccupation with these matters grew directly from his reformist concerns, and ultimately led him (even as they will lead us) to the matter of witchcraft.

CONTEXT, STRUCTURE, AND PURPOSE OF THE *FORMICARIUS*

If the *Formicarius* is a difficult work to summarize and fit neatly into a narrow genre, at least it is fairly easy to date and localize. Internal evidence clearly shows that Nider wrote the work mainly in 1437, beginning perhaps in late 1436 and finishing in early 1438.[9] During this period he was in Vienna as a member of the theological faculty of the university there. Nevertheless, neither the Dominican priory nor the University of Vienna provided the main intellectual context for the composition of the *Formicarius*. The long treatise was, as Nider's biographer Kaspar Schieler aptly put it, "really the work of almost his entire later life."[10] The stories and examples that he related, drawn mainly from his personal experiences and discussions with clerical and lay authorities, reflect the geographic scope of his movements. That is, the *Formicarius* presents a picture of late medieval religious life across the whole southern swath of German-speaking lands: modern Switzerland, southern Germany, Austria, and the Rhineland as far north as Cologne. The stories and exempla related are set almost exclusively in this region, concentrated in areas where Nider stayed for long periods: Cologne, Vienna, Nuremberg, and Basel. This is also the region in which the *Formicarius* had its greatest, indeed almost its exclusive, readership. Of the twenty-seven known manuscript copies of the work, virtually all originated in this area.[11] Yet to describe the context of the *Formicarius* as the entire area through which Nider moved in the course of his life, while in one sense certainly true, seems too broad a categorization to be really helpful or informative.

More narrowly characterized, the real context for the composition of the *Formicarius* was clearly the Council of Basel. Of the many stories that Nider related in this large work, by far the greatest number he either heard or experienced directly during his time at Basel. Particularly with his stories of witchcraft, he must have begun collecting tales, if not composing the actual work in which they would eventually appear, while at the council. Many of the examples of witchcraft that he presented in the *Formicarius* were situated in the Simme valley, which lies some seventy-five miles to the south of Basel, in the Alps of the Bernese Oberland. He heard these stories, so he wrote, from the secular judge Peter of Bern, who had conducted numerous witch trials in the region. Nider maintained that he had conferred with Peter "extensively and profoundly" about the subject of witchcraft.[12] In late 1428 or early 1429, before he came to Basel to stay, Nider visited Bern, and he could have met Peter on this occasion, or Peter might have come to Basel at some point in the following years. Certainly at no other time was Nider so near to Bern for any extended period, and we have no indication that Judge Peter ever traveled extensively beyond Bernese territory.[13] Nider also heard stories of witchcraft from various other sources at Basel, including an account of the famous trial of Joan of Arc from the French cleric Nicolas Amici, a theologian and former rector of the University of Paris, who was attending the council.[14] In turn Nider may well have drawn on some of the material he collected in the *Formicarius* for a series of sermons he delivered when he returned to Basel briefly in the early summer of 1438. Schieler goes so far as to maintain that he actually read out parts of his work to the council fathers.[15] Whatever the case, while the *Formicarius* was not written in Basel, its composition was closely associated with the council. We may well picture Nider as a famous figure in Basel, known for always having an interesting and incredible story to tell and frequently seen going from member to member between the sessions of the great council (which were, after all, mostly held in his own priory) collecting more fantastic tales to include in his sprawling work.

Throughout the treatise, the theologian's lazy but curious pupil acted as Nider's disciple, posing questions and taking in his wisdom. He also served as the learned theologian's excuse for relating contemporary stories of the wondrous, miraculous, or demonic as edifying exempla, rather than expounding learned but dry theological argumentation on the many issues his student raised. With each topic covered in the *Formicarius* and in response to every question the student posed, the theologian would begin by citing biblical, patristic, or scholastic literature. In each case his student, unsatisfied with these responses, would ask the theologian to illustrate his points with contemporary examples rather than ancient authorities. Moreover, it was through the voice of his pupil that Nider was able to raise ideas that were clearly commonly held but that he considered wrong or based on misunderstandings or misinformation. He could then respond to these notions and correct them in the voice of the theologian. It was the student and not the master, for example, who decried the worldliness of prelates and pastors in Germany, the student who complained that the great councils of Constance and Basel had been wholly ineffective, and the student who was shocked by the idea that women, the frail sex, dared to engage in such horrific activities as witchcraft.[16] In each case Nider, in his thin guise as the theologian, then had an opportunity to comment on and refute these common misperceptions.

Nider organized the *Formicarius* loosely around the various forms and conditions of the lives of ants. Thus the first book, dealing with the deeds of good men and women, he organized around the occupations of ants. The second book, dealing with revelations, was based on ants' varied means of locomotion (some crawl and some fly). The third, on false visions, was structured around the sizes of different kinds of ants. The fourth, on the virtues of saints and other holy people, he based on the stages of an ant's life (egg, larva, mature insect), and the fifth, on witches, he structured around the colors of ants (white, black, red). In addition, each of the twelve chapters of each book was based on one of sixty conditions of ants' lives.[17] The reader quickly realizes, however, that this complex organizing scheme has almost nothing to do with the subjects Nider intended to discuss, and in fact all reference to ants generally vanishes after the first few lines of each chapter. Nider began the first book, for example, by dividing the labor of ants into three categories: some engage in productive labor, some stand guard, and some devour the dead. This tripartite structure he then compared to the classic medieval division of society into three orders: peasants, who labored; knights, who fought (or stood guard, as Nider would have it); and clerics, who through their prayers tended to the dead. The lesson that the ants taught here, he concluded, was that all people could and ought to engage in some form of useful activity, whatever their station in life. From this point he launched into his discussion of various specific deeds performed by good men and women, without according ants much further mention.[18]

For inspiration and models for his great work Nider was indebted to a long line of moralistic dialogues, stretching all the way back to the famous *Dialogues* of Gregory the Great. He cited Gregory at several points in the *Formicarius*, and additional evidence of the importance that the last of the Latin fathers of the church held for Nider can be found in a work that may have served as a sort of preparation for the writing of the *Formicarius:* a collection Nider made of numerous exempla from various earlier sources. It exists in a single known manuscript copy stemming from the Dominican priory in Basel and dated to before 1438. Containing more than 350 stories, this large compilation contains no prologue, introduction, or commentary of any kind, so we cannot be certain why Nider assembled the work. What is certain is that nearly a quarter of the exempla it contains are drawn from Gregory the Great.[19] More recent works also served as inspiration and provided models for the *Formicarius*. Anyone familiar with Dominican moral literature will immediately recognize the similarity between a work based on ants and an earlier Dominican treatise based on bees, the *Bonum universale de apibus* of Thomas of Cantimpré, written between 1256 and 1261. Thomas provided a clear precedent not only for the use of insects as an organizing theme but also for the extensive discussion of demons and demonology found especially in the fifth book of the *Formicarius*, and Nider acknowledged his debt to Thomas at the beginning of his great work.[20] In this earlier collection of moralizing stories and exempla, Thomas had been concerned to encourage proper behavior among clerics, both high-ranking prelates and the lower clergy serving under them. Thus, like Nider's treatise, his work can be seen as one of reform. Whereas Thomas dealt only with the behavior of churchmen, however, Nider was concerned more generally with moral reform across all of Christian society. Although he did bring some of Thomas's tales of demons into the fifth book of the *Formicarius*, ultimately he borrowed little directly from the *Bonum universale de apibus*.[21]

Another well-known medieval collection of wondrous stories in the form of a dialogue would have provided an important precedent for the *Formicarius*. This was the *Dialogus miraculorum*, written between 1219 and 1223 by the Cistercian abbot Caesarius of Heisterbach.[22] Nider drew on Caesarius explicitly only once in the *Formicarius,* but given the fame of Caesarius's collection and the similarity of its themes to those of the *Formicarius,* it seems likely that Nider would have seen it as a model for his own work.[23] Like the *Bonum universale de apibus* a generation later, the *Dialogus* was concerned entirely with the behavior of clerics, here solely the monks of the Cistercian order, and was a work of reform. From this tradition of reforming moral treatises the *Formicarius* arose. In his great work, however, Nider pushed the idea of reform beyond cloister walls and even beyond the boundaries of the institutional church to include the entire Christian world. In his concern with moral and spiritual reform among the laity he revealed his debt to another reformist tradition as well, one just reaching its full strength in the late fourteenth and early fifteenth centuries—the tradition of popular reformist preaching.

As a collection of exempla, the *Formicarius* would have functioned as a kind of preacher's manual, a handy collection of ready-made edifying stories for use in sermons. Thus, although he wrote the work in Latin, Nider, an experienced popular preacher himself, would have expected the information contained in his treatise to reach every level of Christian society through the medium of sermons.[24] Preaching, of course, had always been an important means of disseminating religious teachings to the faithful and of correcting any errors in belief among the laity. Saint Dominic had founded the Order of Preachers to combat heresy and spread the true teachings of the faith through sermons. In the late fourteenth and early fifteenth centuries, however, popular preaching had taken on even greater importance.[25] During this period, widely (and wildly) popular preachers reached out to huge numbers of the faithful. The Dominican Vincent Ferrer, for example, traveled through Spain, France, and Switzerland, and the Franciscan Bernardino of Siena preached extensively across much of Italy in the early fifteenth century. For such men, popular preaching became more than a means of spreading the church's message to the people. It became a call for and means toward a general spiritual renewal throughout Christian society (a function it retained until well into the next century, when the Protestant Reformation was driven largely by the direct spread of the reformers' message to a pious and concerned laity).[26] Reformist popular sermons, R. N. Swanson writes, were intended to spread and strengthen the faith "through exhortation, through tales of the saints which provided good examples and showed prospective rewards, through reports of miracles, and with horror stories to warn against following a bad example and the penalties for those who neglected their duty."[27] They achieved their goal as never before in Nider's lifetime.

Nider's *Formicarius* clearly placed him in the popular reforming tradition of moralizing preachers such as Vincent Ferrer and Bernardino of Siena. Nider praised both men in his great work, especially the Dominican Ferrer, noting

their preaching efforts and their work in the conversion of sinners back to
strong faith. In fact, the *Formicarius* was the first written account to devote
significant attention to the life of Ferrer, a future Dominican saint.[28] Like both
Vincent and Bernardino, Nider aimed to effect a moral reform throughout
Christian society by the direct exhortation of believers to good and pious behavior. There seems to have been considerable interest in these men at the Council
of Basel, especially in Ferrer among the Dominicans.[29] The reform programs of
Vincent and Bernardino, circumventing as they did the institutional structures
of the church and carrying the message of reform directly to the people, clearly
appealed to Nider. Although he was also involved in reform on the institutional
level, this was not his principal focus. In his belief that a general reform of the
entire church was impossible he echoed the sentiments of Bernardino of Siena.[30]
Perhaps inspired by Bernardino and Vincent Ferrer, Nider sought through his
Formicarius to work toward the type of societal reform among all believers
that they championed. In many ways, then, the *Formicarius* can be seen as the
literary complement to the reformist tradition of popular preaching that had
developed in the late fourteenth and early fifteenth centuries.

Nider announced in the opening lines of his prologue why he had written the
Formicarius and what he hoped it to accomplish:

> While frequently traveling through certain territories, especially in Ger-
> many, I have sometimes heard the protests of people lax in the faith:
> "Wherefore now among Christians does God not strengthen the church
> with miracles or holy works in order to maintain the faith, and [where-
> fore] does he not illuminate the virtues necessary for living a good life,
> just as he once did with revelations?" For indeed they cry out, with the
> faithless Jews, "Our signs we have not seen, there is now no prophet,
> and he will know us no more."[31]

Imploring the aid of Christ's grace, Nider intended to reassure such people by
citing the many wonders that divine will still worked in the world, by relating
the continuing revelations that God caused to appear, and by describing some of
the virtues of the many truly holy and pious people who lived in this supposedly
forsaken age. Fascination with wonders and marvels of all sorts was particularly
strong in late medieval and early modern Europe, and was certainly not unre-
lated to the growing concern over witchcraft in this period.[32] Such signs and por-
tents were seen as warnings from the Lord and as calls for repentance and
reform, and this was the principal use to which Nider put his stories of divine
and demonic wonders. His self-appointed task, like that of the prophets of
ancient Israel to whom he tacitly compared himself, was to prove to skeptics and

those "lax in the faith" that God had not abandoned his "chosen people," the Christian faithful, or his church on earth. Rather, through examples of the various signs and wonders that continued to occur in the present day, he intended to show that the Lord remained very much active in the world. Through positive examples of the virtues of good people and, unmentioned here, through negative examples of the perils of sin, he would urge and cajole all those weak or idle in faith, the many "sluggards" whose complaints and excuses he had heard throughout Germany, toward a moral and spiritual renewal.

THE WORLD OF THE *FORMICARIUS*: A REFORMER'S VIEW OF LAY SPIRITUALITY

In approaching the religious world of the late Middle Ages through a source such as the *Formicarius,* we must be careful to acknowledge that we are using not only a single witness but a very biased one. Nider was, of course, a member of the elite in that classic dichotomy, elite vs. popular religion or culture. In the stories he collected, while he occasionally turned his gaze to the activities of his fellow clerics, he generally focused on popular religion and religious practice. Much scholarship has pointed out that there was never anything like a strict separation of elite from popular practice and belief in the Middle Ages, and thus it is certainly more accurate to speak of a religious tradition common to all of medieval society, or at least a broad segment of it, around which clustered narrower traditions limited to specific social and cultural groupings.[33] Nevertheless, we must not lose sight of the fact that clerics, while certainly sharing in this common tradition, were also a distinct elite, separated from the masses by their education, by Latin literacy, and, for many, by cloister walls.[34] Also, uniquely clerical concerns often had a profound effect on all of medieval society. For example, the continued relevance of a distinction between elite concerns and more generally held beliefs is certainly evident in the development of the phenomenon of witchcraft. While all groups in medieval society believed in the real efficacy of magic, and while there is no reason to doubt that even ordinary people sometimes conceived of magic as being worked through the agency of demons, it seems clear that the idea of witchcraft—a cult of evil sorcerers who had entered into pacts with the devil and gathered at sabbaths to worship him in exchange for their maleficent powers—was largely a development of the clerical elite that then spread into common culture.[35]

These distinctions, as well as the commonalities between clerical and common religious culture, need to be borne in mind throughout this discussion. Ultimately, however, I am concerned less with the true state of late medieval religiosity than with Nider's particular perceptions of the spiritual state of the world around him, as well as the particular consequences of his conceptions, concerns, and preoccupations. Overall, the material he collected in the *Formi-carius* reveals that he was not so radically pessimistic about the state of the world as might be expected. Although as a reformer he was dedicated to im-provement in the moral and spiritual condition of the faithful, he was gener-ally balanced and reasonable in his estimation of the strength of religious belief and practice in German lands and across Europe, as well as in his perceptions of the problems confronting the faith in the early fifteenth century. He also proved ready to recognize the strong current of popular piety that prevailed in the later Middle Ages. He does not seem, however, to have been particularly interested in most of the major manifestations of that piety. Rather, as a mem-ber of the clerical elite and a reformer, he focused to an extent not found in the common tradition on the virtues of chastity and virginity, on visionary experi-ences, and on the maleficent power of demons in the world. These particular areas of concern helped, in turn, to shape his understanding of witchcraft and in many ways to define how and why he approached that subject as he did.

Despite Nider's conviction that many Christians had become "lax in the faith," in the course of the *Formicarius* he often presented a positive, even optimistic picture of late medieval religiosity and of the late medieval church. Francis Oakley has noted the danger of taking reformist treatises and sermons at face val-ue when one attempts to construct an accurate picture of late medieval religion. Reforming authors, almost by definition, focused on the negative, and their fiery diatribes against the evils of the world often present a falsely bleak picture.[36] Certainly Nider had a great deal to say about heresy, witchcraft, and supersti-tion, but a careful reading reveals another side of the late medieval religious world. True, he wrote in his prologue that he had encountered many people throughout Germany who were generally weak in their faith and who demanded spiritual reassurance in the form of visible signs from God. Clearly, how-ever, even these people had not completely abandoned their faith. Indeed, they remained interested in and concerned about spiritual matters, if in a rather negative and pessimistic fashion. Nider rebuked them, but only because they foolishly ignored the many signs that God was, in fact, continually showing them. In the following books he presented many examples of weak and faithless people, of heresy, superstition, and demonic witchcraft, but he also presented many positive examples of good, pious, and holy people. Indeed, he formally dedicated only two books out of the *Formicarius's* total of five to the explicitly negative topics of "false visions" and "witches and their deceptions." In the other three books he (putatively, at least) focused on the more positive examples of good men and women, good revelations and divine visions, and virtuous works (although in fact both positive and negative stories can be found through-out each book).

Repeatedly in the *Formicarius,* Nider challenged what he perceived to be overly pessimistic evaluations of the state of religious belief and the strength of the faith. Let us consider three criticisms common in the early fifteenth century: that the clergy was hopelessly corrupt; that efforts for reform, focusing in this period on the great ecumenical councils of Constance and Basel, were fruitless; and that because of its internal corruption the Western church was plagued by heretics within and oppressed by infidels without. When Nider's student complained about the worldliness of prelates in the German church, the theologian admitted that there were certainly some clear examples of corruption. This hardly meant, however, that the entire church was corrupt, or that there were not also many good and honest prelates dedicated to God's work.[37] Shortly thereafter, the student criticized the councils of Constance and Basel for their ineffectiveness. The theologian responded by pointing to the major successes of each: Constance had resolved the terrible papal schism and Basel had reached an agreement with the Hussite heretics, ending their threat to the faith. He admitted that the councils had been ineffective in the area of reform, and he doubted that a general reform of the entire church would ever be possible through their agency, but he confidently maintained that many "particular" reforms could be accomplished with great success.[38] Still later his pupil wondered at the suffering of faithful Christians at the hands of the heathen Turks and Saracens, who in some areas were able, as he put it, "to rule and restrict the faithful people of Christ." At first the theologian offered what might be called the expected response. He noted that the Lord often deliberately allowed tribulations to test and strengthen the faithful, citing several biblical passages to support this argument. He then went on, however, to note that the Christian faith, while admittedly losing ground to the Turks in some areas, was actually making good progress against infidels on other fronts, such as in Spain and on the crusading frontier in Poland.[39]

Nider's dispassionate outlook on the state of both the institutional church and the faith as a whole is also evident in his recognition of a strong current of popular piety still focused on the church. The traditional view of the late Middle Ages, articulated in the classic account of Johan Huizinga and others in the early twentieth century, is of course that this was a period of pervasive decay, a steady "waning" of medieval civilization throughout the fourteenth century and especially the fifteenth. This era supposedly witnessed a mortifying stagnation of piety among the clergy and within the institutions of the church, and among the laity an ever-increasing dissatisfaction with official forms of religion, which culminated in the Reformation.[40] More recent scholarship, however, has revealed that the Western church in the late Middle Ages remained as powerful and compelling a force in the lives of its people as it ever had been, perhaps more so. As Eamon Duffy writes in his revisionist history of the English church in the fifteenth and sixteenth centuries, "late medieval Catholicism exerted an enormously strong, diverse, and vigorous hold over the imagination and loyalty of the people right up to the very moment of the Reformation."[41]

Certainly Nider was aware of the widespread popular devotion that flourished at the end of the Middle Ages. His understanding of this devotion, however, seems to have been selective at best. Richard Kieckhefer has identified four "major currents" in late medieval devotion: Christocentric devotion focusing on the passion, Marian devotion, Eucharistic devotion, and devotions to the cults of saints. A fifth current, which he only tentatively classifies as devotional, was increased attention to penance, especially manifested in concern about confessing and receiving absolution before death.[42] Of these five, the only ones that appear clearly in the *Formicarius* are devotion to the Eucharist and concern about confession, perhaps not surprisingly the two devotions tied directly to sacraments, which only priests could administer. I count eight stories in the *Formicarius* that give significant attention to the role and power of the Eucharist. In these tales, the consecrated Host converts sinners, sustains the faithful, drives out demons, points out and punishes sin, and performs other wonders.[43] Nider also clearly reflected the late medieval concern about dying unconfessed, and so in a state of sin. He noted that many people, even the religious, feared death, but he also offered many examples to show that honest confession of even the most terrible sins and at the last moment had absolute power to wipe away fault and ensure salvation.[44]

Nider paid almost no attention to other aspects of popular devotion. The only story in the *Formicarius* at all representative of the profound devotion to Christ's passion that flourished in the later Middle Ages is the brief mention of a woman named Elizabeth in the diocese of Constance. Whenever unforeseen tribulation was about to occur in her life, so she claimed, she received a vision of the passion of Christ on the cross, and this would sustain her through her troubles.[45] Likewise, Nider's two examples of Marian devotion are remarkably brief. In one, a wealthy man in Colmar named Peter gave all his money to the Dominican order after the death of his wife and retired from the world, apparently in a Dominican priory. However, he suffered from visions of an old woman who would come upon him in his bed at night and beat him with a sharp iron fork. To defend himself against this afflicting phantasm, he called upon the Virgin Mary, and the old woman immediately disappeared. The second example of Marian devotion occurred as part of a long story about a knight who fought in the wars against the Hussites. At one point, when the many heretical victories and the terrible cost of the war in human lives were causing the knight to have particular doubts, his faith was strengthened by a vision of the Virgin Mary.[46]

Not only did Nider touch on the power of the Virgin only briefly in each episode, but in neither case was it the real focus of the story. In the first tale he spent far more time on the oppressive power of the nocturnal vision of the old woman; in the second he mentioned Mary only briefly at the very end of a long story that really focused on the crusade against the Hussites.

As for the increased devotion to the cults of saints in the later Middle Ages, Nider related only one story that focused on this aspect of popular piety, regarding the devotion of a simple young man to Saint Barbara. In the course of a conflict between two neighboring nobles, this man was taken prisoner by his lord's foe. Along with other captives, he was thrown into a dungeon and virtually starved. Many of his fellow prisoners died, but this man continued to live "beyond the strength of human nature." When questioned by the astonished guards, he revealed that he had prayed to Saint Barbara to sustain him until he could confess, receive absolution, and partake of the Eucharist. When he was granted the sacraments of penance and Communion, he died peacefully.[47] Thus the story also serves as an example of devotion to the sacraments. The only other example of popular devotion to the cult of a "saint" that Nider recounted was actually a cautionary tale, since, despite popular belief, authorities eventually discredited the sanctity of the supposed saint. There lived in Regensburg a youth who, when he was thirteen years old, died a mysterious death, being found outside the city walls without a mark on his body. The people of the town immediately began to venerate him as a martyr when a man in Regensburg who claimed he had divine inspiration attested that the boy had died for the faith. Eventually Emperor Sigismund came to the place and investigated the issue. He uncovered many "frauds and fallacies" (Nider did not specify what they were) surrounding the case, and declared that the boy was no martyr. He demolished the chapel the people had erected, and apparently the boy's incipient cult quickly faded.[48] No other stories of popular devotion to saints or of manifestations of saintly power appear in the *Formicarius,* although in the fifth book Nider did include pilgrimage to a holy shrine as an effective remedy for people who had suffered harm from witches.[49]

Whatever the commonalties between the religion of the clerical elite and that of the common laity in the later Middle Ages, and there surely were a great many of them, there was also certainly a distance between the two groups, or, perhaps more accurately, educated clerics existed as an elite within the larger tradition of the common religion and to an extent isolated from it. For all his apparent interest in popular piety and belief, Nider seems to have been unaware of most of the major aspects and manifestations of that piety, or at least unconcerned with them. His real preoccupations were shaped by the immediate world in which he lived, and he then projected those concerns onto the religious and spiritual condition of the laity. Of all the major foci of lay devotion, he appears to have concentrated on only two, the sacraments of Eucharist and penance. As a member of the Dominican order, which often exercised pastoral duties, he doubtless administered these sacraments to the laity many times himself, and this perhaps was the reason he wrote about them at any length. In the main, however, his *Formicarius* was dominated by three issues that do not seem to have played such major roles in the common tradition of late medieval spirituality: the (obviously clerical) concern with chastity and praise of virginity, and the two closely interrelated themes of visions and demons.[50] Each of these issues, aside from clarifying the terms in which Nider saw the larger religious world around him, also bears particular relevance to the development of his thought about witchcraft. The relation of demons and demonic visions to this topic is rather immediately apparent. Nider's view of female spirituality and morality, like that of most clerics of his time, was intimately enmeshed with his valorization of chastity and especially the preservation of virginity. Thus his belief that some women might readily become depraved (often sexually depraved) servants of Satan was but a part of his larger concerns about sexuality and particularly female sexual activity.

CHASTITY, VIRGINITY, AND FEMALE SPIRITUALITY

Nider's conviction that women were more inclined than men toward the numerous sins of witchcraft was not based on a purely negative view of female moral capacity. Rather, he presented a dichotomous picture of the female sex as either wholly good or entirely wicked, a view typical of clerics throughout the Middle Ages, and one especially common in late medieval preaching. In this view, when women failed to attain the highest purity, they sank into the basest carnality. They could, in short, be either the Virgin Mary or the sinful Eve, and in either case their moral value was tied almost exclusively to their sexuality.[51] Throughout the Middle Ages women were considered to be more susceptible to the urgings of the flesh because, of course, they were held to be weaker than men at all levels, in body, mind, and spirit. This ideology was based as much on Aristotle and other classical authorities as on biblical and patristic precedents, and in the later medieval period it was developed particularly by Dominican theologians.[52] Repeatedly in the *Formicarius,* Nider fell into this perception of women typical of his order. From Thomas Aquinas, for example, he knew that female physical weakness could contribute to moral laxity.[53] As for the mental shortcomings of the female sex, at the very outset of his work he assured his readers that in collecting and recording wondrous tales, he had always been careful of his sources, especially when the stories originated with women, "whom, unless they have often been proved to be reliable, I always suspect to be delirious in such matters."[54]

Nider justified his suspicion of female weakness by drawing on all the relatively standard medieval misogynist themes in all the standard sources—the Bible, Aristotle, and so forth. Beyond these authoritative precedents, however, his concerns and convictions as a religious reformer led him to see a particular danger in feminine weakness. In the late Middle Ages, religious reformers, with their heightened moral concerns, were convinced that the laxity of women was a major hindrance to the moral and spiritual progress they sought. Nider noted that not a single female religious house had been reformed in the previous six years in which the Council of Basel had been in session, even when the reformers had the full support of all local authorities.[55] A manuscript copy of the *Formicarius* from the Dominican priory in Basel may indicate his more specific concern here: in the margin stands the single word "Clingental."[56] Remember that the nuns of the large and wealthy Dominican convent of Klingental, located just across the Rhine in Lesser Basel, had refused to be reformed when Nider introduced strict observance into the male priory in 1429, and they had stubbornly resisted reform for all the years since then.[57] The obstinacy of the sisters doubtless proved a great embarrassment to the male Dominicans, and might have been taken as an affront to the council as well.

Observant leaders often saw women, either lay or religious, as presenting a dangerous temptation for reformed brothers. In his ordinances for the reform of the Basel priory in 1429, the Dominican master general, Barthélemy Texier, was in no way atypical when he ordered that no friar was to leave the priory without the express permission of the prior, even to go to other Dominican houses, and "especially not to the convent of Klingental." He also ordered, we recall, that none of the friars should go to those parts of their own priory, such as the vineyard, when women might be working there, and that they must refrain from using the public baths, "because it is exceedingly irreligious for the brothers to enter a bath where both men and women bathe."[58] In *De reformatione status cenobitici* Nider listed the "reckless clinging of women," whether ordinary laywomen or professed nuns, as one of the main causes of decline in the religious orders.[59] That this "clinging" was sexual in nature is revealed by the fact that he immediately cited Moses' question to the officers of the Israelite army after their victory over the Midianites, recounted in Numbers 31: "Why have you saved the women? Are these not they who deceived the children of Israel by the counsel of Balaam and made you transgress against the Lord by the sin of Phogor, for which the people were also punished?" The sin of Phogor was fornication, into which the daughters of Moab had seduced the men of Israel, thereby corrupting them in the eyes of the Lord.[60]

Despite his clear suspicions of women, however, Nider also felt a certain sympathy for them. After all, he had reformed several female houses of his own order and he continued, through letters, to oversee and advise his spiritual daughters there.[61] He was surely reflecting his own experience when he had his student note that the sisters in the Dominican convent of Schönensteinbach, near Colmar, had complained to him that Scripture and patristic writings warned incessantly against the deceits of women, but never cautioned women about the lies told by men. "If we had had the ability to write and speak like you [men]," the nuns had told the young man, "we would already have related honestly your [male] vice."[62] Having presented this challenge through the voice of his student, Nider responded in the voice of the theologian that no wise man would ever condemn the female sex per se, for it had been created by God. Like earlier authorities, he sought only to criticize the "foolishness" (*stulticia*) so often associated with women.[63] Nider was convinced, however, that when typical female foolishness was overcome, women were capable of much good. For example, he related that at Nuremberg, pious women received the Eucharist far more often than men did. Also, he twice mentioned that in the lands around Basel and in the diocese of Constance, there were so many good and pious women seeking to lead lives of religious devotion that there were not nearly enough nunneries or even beguinages to hold them all. He specifically praised Colette of Corbie, a contemporary Franciscan nun and reformer, later to be canonized. He presented her, along with the Dominican Vincent Ferrer, also later elevated to sainthood, as primary examples of individuals whose efforts for reform were to be emulated.[64]

Nider presented numerous individual cases of good and pious women, both religious and lay. His examples are quite diverse, yet even a cursory glance through his descriptions of good women reveals a single characteristic that dominates all others—their chastity. Even most of those who were not nuns or beguines vowed to celibacy were described at some point as *virgines*. It would be unfair to say that only by chastity could women attain moral worth for Nider. He did describe numerous women who were admirable though married. Yet he also called certain clerics in German lands worse than heretics when they argued that no laywoman should ever seek to maintain her chastity, but should marry in order to avoid falling into sin.[65] Clearly, female moral value was closely associated in his mind with female abstinence from any sexual activity.

Of course, Nider did not value chastity only for women. Men too should seek to remain pure. He wrote, for example, of a certain man in Nuremberg who slept with his wife only once a year. Even this was not severe enough discipline for the couple, however, and together they both sought to live in complete chastity within marriage. Nider mentioned three other married couples who sought to live likewise,[66] and the theme of chastity in marriage recurs through-out several of his works. Several chapters of his *De lepra morali,* a moral treatise written some years before the *Formicarius,* discuss the place of sex in marriage, always concluding that continence is the most laudable course.[67] We also have a German sermon that he apparently preached to the people of Basel sometime during the council, in which he stressed the value of complete abstinence from intercourse in marriage.[68] In the *Formicarius* he set out three grades of matri-mony. In the first, the couple engaged in sex, but only for procreation. In the sec-ond and higher grade, the couple gave up sex entirely, following the example of Abraham and Sarah. The highest grade of marriage was attained by couples who never lost their virginity, following the example of Mary and Joseph.[69]

While such discussions of sexual abstinence within marriage in the *Formicar-ius* dealt with the value of chastity for both men and women, other stories reveal that Nider was far more concerned with female than male sexuality. Even more than the value of chastity reacquired late in life, he stressed the value of virgin-ity never lost for women in a way that he never did for men. His advice for good and pious women focused less on attaining the status of chastity than on pre-serving unblemished the condition of virginity.[70] Since virginity, once lost, could never be acquired again, women were advised to undertake the most extreme measures to protect themselves from irredeemable corruption, as exemplified by a young woman named Anna who lived in Basel. When she reached maturity, her parents wanted her to marry, but she refused and even considered fleeing the city to avoid this fate. Her commitment to preserving her virginity won Nider's approval. Another example concerned a young woman named Agnes who actually did flee from her home near Basel when her lord tried to force her into marriage.[71] The student interlocutor was quite shocked to hear his master defend and even praise women who were so disobedient to their superiors. The theologian, however, responded that women had the right to defend their chastity even as they had the right to defend their lives.[72]

In fact, not only could women defend their purity as their lives, they should defend their virginity with their lives if necessary. The motif of a holy woman dying instead of sacrificing her maidenhood was long established, stretching all the way back to the female martyr saints of early Christianity. Since for women virginity was a pinnacle from which they could only fall, an early death that eliminated the possibility of eventual corruption was laudable, even advis-able, in a way that was unthinkable for men.[73] Nider referred to this long tradi-tion when he wrote that "formerly there were many maidens . . . [who] gave up their lives to defend their chastity."[74] He also presented several modern exam-ples. One he heard from the dean of the church in Isny, his hometown. This man was related to a beautiful young woman of marriageable age who felt herself divinely inspired to dedicate her life to Christ. She pleaded with her family to let her remain unmarried, but her father was unmoved, convinced that if she did not take a husband, she would eventually fall into the sin of fornication. The girl then prayed to be married to Christ and to remain a virgin, "either in life or in death, to which she was indifferent." Shortly thereafter her prayer was answered. She fell ill and soon died. Another example came from Colmar. The parents of a young woman named Anna had determined that she should marry. Since she refused all suitors, they arranged her betrothal secretly. Eight days before the wedding, the girl, who was completely ignorant of her parents' scheme, contracted a fever. A certain Friar Peter of the Colmar Dominicans was called to hear her confession. He knew of the arrangement her family had made, and when he asked her if she would rather face death than marriage, she replied, "Gladly, I would rather die," and then expired.[75]

Medieval authorities traditionally tied female moral value to female sexuality, and Nider certainly fits this pattern. In his dichotomous view of women, in which they could attain either the pinnacle of sanctity or the depths of depravity, sexuality served as the most obvious criterion for assignment to these two extremes. Not surprisingly, then, when he needed to explain the apparent female proclivity for witchcraft, he turned to the widespread perception that women were weaker than men physically, mentally, and spiritually, and he focused above all on uncontrolled female sexuality. If the best women were those who never lost their virginity or sank into any carnal activity at all, then the worst, witches, engaged regularly in demonic orgies and often fornicated with the devil. Some fifty years later the *Malleus maleficarum* stated the position definitively: "All witchcraft comes from carnal lust, which is in women insatiable."[76] Yet, although Nider's ideas about female sexuality and female spirituality certainly informed his views on witchcraft, they did not motivate his interest in this subject. In some ways his view of women's sexuality actually privileged them over men, at least potentially, for he seems to have charged female virginity with a moral value far exceeding anything attributed to male chastity.[77] By maintaining their virginity—that is, by overcoming their natural weakness and above all by sublimating their dangerous and threatening sexuality—women could become extremely praiseworthy moral figures. This view can, of course, be seen simply as a kind of reverse misogyny: standard criticisms of female weakness were employed to praise those few women who overcame their "natural disadvantage" to achieve the same moral level as men.[78] At the same time, women could be praised for excellence in their own specifically feminine virtues, such as obedience and submission, although these too only served to emphasize their ultimate weakness and inferiority to men.[79] Thus a positive view of some women in no way undermined, and in some ways even supported, the condemnation of countless others for witchcraft. Yet Nider's real concern over witchcraft did not revolve around the gender of supposed witches; his concern was rooted in another aspect of his view of the moral and spiritual state of the world around him: his preoccupation with visions, both divine and especially demonic.

VISIONARY AND DEMONIC EXPERIENCES IN THE *FORMICARIUS*

Visions, both positive and negative, both divine and demonic, come closer than any other element to being the central theme of the wide-ranging *Formicarius*. Nider formally dedicated two of the work's five books to "good revelations" and "false visions" (the second and third books, respectively). In its final early modern printing in Helmstedt in 1692 the *Formicarius* appeared under the title *De visionibus ac revelationibus* (On visions and revelations). Not in any sense a "devotional" practice and by no means a common occurrence for the vast majority of the laity, visionary experiences were nevertheless an important part of the late medieval religious scene.[80] The *Formicarius* abounds in stories of visions, dreams, and revelations, some coming from God and others inspired by the devil. The theologian's lazy interlocutor was initially dubious about the value of any visions, fearing that they were all demonic deceptions, and in this attitude he surely represented the ambivalence that medieval clerical authorities felt toward visionary experience.[81] At the very outset of Nider's discussion of good revelations, for example, he had the pupil note that more women than men seemed to receive visions and revelations, and, suspecting that many of these visions in fact came from the devil, the young man assumed that women's weaker natures, both physical and moral, made them more susceptible to the devil's deceptions.[82] The theologian, however, cautioned his student against spurning all visions, because some did indeed come from God to strengthen the faith of good and pious people.

As an example of one such divine revelation, Nider related a story about his old mentor in the Dominican reform movement, Johannes Mulberg. Long after Mulberg was dead, his sister Adelaide, who at the time was in her nineties and still living a chaste and devout life in the city of Basel, told Nider that in her youth the family had moved to a new house. Each of the three children—Adelaide, Katharina, and young Johannes—ran through the house and the yard behind, and each picked a certain tree in the yard as his or her favorite, "in the manner of children." That spring the trees began to bloom, but in a different manner than was natural for them. The two girls' trees brought forth white flowers, which they took to mean that they should devote their lives to chastity. The tree that Johannes had selected bloomed red. He too maintained his virginity until his death, but when he was about twenty years old he was called to a more active form of religious life in the Dominican order.[83]

Nider was convinced that revelatory experiences such as Mulberg's were messages commonly sent by God to strengthen and guide the faithful. When a pious woman named Sophia, for example, became the abbess of a house of secular canons in the diocese of Strassburg, the house was in great need of reform, and she was forced to labor long and hard to introduce correct observance there. Later she reported to Nider confidentially (*confidenter*—perhaps meaning in confession) that she had been sustained through her long ordeal by nightly dreams in which she received a vision of a chalice containing the Eucharist. Nor were such visions confined to the religious. I have already touched upon the visionary experience of a certain married laywoman named Elizabeth, in the diocese of Constance, in relation to Christocentric devotion. In times of hardship she was accustomed to receive visions of the passion of Christ on the cross, and these visions strengthened her moral resolve.[84]

Despite this range of positive examples, however, Nider was often skeptical about visionary experiences, and apparently with good reason, for the possibilities of deception were manifold, ranging from simple human iniquity to demonic intervention. As an example of a purely human deception, he related the story of a certain "*fraticellus* and semibeghard" in Bern who managed to convince people that a spirit dwelled with him in his house and granted him visions, and that he could converse with the dead.[85] The beghard's purpose was to augment falsely his own spiritual reputation and ultimately to persuade people to pay him for his supposedly supernatural services and advice, but such deceits were not always motivated by greed or malevolence. Nider told a story about a monastic hospice in Germany in which one of the rooms was thought to be haunted by a ghost or demon. A certain knight, however, doubted the reality of the spirit. Standing watch one night, he saw what appeared to be a ghost enter the room and struck at it with his sword. The "spirit" vanished, but in the morning a trail of blood was visible, and it was revealed that the ghost had been only a young *conversus*, or lay brother, who had used a secret door from the cellar to enter the room at night and fool people into thinking he was a spirit. No motive was given, and the whole event bore the appearance of a youthful prank. Unfortunately, the knight's blade had struck true, and the *conversus* paid for his joke with his life.[86]

Some people might truly be unaware that their visions were false. Witness the case of a young religious woman, Magdalena. Shortly before the beginning of the Council of Basel, she entered a convent in the town of Freiburg, only a short distance north of Basel along the Rhine, and very soon she came to be revered by the other sisters in the convent for her visions. One day she had a vision predicting her death, which was to occur around the next Epiphany, and she piously began to make arrangements for her funeral. Word spread to all the surrounding area, and many people traveled to Freiburg to see if the woman's prediction would come true. Nider himself, as prior of the Dominicans in Basel, sent a friar to observe the event. On the day of the predicted death, the convent church was full of the devout, the suspicious, and the merely curious. When Magdalena entered the choir, she immediately fell into a trance and lay completely immobile. A doctor was present, however, and he confirmed that she still lived. People waited for a time, but eventually it became clear that she was not going to die, and thus her mystical visions were proved to be false. Upon hearing this story, Nider's pupil asked whether her visions resulted from natural causes, were sent by some demon, or were simply a deceit on her part. The theologian replied that the cause could have been any of the three.[87] The *Formicarius* contains a similar story involving a female recluse living near Constance at the time of the earlier council there. This woman was renowned for her holiness and for her visions, and many clerics from Constance went to consult with her. She would enter a trance and then report to them on the visions she had received. One day she predicted that she would receive the stigmata. As in the later case of Magdalena of Freiburg, people were curious, and on the appointed day many clerics and other people crowded into the recluse's cell. The woman went into a trance, but no sign of the stigmata appeared. Again Nider offered no explanation as to the cause of her false visions, but apparently not long after this event she became "suspect" before the Council of Constance. She was forced to recant her claims of receiving visions and do penance.[88]

We do not know the source of these two women's visions, but inasmuch as one of them was declared suspect by the council fathers at Constance, we may well suspect the agency of a demon. The *Formicarius* contains numerous examples of false visions brought about by demons, and in such demonic activity we can see the close connection between Nider's interest in visionary experience and his concern over witchcraft. Perhaps this relationship is most clearly seen in his tale of a demonically inspired nocturnal vision that echoed the famous tenth-century canon *Episcopi* and its description of women who believed that they flew at night with the goddess Diana.[89] In Nider's time a woman was similarly convinced that she flew at night with other women in the train of the goddess. One day a Dominican friar approached her and asked if he could observe as she undertook her supposed journey. She assented, and that night he watched as she covered herself with ointments, recited magic words, seated herself in a large pot balanced on a stool, and fell asleep. Throughout the night she never moved from the pot, but only shook violently back and forth so that she finally tumbled from the stool to the ground. When she awoke, she claimed that she had been with the goddess in flight. The friar, however, was eventually able to convince her that her journey was merely a delusion brought on by demons.[90] This case obviously bears a close relation to the supposed night flight of witches, although Nider placed this story in the second book of the *Formicarius,* on revelations, not in the fifth book, on witchcraft. Immediately after this tale he presented a similar story taken from the legend of Saint Germanus of Auxerre concerning a family that set out food in the evening for the "good women of the night." The family feared that these women, who appeared to be their neighbors, would work great harm upon them if they were not placated by such offerings. Germanus, doubting the story, observed the event one night and recognized that the women were in fact demons in disguise. Commanding the demons not to flee, he woke the people who had set out the food and showed them that their neighbors were all still asleep in their beds. He then commanded the demons to reveal themselves and their deceit.[91] Similar tales of night-flying creatures, usually female, who plagued their neighbors and demanded to be placated by offerings were a typical feature of medieval European folk culture, and would come to contribute much to the stereotype of witchcraft.[92]

The use of demons and demoniacs in moral fables and exempla had, of course, a long tradition in the religious literature of edification, in which Nider was simply following. The tales collected by Gregory the Great in his *Dialogues* had extensive demonic elements, and more recent literary models for the *Formicarius* such as Caesarius of Heisterbach's *Dialogus miraculorum* and Thomas of Cantimpré's *Bonum universale de apibus* contained many stories focusing on demons and demonic power. Yet Nider's demons, I suggest, were of a slightly more sinister sort. The demons in earlier exempla collections had been horrific, to be sure, but overall they had served to make moral points colorfully, and in some cases even to validate holy power.[93] Churchmen seemed more confident in their authority over demons in the thirteenth and early fourteenth centuries than they became later. Now the demons, while still of course able to be bound by the cross or the name of Christ or other holy means, came to be seen as far more sinister and implacable enemies. This shift is representative of the growing fear of the devil and his servants in the late Middle Ages, which ultimately fed into the frenzy of the witch-hunts.[94] This increased fear of demons and of the devil as real and effective actors in the world was grounded in scholastic theology, and thus, at least initially, was primarily the province of the learned elites.[95] Of course, all groups in medieval society believed in demons and their power, and Eamon Duffy has provided evidence that fear of the demonic may have been on the rise among the common laity as well as the clerical elites in the fifteenth century. I think the overall evidence remains strong, however, that a vivid concern over the demonic existed particularly among the learned classes.[96] Certainly the most reliable evidence suggests that the diabolic elements of witchcraft were almost exclusively the creation of learned judges, lay or clerical. Average

lay people of the fifteenth century might well have been concerned about harmful magic that other people could use against them, but it was learned authorities who saw demonic agency in this magic and postulated a diabolic cult of
witches behind it.[97]

Even before he turned to the subject of witchcraft, Nider gave ample evidence
of his profound concern over demonic power. He had double cause to fear
demons, not only as a theologian but also as a reformer. For demons, he was
convinced, were the particular foes of reform and the special enemies of the
reformed or observant religious orders.[98] One of the first demonic tales he
related in the *Formicarius* took place in the observant Dominican priory in
Nuremberg. A young novice was sorely vexed and tempted by a demon that
tried to prevent him from taking his vows and entering the order. "But the grace
of Christ won out in him," Nider wrote, "for he professed, and afterward
was made [our] gracious procurator in the reform of the Basel priory."[99] Nider
made his point about demonic opposition to religious reform more explicitly
at another point in the *Formicarius*. Just as anthills were often attacked and
destroyed by certain large animals, he explained, so demons often sought to
afflict observant religious houses, and he presented a particularly horrific example. A "malign spirit" began to torment the brothers at a reformed Dominican priory in Savoy. The spirit broke windows, upset tools and utensils, and
destroyed jars of wine. It cut the bell ropes in the tower and carried off the bells,
and then rang them throughout the night. As in Nuremberg, the demon particularly afflicted a young novice. One day it appeared to the young man in the
form of a black cat and said to him, "Unless you put off the habit of the order, I
will kill you in three days." The novice adjured the creature to depart in the
name of Christ, but the demon was powerful enough to resist this command and
possessed the novice instead. With great effort the other brothers managed to
drag the demoniac into the priory church and before the altar. Here the demon
broke free from their hold and flung the boy's body all about the church until
they thought he must be dead. After many prayers to the saints and the Virgin
Mary, the friars finally were visited by a vision of Saint Dominic. Only then did
the demon flee.[100]

Elsewhere in the *Formicarius*, in relating how he and Barthélemy Texier had
reformed the Dominican convent of St. Catherine in Nuremberg, Nider told
another tale of demonic assault. When a few nuns still did not wish to submit
entirely to strict observance of the rule after the convent had been reformed, a
demon entered the place and began to plague the sisters by making strange
noises at night. They complained to Nider, their vicar, but at first he did not
believe them; the noises were being made by mice, he told them. In fact, he suspected a form of delirium among the nuns. The demon continued to plague the

convent until the sisters were too terrified even to walk through its halls alone. Nider told the nuns to pray and meditate on the Lord, but still the demon persisted, attempting to terrify the women into rejecting the reform outright. Ultimately the demon failed in its purpose, Nider noted with satisfaction: "But nevertheless through the grace of God the devil lost more in this game than he won, because some of these women, whom he did not want to obtain the full piety of the reformers, he terrified so much by this phantasm that they confessed the misdeeds of their entire lives, put off their old clothes, and donned new ones following the form of the order."[101] Only when the demon saw that its hopes of halting the spread of strict observance would not be realized, and that it was in fact contributing inadvertently to the progress of reform, did it depart the nunnery of its own will. In the course of this story, Nider explicitly referred to himself and other reformers as "we who bore the burden of the struggle against the wrath of the demons."[102]

Visionary experience, while an important and widely accepted part of the late medieval religious world, was hardly a common occurrence in the spiritual lives of most people, and direct encounters with demons were likewise rare. Yet these elements figured prominently in Nider's perception of the state of the world around him. Doubtless to some extent he focused on such stories in his *Formicarius* precisely because they were extraordinary, and thus carried extraordinary power. Yet his inclination to see and describe his world in such terms certainly also reflects the way he perceived that world to be. As a cleric and especially as a reformer, he saw a world filled with manifestations of supernatural power and beset by the evil of demonic forces. From here only a short step was needed to carry him into the world of witchcraft.

Many scholars, focusing too exclusively on the material on witchcraft contained in the *Formicarius* and tending to quote isolated episodes rather than analyze them in any larger context, have regarded Nider's great work simply as an incoherent jumble of collected stories.[103] Taken as whole, however, the work does reveal certain clear precedents. It was a moralizing dialogue following the pattern set by Gregory the Great, Caesarius of Heisterbach, and Thomas of Cantimpré. As a collection of exempla for use in sermons, it was also a work of reform in the tradition of such popular preachers as Vincent Ferrer and Bernardino of Siena. Thus the subject of the *Formicarius* can be seen as the moral renewal and spiritual rejuvenation of all of Christian society in the early fifteenth century. Clearly Nider never intended to fashion a unified treatise from all the diverse material he collected, but nevertheless several distinct themes are apparent. As a moral reformer, he was not so pessimistic about the state of the Christian faith or of the fate of Western Christendom as might be expected.

He recognized that piety continued to flourish among the laity, but strangely he seems to have missed most of the major manifestations of late medieval popular devotion. His focus, fed by his particular concerns as a cleric and religious reformer, fell instead on issues of chastity, visionary experience, and demonic power. Each of these concerns, in turn, helped to shape Nider's accounts of witchcraft in the fifth and final book of the *Formicarius*. His notions of female weakness, especially sexual weakness, helped him explain why women were particularly inclined to become witches. But above all his concern over witchcraft was rooted in his larger concern over demonic power. He feared demons as the servants of Satan and the opponents of God's church on earth. More specifically, however, he feared them as the opponents of reform.

The connection that Nider perceived between demonic activity and religious reform is clear in his several examples of demons' opposition to the spread of strict observance in religious orders, as they infested monasteries and convents and attempted to prevent young friars from taking on the religious habit or nuns from donning the new habit of the reform. Just as his concept of reform in the *Formicarius* was not limited to the religious orders but extended to all of Christian society, however, so his fear of demons was also extended. If demons worked to hinder reform among the religious orders, they also endeavored to prevent any moral or spiritual renewal among all believers. And if even the devout monks and friars were seriously threatened by these attacks, how much more vulnerable must the laity be?

In the early decades of the fifteenth century, the Christian faithful faced a new enemy as well. As men and women who had traded away their very souls to the devil in exchange for magical powers, which they then used at his command, witches must have appeared to Nider as yet another battalion in the diabolic army that threatened the reform of the world. His concerns over demonic power, rooted in his theological education and especially in his work as a reformer, made easy the acceptance of an idea like witchcraft. Moreover, his reforming impulses provided him with a motivation to write about witches. Just as he related tales of demons as moral exempla to discourage people from improper behavior and inspire them to greater faith, so he would warn them about the threat posed by satanic cults of witches, and in so doing he would partake in the creation of the pious terror that would grip Europe for the next three centuries and lead tens of thousands to the stake.

6

WITCHCRAFT AND REFORM

Witchcraft was only one of the many issues that Johannes Nider addressed in his writings. Yet to judge from the amount of space he devoted to this subject in his *Formicarius,* it was an issue that occupied much of this thought and raised some of his deepest concerns. Why? In all other areas Nider was a cautious thinker, not prone to unwarranted pessimism or unfounded alarm. Confronted with other heretical threats to the faith, which are sometimes too easily associated with witchcraft in modern scholarship, he exhibited only moderate concern. Indeed, real heresy seems to have been something of a side issue for him, despite his intense involvement with the Hussites at the Council of Basel. Witchcraft, however, played on his deeper anxieties and interests. At the heart of Nider's thought lay an abiding commitment to reform. Although he engaged in institutional reform among the religious orders, ultimately his conception of reform entailed an internal spiritual renewal. Not content to limit his activity in this area to his own religious order or even to the institutional church, in his greatest work he pressed for a reform in this broad sense among all believers. This was the primary thrust of the *Formicarius.* How, then, did the idea of witchcraft fit into that larger framework? What reformist function did Nider hope to fulfill by collecting and recounting such extensive tales of witches, and how was his particular but extremely influential vision of witchcraft shaped by his desire to promote moral and spiritual reform?

Witches, of course, were perceived as a serious threat to other individuals through the harmful sorcery that they supposedly practiced against their neighbors. Moreover, as members of a secret cultic army organized by Satan and wholly in his service, they were a threat to the entire Christian faith. Part of Nider's purpose in the *Formicarius* and his other works on witchcraft was simply to inform people, both clerics and the laity, about these dangers. Far more important, however, he sought to instruct people as to how they should respond to these sorcerous and ultimately satanic assaults on their bodies, their worldly goods, and their very souls. Again and again he returned to the notion that against the terrible threat represented by witches stood the power of the true faith. His tales of witchcraft, and especially the defenses against bewitchment and the remedies that he prescribed, became exhortations to proper belief and pious living. Here his concern over witchcraft coincided most completely with his reformist agenda. And here, not surprisingly, his descriptions of the horrors of witchcraft became most florid. It is informative to note, however, that in respect to other traditional magical practices, which many moralizing reformers saw as dangerous superstitions, Nider appears to have been much more cautious in his conclusions, and he allowed for and sometimes even advocated a variety of popular spells and charms that the laity could use to counter the effects of demonic witchcraft. Writing as a reformer, he was concerned above all to define licit and proper behavior, to separate valid practice from vain superstition, and to encourage lay people to conform to these strictures through positive examples of the benefits they would enjoy if they heeded clerical instruction and through negative examples of the terrible punishments they would incur if they strayed.

The connection between the rise of witchcraft and the desire for reform in the late Middle Ages has long been recognized. As Richard Kieckhefer noted, "if we need to locate a spark [for the rise of witch trials], at least one source is clear: the vigorous drive for reform of the Church in head and members, found throughout Western Christendom in the wake of the Council of Constance."[1] In the early fifteenth century, many reform-minded clerics, including such prominent theologians as Jean Gerson, Johannes of Frankfurt, Nikolaus of Jauer, and Heinrich of Gorkum, began to look more closely at popular religious practices and found them replete with harmful and condemnable superstitions.[2] Some of these superstitious practices, which could include anything that might appear "false" or "vain" to clerical eyes, fed into notions of witchcraft. People uttered strange names, performed mangled prayers or blessings, or attributed occult powers to certain words or objects.[3] Concern over such matters was particularly strong at the great councils of the early fifteenth century, Constance and Basel. As centers of reform they served also as centers of discussion for like-minded clerics from across Europe, and Basel especially was a focal point in the development and spread of the idea of witchcraft.[4]

Recognizing the concern among such clerical authorities with eliminating superstition and promoting correct religious practices among the laity, scholars have seen reformers as natural opponents of heresy, sorcery, and ultimately witchcraft. Certainly, through their efforts to spread heightened morality and strict religious practices, popular reformers especially could become leading fomenters of the persecution of heretics and witches, either by direct action or indirectly through the zeal they inspired in others. The Dominican observant leader Johannes Mulberg, for example, played a key role in instigating the persecutions of beguines in Basel in the early fifteenth century, driven mainly by his commitment to reform and by his conviction that the lay religious mode of life represented a dangerous aberration that needed to be eliminated. At nearly the same time, the fiery Dominican preacher and reformer Vincent Ferrer stirred fears that contributed to rising accusations of sorcery as he passed through Dauphiné, and he delivered a series of sermons in the city of Fribourg, in western Switzerland, shortly before a wave of persecutions broke out there, directed initially against Waldensian heretics but later shifting into charges of witchcraft. Only slightly later in Italy the Franciscan popular reformer Bernardino of Siena, another incendiary preacher, helped trigger waves of persecutions and trials for sorcery and witchcraft in Rome and Todi by his impassioned attacks on immorality and sin.[5] The evidence seems clear. Wherever such reformers went, bonfires and burned flesh appeared in their wake. The pattern would continue throughout the fifteenth century, culminating perhaps most famously in the figure of the Dominican reformer Girolamo Savonarola and his campaign for stricter morality in the city of Florence at the very end of the 1400s. Ultimately, of course, Savonarola achieved tremendous influence over the city, instituting his famous "bonfire of the vanities," before the Florentine population eventually bridled under his extreme reformist message and he himself was finally sent to the flames by his political and religious enemies in 1498.[6]

While such examples point rather compellingly to a close connection between reforming impulses and persecuting ones, scholars have generally not probed this connection very deeply. Content with the idea that moralizing reformers spurred attacks on all forms of immorality, superstition, and deviant religious practice as a matter of course, they have not sought to explore other intellectual underpinnings linking witchcraft to reform. Certainly the perception of a relationship between the desire for reform and the zealous persecution of witches, as well as of heretics and those guilty of superstitious beliefs, is broadly correct. Concerned with the proper reformation of the church and the world, men such as Nider were naturally also concerned with eliminating any perceived deformations in Christian society. A close consideration of Nider's approach to witchcraft, however, both augments and modifies this basic picture. For the comparison between witchcraft and other forms of heresy and superstition, while valid in one sense, fails in another. Heresy and superstition represented corruptions within the faith, and the most effective remedy for such malignancy was excision. Reformers therefore sought to eliminate such errors by all means at their disposal, whether that meant correction, conversion, or ultimately combustion. For Nider, however, reform was not just a negative activity, focusing only on the elimination of deformation. For him the more important aspect of reform was positive, internal, and spiritual, a progressive rejuvenation of faith within individual believers. Such reform was intended not just to correct abuses but also to lead to a new and improved state. Here simple opposition to and elimination of error played only a small role. Certainly the negative and positive aspects of reform could complement one another, but where they conflicted, Nider tended to emphasize the positive, as when he stressed the value of the lay religious mode of life over the potential dangers of sinful beguines or the heresy of the Free Spirit. In short, a persecuting impulse was not the only reaction to which reformist concerns could or did lead. This fact is particularly apparent in regard to witchcraft.

More threatening than simple superstition, witchcraft was also more than just another form of heresy. Witches were maleficent sorcerers who wielded tremendous supernatural power. The danger they represented was not just corruption of the faith by terrible error (idolatry and apostasy) but very real harm worked in the physical world—withered crops, aborted pregnancies, murdered babies, pestilence, and disease. Thus witches appeared far more threatening to average Christians than the proponents of any other heresy or error, and so they became far more useful to reformers such as Nider. Studies of witchcraft often, and entirely correctly, stress that for clerical authorities the real horror of witchcraft lay in the witches' rejection of the true faith, not in their acts of harmful sorcery. Errors of faith aside, matters of simple *maleficium* could be left to secular authorities, and theologians throughout the Middle Ages, indeed theological authorities since the time of the early church fathers, had all stressed the necessary heretical implications of demonic sorcery, rather than the worldly harm it could cause, as their principal grounds for opposition to such practices. Yet Nider did not treat witchcraft exclusively, and in a sense not even primarily, as an error of belief. Tellingly, he was in no way concerned with the correction and salvation of witches themselves, or with preventing the spread of their pestiferous sect. Indeed, while he obviously approved of the prosecution of witches by both secular and ecclesiastical authorities, he was not involved in this activity in any way, either directly or through his writings. Rather he was very much concerned with the effects wrought by witches in this world and the means that could be used to combat them. In this sense the closest parallel to witches, in his mind, was provided not by human heretics but rather by demons. Witches, of course, commanded demons to work their magic, but, like these fallen spirits, they were also themselves bound to the service of Satan. Thus, just as clerical authors had long been accustomed to employ tales of demonic power to demonstrate the consequences of weak faith and improper acts and to encourage proper belief and behavior, so now they might use accounts of the horrors of witchcraft as a powerful tool in an essentially reformist effort to encourage a spiritual renewal among the laity.

RESPONSES TO WITCHCRAFT: A RENEWAL OF FAITH

Throughout the *Formicarius*, Nider's moralizing stories and exempla performed two functions. Accounts of the lives of saints and the deeds of pious men and women presented positive examples for the laity to follow, while negative stories of impious behavior, heresies, and superstitious beliefs served as negative examples for them to avoid. His extensive accounts of witchcraft, however, in a sense served both functions at once. Certainly these stories presented the negative example of people who had been seduced into the service of Satan, and thus Nider instructed the laity about the nature of witchcraft and made clear why it was such a terrible crime. At the same time, however, he sought to encourage proper behavior and renewed belief among the laity by using the menace that witches represented—that is, the threat of *maleficium* that could afflict any Christian at any time—to reinvigorate devotion to Christ and encourage closer adherence to the rites and practices of the true faith as laid out by the clergy. Here the two views of witchcraft outlined in Chapter 2—the common conception of harmful sorcery and the elite concern over diabolism and apostasy—again come into play. Religious authorities sought to establish and enforce correct belief and pious behavior. Their harsh opposition to witchcraft arose because of its supposedly demonic nature, which in their view necessarily entailed idolatry and ultimately the complete rejection of the Christian faith. The laity was concerned, more basically, about the dangers of harmful sorcery worked by witches—hailstorms, withered crops, impeded fertility, disease, and the deaths of animals and children. While in no way rejecting the clerical message that most sorcery was demonic, the greater part of late medieval society did not share in the full diabolical and conspiratorial fantasies of the elites. Nider, however, clearly realized that he could use the basic fear of *maleficium* to his own more spiritual ends.

A story told to Nider by Peter of Bern perfectly illustrates this connection between the threat of *maleficium* and exhortation to proper faith. A witch captured by Peter confessed that sometimes he was unable to work his evil sorcery entirely as he wished, for he could not harm those who were strong in faith. As he confessed: "I myself called the little master, that is, the demon, who told me that he was able to do nothing. 'Does he [the intended victim] have good faith,' he [the demon] asked, 'and does he diligently protect himself with the sign of the cross? Therefore I cannot harm him in body, but [only] in the eleventh part of his yield in the field, if you wish.'"[7] Witches often tried to injure or kill

Peter himself, but they never could, "because he acted in good faith and was accustomed diligently to protect himself with the sign of the cross." On one occasion, however, he failed to "guard himself entirely by the Lord," and witches were able to assail him. At some point after he had stepped down as the Bernese official in the Simme valley, the scene of his major witch-hunting activity, he was again traveling through that region and spent the night at his former official residence in the castle of Blankenburg. He went to sleep, having dutifully protected himself with the sign of the cross, intending to rise early the next morning to write some letters and then depart. In the middle of the night, however, a group of witches, having learned that their old persecutor was again in the region, were apparently able to deceive him with a "fictitious light." Waking and thinking he had slept past the dawn, Peter was in such a hurry to get dressed that he failed to make his customary sign of the cross. Descending from his bedchamber to the lower chamber where he had stored his writing materials, he found the place still locked for the night. Angered, he began to climb back to his room, cursing to himself, and perhaps (so Nider suggested) even uttering the name of the devil. Because of this moral lapse, Peter fell into the power of the witches. Through their magic they immediately struck him with a temporary blindness, and as the complete darkness overcame him, he tumbled down the stairs, injuring himself severely.[8]

Viewed from a modern perspective, what Nider described as a threatening assault by witches appears to have been merely a case of a man stumbling angrily up and down narrow castle stairs in the dark of night, only half awake, and slipping and falling down. Our skepticism should not be projected back on Nider, however. There is no indication that he did not completely believe the stories he presented in the *Formicarius*. In the prologue he asserted that he had been careful to include accounts only of such wonders as he himself had experienced or of which he had learned from reliable sources. He was a theologian, after all, and as he noted, theology "detests falsehood."[9] Moreover, the power of demons to harm people was proved and accepted by theologians and the laity alike in the Middle Ages. Witches were both the masters of demons and, in their subservience to Satan, their servants. It was accepted that demons actually preferred to work harm through witches, since in this way they could not only achieve whatever evil ends they desired but corrupt a human soul in the bargain. The witches described by Nider, in performing their magic through demonic agency and under the direction of Satan himself, became in effect surrogate demons. That is, they functioned in his exempla essentially as demons functioned. Nider truly feared demons as active forces for evil in this world, as terrible foes of God's church, and especially as bitter opponents of reform. Likewise he honestly feared the power of witches and clearly saw them as opponents not just of the proper spiritual order but, through their assaults on officials such as Peter of Bern, of secular justice as well. There is no indication that his use of witchcraft stories essentially to frighten the laity back to proper behavior and belief was in any way cynical. Rather, he was warning about a serious threat that he honestly believed to exist.

Of course, for all the malevolent power that witches commanded, Nider was convinced that ultimately they were subject to the far greater power of God. Repeatedly throughout the *Formicarius* and other works he stressed that witches and demons could work their evil only by God's consent.[10] For all their hostility to the Christian religion, they actually served a divine purpose by testing and strengthening the faithful. I might note here that, to the extent that Nider employed accounts of heresy in his reform agenda (which was not much), he depicted heretics in a similar light, especially the militant and extremely threatening Hussites. Many people in the early fifteenth century, both clerics and members of the laity, were moved to question why God would allow such a terrible error to exist in the world, and as Bohemian armies defeated crusade after crusade directed against them and mounted their own successful campaigns into bordering lands, many asked how God could grant heretics such fortune. Nider responded in the *Formicarius* with the standard passage from I Corinthians that "there must be heresies, so that they who are approved may be made manifest." In his treatise *Contra heresim Hussitarum* he also noted that adversity tested the faithful so that they might gain greater merit in the eyes of God. Slightly later he wrote, "Persecution or tribulation increases and adds to virtue, which can hardly ever or never be acquired in times of peace and prosperity." Indeed, if there were no evil on earth, "the world might become overly sweet to us," and we might wallow in temporal pleasures.[11] As a curative for the seductions of this world and as a test to hone the piety of the faithful, demons and witches were obviously superior to heretics in that they could strike covertly at any moment of weakness and anywhere in Christendom.

Not surprisingly, given Nider's belief that witches served God's purposes by strengthening true belief, the best defenses against witchcraft, as against demons directly, were to be found in officially sanctioned ecclesiastical ceremony and prayer. He presented several lists of such remedies in the course of the fifth book of the *Formicarius*, and in fact the first list concerned protecting a home or habitation directly against demons, not against witches. At the outset of the second chapter of the fifth book, Nider meditated on the fact that ants that foolishly build their nests in areas inhabited by men or other beasts often have their habitations destroyed by these larger animals. In these ants he saw the condition of people who did not "studiously protect their home and habitation against the plots of the devil by means of the ceremonies of the church." He then listed the steps that all the faithful might take to avoid the threat of possible demonic assault: "Every Sunday holy water ought to be sprinkled in the homes of the faithful (just as is indicated for an exorcism), and exorcised salt ought then to be taken faithfully every morning by both men and women, and every one of the faithful should frequently be marked with the sign of the cross to keep them safe from grave sin, and they should often call upon their particular angel for protection with divine aid."[12] Clerically sanctioned religious ceremony, prayer, and avoidance of sin were the surest ways to escape the snares of demons. Such acts would, of course, also protect against witchcraft by negating the demonic power that witches employed to work their dark sorcery.

Several times in his writings on witchcraft Nider listed specific means of protection and remedies against the harmful magic of witches. One such list included five means of impeding the power of witches, very similar to the devices for protection against demons. First, and probably most important, simple integrity in the faith and proper adherence to divine precepts were enough to protect the faithful against witchcraft. The sign of the cross and prayer were also effective means of defense. Attendance at ecclesiastical rites and ceremonies could also shield one from the assaults of witches, as could simple adherence to secular law and public justice. Finally, ruminating on the passion of Christ in both word and thought could help ensure one's safety.[13] In a later chapter of the *Formicarius* he listed means for undoing or relieving an evil spell. These remedies, too, centered mainly on ecclesiastical ceremonies and pious devotional acts. People who felt themselves bewitched might undertake a pilgrimage to the shrine of some saint. They could pray or make the sign of the cross. They could also turn to the sacrament of penance or to the rite of exorcism (by which Nider did not necessarily mean to imply a formal exorcism, but simply commanding the demon responsible for the *maleficium* to depart in the name of God). A fifth possible remedy was the "cautious removal" of the maleficent material.[14] As mentioned in Chapter 2, for example, the witch Staedelin had once rendered an entire household infertile by burying a lizard beneath the threshold stone of the dwelling. After authorities discovered and removed the lizard, the spell was broken.[15] Nider repeated these five remedies almost verbatim in another work dealing with magic and superstition, his *Preceptorium divine legis.*[16]

In these defenses against witchcraft and remedies for maleficent spells the relationship between reform and witchcraft becomes clearer. Fear of witches and their harmful power provided a powerful theme that a preacher could use to encourage the laity toward stronger faith, frequent prayer, regular participation in the sacraments of the church, and regular attendance at ecclesiastical ceremonies. That most of Nider's recommended defenses and remedies consisted of external acts should not disguise the spiritual good he hoped to achieve. Recall that for Nider, as for other late medieval religious reformers, external reforms were the necessary basis for internal change and spiritual rejuvenation. Tales of sorcery and witchcraft similar to those found in the *Formicarius* were used to great effect in the early fifteenth century by such reforming preachers as Vincent Ferrer and Bernardino of Siena, and they continued to be employed by reformers, both Catholic and Protestant, well into the early modern period to encourage repentance and spiritual renewal.[17] Likewise, people afflicted by the spells of witches, presumably having been made vulnerable by some moral lapse, could be encouraged to turn to the church and seek relief through prayer, confession, and pilgrimage. Such tactics may seem cynical to modern minds, but we must remember that the real efficacy of religious rites was never in doubt in the Middle Ages. Church bells rang to summon the faithful to prayer, for example, but they also had the power to avert storms and protect crops.[18] As Keith Thomas has noted in his magisterial study of religion and magic, the medieval church was "a repository of supernatural power which could be dispensed to the faithful to help them in their daily problems."[19] Obviously, however, this power would have been accessible only to those who adhered to God's commands and those of his clergy, and who above all did not allow themselves to grow "lax in faith," as Nider had complained at the very outset of the *Formicarius*.

One aspect of such laxity in faith that clearly concerned Nider was the fact that people afflicted by witchcraft or suffering from other sorts of hardships or troubles would often actually turn for relief to witches instead of to the clergy and prescribed religious ceremonies. People of almost every sort employed a wide variety of common magical practices, and some did so quasi-professionally. Serving as healers or diviners, as cunning men or wise women, these practitioners of the common tradition of medieval magic offered their services to the faithful, often under conditions far less restrictive than the clergy's. Thus they constituted a sort of magical competition against the church's divine power.[20] To trained theologians, this rival power was clearly that of Satan himself. Many lay people seem to have been less aware of the distinction. This is not to say that the common folk did not believe in the power of demonic magic, or that they did not understand its evil nature as well as educated clerics did. Rather, many people seem to have been unaware or at least unconcerned, before preachers and inquisitors began to stress the point, that many of the traditional magical services they sought to utilize might well be demonic. They were more immediately concerned with the positive or negative effects achieved by magic than with the mechanism by which the spell might operate, and they often moved easily from clerically sanctioned prayers and ceremony to suspect sorcery and condemned witchcraft as they sought solutions for their problems.[21]

In all his writings on witchcraft, Nider clearly worked to combat this tendency to turn to illicit sorcery in addition to or instead of approved religious ceremony. He admitted in the *Formicarius* that acts of witchcraft "can be removed through another spell, or through the illicit rites of another witch," but he immediately stressed that any such remedy "is known to be illicit." He then added emphatically, lest someone miss his point, "rather a person should die than consent to such things."[22] Likewise in a later chapter he acknowledged that any type of *maleficium* might be undone through further witchcraft, as many witches had themselves admitted. He again stressed, however, that even "if a remedy can be administered by a witch, nevertheless it should universally be reckoned a sin, for by no means should anyone invoke the aid of a demon through witchcraft."[23] In his *Preceptorium divine legis* also, immediately after he listed licit remedies for acts of *maleficium,* he wrote that witches' spells could not otherwise be undone "except through a superstitious method or through new works of witchcraft, and this is illicit."[24]

Resorting to witchcraft might appear easier than adhering to approved religious remedies, or might promise more immediate results, and thus appeal particularly to those of weak spiritual resolve, but such methods carried great risks. As an example of the danger inherent in turning to witches for aid rather than to the power of faith, Nider related a story drawn from the *Dialogues* of Gregory the Great. A demon had possessed a young woman. Her family tried to cure her by taking her to some "witches" who were to drive out the demon. Through their magic they succeeded in freeing the woman from the single spirit that had possessed her, but because of the illicit and sinful nature of this cure, an entire legion of demons immediately entered the woman in the departing spirit's place. Ultimately she had to be brought to Fortunatus, the saintly bishop of Todi, who was able to cure her legitimately, but only through many days of pious prayer. Nider felt so strongly about this example that he presented it twice in the *Formicarius*.[25]

Another example, and happily a somewhat more lighthearted one, shows how people beset by injury or suffering may have had recourse (or think they have had recourse) to some form of traditional magic or witchcraft. To convince the laity that they should turn only to religious remedies in their troubles, and that prayer and faith were far more powerful than illicit sorcery, Nider related a story about a very pious old woman named Seriosa (the English rendering of her name would, I suppose, be Ernestine) who lived in the diocese of Constance. A friend of hers (who was clearly not so earnest a fellow) was magically assaulted by witches and suffered a severe injury to his foot. The man tried many remedies but could find no relief. Finally he visited Seriosa and asked her to say a blessing over his foot. She silently said the Lord's Prayer and the Creed and made the sign of the cross, which immediately overcame the witchcraft and healed her friend's injury. Needless to say, he was delighted, but, not realizing exactly what she had done, he asked her what "incantations" she had used, so that he might employ them himself in the future. The old woman, only moments before full of concern for her injured and suffering friend, turned on him in anger. "Owing either to bad faith or to weakness, you do not adhere to the divine and approved rites of the church," she chided him, "and often you apply spells and prohibited remedies to your illnesses." She warned him that such practices were extremely harmful, and that because of them he had suffered gravely, "sometimes physically and always in spirit."[26] She then explained how she had cured him by the approved means of prayer and the sign of the cross, with no need to resort to any of the illicit spells or incantations of which he was apparently so fond, but which were so perilous to his soul.

When Nider argued that piety and strong faith provided the best defenses against the evil works of witches, and when he prescribed ecclesiastical cere-monies, sacraments, and prayer as the best remedies for witchcraft, his goals seem fairly clear. Writing as a reformer, he sought through his tales of witchcraft to present exempla that would "define sin, castigate, urge penance and a return to something like pristine innocence by the rejection of sin, and offer hope of salvation by acceptance and enactment of the requirements of the Christian life."[27] Thus his ultimate goal in the fifth book of the *Formicarius* was really no different from his purpose elsewhere in that work, and tales of witchcraft were merely one tool that he used in his efforts to effect a moral rebirth and a spiritual reform throughout Christian society.

Yet while witches might indirectly provide others with an impetus for reform, they clearly were beyond any hope of reform themselves. Witchcraft was not simply another form of heresy that could be recanted, nor was it merely a form of superstition that could be corrected by proper instruction in the faith. The greatest crime of witchcraft, in theological terms, was apostasy. Witches renounced their faith entirely and surrendered their souls to the devil in ex-change for magical powers and command over demons. So severe was this devi-ation that no authority, ecclesiastical or secular, could offer pardon, and only death by fire would serve to remove the corruption from the world. The French secular judge Claude Tholosan, a contemporary of Nider, wrote very clearly on this point in his own treatise on witchcraft, comparing the apostasy of the witch to a form of treason against God. Such a crime demanded the execution of the guilty party.[28] In the *Formicarius* Nider indicated that witches should be encour-aged to confess and repent, and they might even attain forgiveness for their sins. Nevertheless, they still had to be put to death. To illustrate this point, he related a story of a young married couple who were both witches. Captured by Peter of Bern, the woman proved obstinate and refused to confess, even when the flames were lit under her. The husband, for his part, confessed all he knew about witchcraft in order to gain forgiveness. Even though he had confessed, however, he knew he would still be executed, and indeed he was burned, "although in the end, so I believe," Nider wrote, "he was truly penitent."[29]

For Nider, not only was witchcraft far more terrible an error than any other heresy or superstition, but witches were far worse than other sorcerers, even necromancers. For those who practiced demonic magic but did not enter into the diabolical sect of witches, repentance and reform were clearly possible. Take the monk Benedict, with whom Nider was acquainted in Vienna. Earlier in his life, before taking religious vows, this man had been a renowned necromancer, yet he was able to save himself and abandon his former error by entering a reformed monastery. Nider wrote:

> While living in the secular world, this man was a very famous necromancer ... [and] he lived very miserably and dissolutely for a long time. He had, however, an extremely devoted virgin sister in the Order of Penitents, by whose prayers, so I think, her brother was rescued from the grip of the demon. For, driven on, he came to various reformed monasteries in diverse places, seeking to take up the monastic habit. But ... hardly anyone had any faith in the man. Finally, however, received into the aforesaid monastery [in Vienna], he changed both his name and his life by that entry. For he began to be called Benedict, and, following the rule of the blessed father Benedict, he made such progress that within a few years he became a model of the religious life.[30]

Clearly reform was possible for those who practiced demonic magic, and in this case the means to individual reform and redemption was entry into the observant religious life. Witches, however, did not enjoy such possibilities; Nider's reformist impulses seem not to have extended to them at all. In none of his stories did he indicate that clerics or other authorities were to give any thought to saving people who had become witches. Witchcraft appeared to be an absolute evil from which there was no recovery, and tales of witchcraft were used exclusively to exhort other people to reform themselves and to turn for protection and aid to the clergy, to the rites of the church, and to the faith they represented.

RESPONSES TO WITCHCRAFT: THE BOUNDARIES OF LICIT MAGIC

Aside from the diabolical threat posed by witches, many late medieval clerical authorities were deeply troubled by a wide variety of what they considered to be superstitious practices among the laity.[31] These practices often involved various aspects of traditional magic—common spells, blessings, or charms—which could in some cases lead to charges of witchcraft. In theory, the line separating officially sanctioned blessing, prayer, and ceremony from illicit demonic sorcery was fairly clear. Blessings and prayers drew their power from God while witches and other sorcerers called upon devils to work their spells. In practice, however, the boundaries between these two areas of supernatural operation were not always so apparent, and confusion could easily arise. Take Nider's account of the pious old woman Seriosa and her friend whose foot had been injured through witchcraft. Nider clearly intended the story to illustrate the superiority of "religious" cures worked through prayer and the supplication of divine power over "magical" cures achieved by invoking demonic forces. Yet the man in this case was cured not by visiting a saint's shrine or even by his local priest. Rather he was healed by his friend, an elderly laywoman who might easily have seemed like a practitioner of traditional magic or even a witch. In fact, although she actually worked her cure through prayer and the sign of the cross, the man's first thought was that she had used some sort of spell or incantation. This confusion may serve to introduce the vast gray area of common or traditional magical practices that existed between approved religious ritual and demonic witchcraft in the late Middle Ages, and on which, given his concern over witchcraft, Nider obviously had to comment.[32]

Clerical authorities were often deeply suspicious of the use of popular spells, prayers, blessings, charms, and other elements of the common magical tradition, even when they did not suspect that these practices entailed actual witchcraft, because such actions seemed to be superstitious—that is, based on false or incorrect beliefs—and they often appeared to circumvent or subvert proper religious rites. Warnings against reliance on such spells and charms were frequently on the lips of popular preachers throughout the late Middle Ages and early modern period.[33] Nider, however, was not so opposed to the use of such devices as his intense concern over witchcraft might lead us to suspect. In this area he again appears cautious and moderate. He certainly did not allow his fears of demons or commitment to reform to lead him into any expansive or unfounded condemnation of such activity. Rather, in the uncertain zone between clearly approved and obviously illicit practices, he sought to draw a sharp boundary, distinguishing as precisely as possible permissible spells and charms to which the laity could legitimately turn for aid from condemned superstition and sorcery that would imperil their souls. On the whole, he seems to have been inclined to allow even somewhat questionable practices to continue, so long as there was no obvious possibility of involvement of demons.

The subject of popular spells and charms, while clearly related to the topic of witchcraft, has not received anywhere near the amount of scholarly attention that witchcraft has enjoyed. In his seminal book *Religion and the Decline of Magic*, Keith Thomas examined both subjects in early modern England, but generally maintained a sharp distinction between the practitioners of traditional magic and witches.[34] Richard Kieckhefer treats common spells and charms at length in his survey of medieval magical practices, but he has little to say about them specifically in relation to witchcraft.[35] An extended discussion of the widespread use of spells, blessings, charms, and prayers in late medieval Europe also appears in Eamon Duffy's broadly revisionist study of late medieval and early modern English religiosity, *The Stripping of the Altars*. As Duffy's intention throughout this work is to argue against previous scholars' overly intense focus on heresy and superstition—the extreme fringes of late medieval religion—he does not treat witchcraft at all, focusing instead on the relation of popular spells and charms to liturgy and established religious ceremony. "Such incantations," he writes, "represent the appropriation and adaptation to lay needs and anxieties of a range of sacred gestures and prayers, along lines essentially faithful to the pattern established within the liturgy itself."[36] The point is certainly valid, and many popular spells and charms did indeed incorporate liturgical elements, standard blessings, and prayers. So too, however, did many clearly illicit conjurations of demons. The rituals of necromancy especially were often profoundly liturgical.[37] Thus even when they incorporated significant religious elements, common spells and charms had at least as much to do with the shadowy, illicit world of sorcery and witchcraft as with the pious world of late medieval devotionalism. In fact, in some ways they represented the meeting point between these two worlds, where intensity of religious devotion balanced on the tenuous line between extreme but allowable practice and illicit superstition. Religion and magic were by no means one and the same in the Middle Ages, but they did often enough intermingle with and serve to reinforce each other.[38] To separate popular spells and charms completely from illicit practices is to miss this crucial connection, as well as to obscure the fact that there was much confusion between the two even in the medieval world.

In the Middle Ages, blessings, prayers, the names of God, the sign of the cross, and other approved formulae were all considered to have real power in their own right, *ex opere operato*. That is, invoking or performing them was widely thought to produce more or less automatic effects, independent of who used them or in what context they were employed.[39] Spells or charms that included such elements, therefore, might be perfectly effective and legitimate even when uttered by an illiterate peasant, and even when used to protect crops in a field rather than to praise and glorify the Lord in heaven. Nider presented one such effective spell in his *Formicarius*. After the witch Staedelin had confessed to Peter of Bern that he had raised hailstorms by demonic means, he revealed that all his efforts could be brought to naught by a simple charm: "I adjure you, hail and winds, by the three nails of Christ, which pierced the hands and feet of Christ, and by the four evangelists, Saints Matthew, Mark, Luke, and John, that you should fall dissipated into water."[40] Staedelin believed the charm to have been effective, and Nider gave no indication that he thought otherwise, or that he feared a farmer who used this spell to protect his crops from storms would be committing an illicit act in any way.

Many authorities did believe that such counterspells constituted illicit sorcery, however, or at least they were deeply suspicious of them. Employment of divine names and blessings in strange or unconventional ways raised concerns that some form of error might creep in and corrupt the otherwise wholesome charm. The greatest danger was that the invocation and supplication of demons might enter the formulae, either inadvertently or by deliberate interjection. Nider specifically warned against the blessings and charms that some old men and women performed over sick people. Such cures, he wrote, resembled the blessings and ceremonies of exorcism used by clerics. Originally they had been entirely licit, and indeed remained so when employed by "educated men and doctors of sacred theology." He feared that in the hands of the uneducated laity, however, the cures had become corrupted through the agency of demons.[41] Although he referred to the lay practitioners of such cures here only as "old women and certain men" (*vetule … et viri quidam*), these figures could easily be interpreted as witches by any authority so inclined. Whether or not Nider thought such activity was an aspect or indication of witchcraft, clearly he was concerned that otherwise legitimate spells and charms were being perverted by incorrect use among the uneducated and ill informed.

Nor was such confusion between licit spells and charms on the one hand and illicit superstition and witchcraft on the other limited to the uneducated laity. Trained clerics were often uncertain of the boundary between holy blessing and demonic curse. Consider the case of the Augustinian friar Werner of Friedberg, put on trial in Heidelberg in 1405 for certain of his professed beliefs. Decades later his case was still serving as a model for discussion about the validity of certain spells and charms.[42] In the course of his interrogation, Werner was asked if he was familiar with any superstitious blessings. He replied that he knew one: "Christ was born, Christ was lost, Christ was found again; may he bless these wounds in the name of the Father and the Son and the Holy Spirit." He did not believe this particular blessing had any power to heal wounds, he said, but he had nevertheless employed it successfully several times to cure himself, apparently of ailments other than wounds.[43] Although we do not know whether any harm came to Werner as a result of his rather uncertain beliefs, for many others the consequences of such uncertainty were very serious indeed.

As a reformer, Nider was deeply concerned to promote proper belief and practice among the laity. He used the perceived threat posed by witches to achieve this end, and his concern over witchcraft and illicit sorcery naturally led him to address the related issue of the widespread use of popular spells and charms. Despite his ready acceptance of all the horrors of witchcraft, he was relatively restrained in his judgment concerning common magical practices. While he utterly condemned any practice that might be perceived as containing demonic elements, he was otherwise prepared to allow almost any type of popular spell or charm. In writing about possible responses to witchcraft and the power of demons in his *Preceptorium divine legis,* for example, he noted that certain herbs and stones had natural but occult properties that could be used to restrain demons and heal the sick. Prayers and blessings containing holy words might also be used to this effect. Moreover, these two elements could be combined in a ritual that begins to appear as more magical than religious, so that "if someone gathers medicinal herbs with the divine Creed or with the Lord's Prayer, or writes on a paper the Creed or the Lord's Prayer, and places this over some sick person . . . it is not censured, provided that no other superstitious practice is involved."[44] Later in the same work Nider provided a more detailed account of what he felt such "superstitious practices" would entail. Following the great Dominican authority Thomas Aquinas, he wrote that blessings and charms of any sort were generally permissible so long as they met several conditions. Most critically, they could contain nothing that might suggest the invocation of demons "either expressly or tacitly." Thus they could employ no unknown words or names that might secretly supplicate demons. They should also contain no "falsehoods"; that is, they were not to seek or produce any effect that could not legitimately be asked of God. Moreover, they must not contain "vanities"; that is, devices or formulae that theologians had determined could have no real power or effect, such as characters written across the sign of the cross. Nider also stressed that so long as the intent of a spoken or written blessing or charm was pious, its form was of no importance. Demons might be compelled by certain ritualized invocations, but divine power could only be supplicated, and the specific form of the supplication was less important than the pious intent. Nevertheless, in calling on divine aid through blessings or charms, people should be careful to employ holy words respectfully and with an understanding of their meaning so that they would not commit any irreverence.[45]

With these few (although not inconsiderable) restrictions in place, Nider was willing to allow the laity the use of a broad range of traditional spells and charms. Some scholars have suggested that much of the elite response to traditional magical activities was "dictated by realism in the face of popular practice."[46] That is, such practices were foolish or improper, but they were too deeply embedded in the common culture to be rooted out. This was undoubtedly one factor in the clerical acceptance of certain common practices. Nider's arguments here, however, based as they were on Aquinas and other authorities, reveal a different rationale at work. He was not immediately concerned with whether traditional spells and charms were effective or not, proper or not. Nor did he regard them as some quasi-pagan challenge to clerical authority or to basic Christian belief. Indeed, by the late Middle Ages almost all such magical practices were thoroughly Christianized.[47] Rather, he had fixed and logically coherent criteria for separating licit from illicit magical practice based on the supposed methods employed. Above all, he suspected and feared that invocations of demons might lie hidden within otherwise seemingly permissible ritual formulae. Hence his repeated admonitions against the inclusion of unknown words or names in prayers, charms, and blessings, since they might indicate a summoning of some demon.[48] Again, as with witchcraft, Nider's concerns were rooted in his fear of demonic activity in the world and his conviction that demons were waging a very real war against the Christian faith.

Against such demonic enemies, however, the faithful had a variety of weapons, and Nider was convinced that certain elements of the common magical tradition could be numbered among them. People might employ spells and charms expressly directed at demons quite licitly, he conceded, so long as they avoided the crime of "necromancy." That is, they must be careful always to command the demon throughout the course of the magical operation, and never to supplicate it. For one could conjure or adjure demons in either of two ways, according to Nider: by "soliciting" (*deprecando*) them or by "commanding or compelling" them (*imperando seu compellendo*).[49] The first method was used by necromancers and witches, since both witchcraft and necromancy, according to Nider, functioned in essentially the same way. Needless to say, such spells were entirely illicit, because the only way to "solicit" a demon was to offer it some form of sacrifice or worship. The second method, however, was sometimes allowable, since the faithful could in fact command demons through divine power, even as Christ and the Apostles had done.[50] In such cases, Nider cautioned, a further distinction needed to be drawn as to what ends the demons were being commanded. It was permissible, for example, for someone to command a demon by the power of the divine names to cease its harmful activity and depart, but one must never summon a demon, even by means of command, in order to learn something from it, or to have it perform some task. To do so would be to fall into a sort of "fellowship" (*societatem*) with demons, which was the chief crime of necromancers and witches.[51]

The power to command demons in the name of God or of Christ was obviously akin to the clerical power of exorcism, yet Nider granted this power not

just to members of the clergy but to all believers. In fact, throughout the Middle
Ages "exorcism" did not necessarily refer only to the official rite of the church.
The verb *exorcizare* could mean simply "to command" a spirit or demon, and
it was often used almost interchangeably with such terms as *conjurare* and *adju-
rare* in necromantic spells.[52] It was in this sense that Nider listed exorcism as
one of the possible remedies for bewitchment in the *Formicarius*. In his *Preceptorium divine legis* he stated explicitly that the laity could "exorcise" demons,
although they of course could not employ the full and formal rite of exorcism,
which only a cleric was allowed to perform *ex officio*.[53] Still, against the dark
power of witches, who sold their souls to Satan in exchange for the ability to
command demons, every Christian who remained strong and true in faith had
a divine power to command demons and drive them out in the name of Christ.
One only had to be careful, Nider warned (again), that no unknown characters,
strange words, or other "superstitions" crept into the adjuration, for they could
turn a licit command into an illicit supplication.[54]

Despite the dangers of superstition, Nider was willing to allow the laity to
continue to use a wide range of traditional spells, prayers, blessings, and charms
to heal themselves and to protect their persons and their possessions from
demonic assault. Ultimately, he was concerned only that such practices not
lapse, deliberately or inadvertently, into the crimes of necromancy and witchcraft; that is, of supplicating demons, worshiping them, and forming a "fellowship" with them. Of course, one might argue that all these narrow distinctions
between allowable magic and illicit witchcraft were purely theoretical, and that
in practice they probably kept few practitioners of traditional magic who had
fallen under suspicion from being sent to the stake at the hands of zealous
authorities. Certainly there is a dismal truth to this surmise. But it remains
important to acknowledge that the distinction did exist, at least in theory, and
to understand the basis on which that distinction was made. As a reformer,
Nider did not fear all popular magical practices as automatically and inevitably
superstitious, and his zeal for reform would not have driven him to accuse every
peasant who employed a blessing or charm of being an agent of Satan. Rather,
his concerns in this area, as with witchcraft itself, were informed mainly by his
fear of demonic power operating in the world, and his clear perception of a
war being waged between those demonic powers and the Christian faithful on
earth. Within the church militant, he was quite explicit, reformers bore the brunt
of that struggle, and the stakes were nothing less than the souls of the entire
Christian world.

Johannes Nider was not an inquisitor working actively to extirpate the crime of
witchcraft from the world (although he had no doubt that witches deserved to

die, and certainly shed no tears for them when they went to the stake). Rather, in his *Formicarius* and other works he approached witchcraft as a reformer, and above all he regarded witchcraft as a crucial exemplum for the instruction of the faithful and as a means to spiritual reform. He was concerned, as were many other reform-minded theologians and preachers, with superstitious practices and errors of belief among the laity, but this does not seem to have been the chief cause of his preoccupation with witchcraft. Although he dwelled on the horrors of the sabbath and other aspects of witchcraft at great length and in considerable detail, he was not primarily concerned with explicating the many sins that witches committed or with correcting the terrible errors of which they were guilty. For him the crimes of witchcraft were so heinous as to place witches beyond salvation. He saw them as very similar to the demons they commanded, as committed servants of the devil and soldiers in his war against the Christian faithful. He readily accepted the horrors of witchcraft because he was thoroughly convinced of the reality, scope, and power of this diabolic assault on the world, and he used tales of witchcraft, even as he used stories of demonic malevolence, possession, and so forth, to illustrate the moral laxity not of the witches themselves but of the people they assaulted. Thus through his accounts of witchcraft, as with all of the material he presented in his *Formicarius*, he sought to encourage a renewal of faith and a closer observance of true religious precepts and practices among all believers.

Witches represented a terrible threat to all those who believed in their power. Most people, the average laity, were concerned with the potential harm that could be wrought by *maleficium*. Dead babies, sudden illness, blighted crops, and destructive storms were all indications of the power of witches. Clerical authorities recognized the demonic agency and indeed the diabolic conspiracy that underlay such occurrences. Awful as this demonic assault was, however, Nider was confident that the Lord had given his faithful more than adequate means of defense. The most basic defense was to remain strong in the faith. Faith alone would protect true believers from the dangers of witchcraft. To bolster this personal faith the clergy provided a whole range of institutions and services—sacraments and ceremonies, blessings and prayers, pilgrimages to saints' shrines, and the simple sign of the cross—that could be used as defenses against witchcraft or as relief from bewitchment. Thus Nider used tales of witchcraft to urge and cajole (to terrify and coerce, if one is inclined to see matters less charitably) a sometimes lax laity to adhere more closely to official precepts and the institutions of the faith. Yet the laity could also have recourse to many common spells and charms, so long as they took care to avoid obvious superstition, which for Nider meant mainly any possible indication of summoning of demons. In several cases he explicitly acknowledged the effectiveness of such spells. Christ gave his disciples power to exorcise demons, and this power devolved not just on the clergy but on all the Christian faithful.

Writing as a reformer, Nider saw witchcraft not simply as a corruption in the faith that needed to be eliminated, as were other heresies or superstitions. He also saw in the threat that witches represented a means to encourage reform in others. The devil and his demonic minions were fiercely opposed to reform at all levels and used all their powers against it, but ultimately the Lord would allow nothing that did not serve his greater purpose. As when a demon had assailed the nuns in the newly reformed Dominican convent of St. Catherine in Nuremberg, so with the far greater demonic conspiracy of witchcraft Nider was convinced that Satan could be made to lose "more in this game than he won." Reformers could turn witchcraft to their own ends and through this dire threat to Christianity bring about a further strengthening of the faith.

Nider did not invent witchcraft. Numerous factors on all levels of medieval society contributed to the construction of this terrible concept in the early fifteenth century, and numerous sorts of people played their roles in the process. Clerical inquisitors and lay judges, theologians and preachers, poets and troubadours, those who accused their neighbors in the courts, and of course the accused themselves all contributed to the development of this multifaceted crime. Yet Nider was one of the earliest and most important authorities to describe this fateful stereotype systematically and thereby transmit it to others. The reasons that he seized so tenaciously on this new and horrific idea were complex but ultimately clear. Witchcraft played to all his concerns as a reformer—his fear of demonic power, his sense of the corruption of the church and the world, and above all his desire to call for renewed faith and spiritual reinvigoration. Had he sat down deliberately to invent a concept that would both sum up and symbolize his greatest fears about his world and also provide him with a means, a powerful and universally applicable rhetorical point, with which to combat those fears, he could scarcely have conjured a better image than that of the witch. That others saw matters differently I have no doubt. As one study has noted, every early authority who wrote about witches did so for a different reason and aimed at a different objective, drawing on his own particular environment, culture, and imaginative universe.[55] Yet Johannes Nider was the most important of these early authorities, and his accounts were the most extensive and influential. Thus understanding his particular approach has broad importance. The terrible idea of witchcraft did not stand alone in his thought, but was affected and influenced by all his concerns as a theologian and a reformer.

CONCLUSION

WITCHCRAFT AND THE WORLD OF THE LATE MIDDLE AGES

The figure of the witch haunted Europe for several hundred years. From the early 1400s until well into the eighteenth century, witch trials appeared regularly, although of course with wide variations in frequency and degree of severity, in every region of the continent and in European settlements in the New World.[1] All too often a trial generated a full-fledged witch-hunt. Needless to say, given such a wide expanse of space and time, the factors behind these waves of persecution were extremely complex and varied, and patterns of persecution were by no means identical in all regions or in all centuries. The phenomenon of witchcraft had so many facets and encompassed so many factors that it invites a wide range of interpretations. Scholars of religious history, social history, and economic history, of law, gender, and culture have all contributed to our understanding of an issue that manifested itself in so many areas of European life. Even when we limit our focus to the origins of this phenomenon in the late Middle Ages, the situation becomes scarcely less complex. As Richard Kieckhefer has noted, medieval magic in general was a sort of crossroads where religion and science met, where learned thought and theology combined with common belief and popular superstition, and where fiction and reality merged.[2]

Despite its impact on so many areas of late medieval society and culture, witchcraft is still too often regarded as a thing apart, a separate and somewhat outlandish sideshow in the larger drama of the late Middle Ages and early modern period. Although it has been the subject of much focused and often excellent scholarly inquiry, the rise of witchcraft in the fifteenth century has still not been fully and successfully integrated into the overall religious, intellectual, and cultural history of that period.[3] By examining Johannes Nider's appropriation of witchcraft, his understanding of that new phenomenon, and the use he made of it, I have sought to contribute somewhat to this integration. We have seen that witchcraft was not an isolated concern of Nider's; his particular interest in witches and their malevolent activities was closely related to his other religious concerns. Thus we cannot fully or accurately understand his approach to witchcraft unless we place his accounts within the context in which he wrote them. Here his writings on heresy and especially on religious reform are of as much interest as his tales of magic, witchcraft, and superstitious practices. These issues shaped the contours of the mental world in which he lived, and were as real and stark to him as the Alps from which so many of his tales of witchcraft emanated. In the towns and villages where individuals were actually accused, tried, and burned, witchcraft was a terrible social reality, rooted in the social, legal, and economic developments of those particular locations. For Nider, however, witchcraft was an intellectual problem, no less terrible for being mainly abstract, and was rooted in the larger intellectual, cultural, and spiritual crises that for him shaped the religious world of the early fifteenth century.

Nider's outlook on the issues of his day was obviously that of a cleric, a university-educated theologian, and a reformer. I have set forth elsewhere in this book my thoughts about the advantages and disadvantages of focusing on the learned clerical elite's understanding of witchcraft and their contributions to the construction of that idea, and I will not rehearse them here. I will, however, address Nider's importance as a source, the degree to which his accounts are specific to his thought and the degree to which they reflect wider concerns. His writings represent perhaps the most important single source we have on the origins and early development of the idea of witchcraft. No other authority from this period, the crucial period of initial formation, wrote such extensive, detailed, varied, or influential accounts of this new phenomenon. Only recently, however, has he begun to receive his due as an important historical figure (and not only in respect to witchcraft).[4] Yet Nider's importance lies not simply in the volume and richness of the material he produced. Such factors mark him as extraordinary, but his real importance, in respect to both witchcraft and the many other subjects on which he wrote, lies in the extent to which he was also quite ordinary. Even when he wrote about relatively new and largely fantastic developments such as the idea of witchcraft, or when he advanced his own particular arguments on certain points, the beliefs he held and the basic concerns from which he operated were all fairly typical of his period. As a theologian and even as a reformer, he seems by inclination to have been moderate, tempered, and reasonable.[5] He can therefore serve as a fairly representative figure of his time, or at least of the clerical elite of his time. His concerns were their concerns. His opinions and perceptions were (most often) generally held. His descriptions of demonic *maleficium*, of diabolical cults, and of the horrors of the witches' sabbath were, in their essentials, quite similar to those of other authors writing in the early fifteenth century. These notions were widely accepted not because they were shocking but rather because, after the initial shock, educated and reasonable men saw them as logically coherent and readily comprehensible.[6] Witchcraft as he depicted it fitted easily into the larger mental world that ecclesiastical authorities, and increasingly secular ones as well, had constructed for themselves in the early fifteenth century.

When we seek to situate witchcraft within that larger mental world, Nider provides an ideal subject and a unique opportunity. For not only did he write extensively on sorcery and witchcraft, but he wrote at great length on many other subjects as well. Moreover, he never wrote exclusively about witchcraft, but always situated his accounts within some larger work—the wide-ranging *Formicarius,* for example, or his accounts of basic moral law and the Ten Commandments in *De lepra morali* and his *Preceptorium divine legis.*[7] We are virtually required, then, to place witchcraft in the larger context of his more general thought. Yet until very recently no one has ever done so. For the most part, studies focusing exclusively on witchcraft have excerpted passages from his *Formicarius* and treated them as if they were isolated aspects of his thought, or as if he himself were somehow isolated from other religious issues and concerns of his day.[8] Nider, however, was by no means an isolated figure. He was an important leader within his own religious order and also within the church as a whole. His concern over witchcraft developed particularly while he was a member of the great ecumenical Council of Basel. Here he collected stories of divine wonders and miracles, as well as of demonic activity, sorcery, and superstition, from across Europe. Most of his accounts of witchcraft came from lands just to the south of Basel, in the high Alpine valleys of the territory of Bern and elsewhere in the diocese of Lausanne, very much the birthplace of the European witch-hunts. Yet witchcraft was not Nider's only preoccupation while he was at the great council. All of his other major treatises considered here also stemmed from his time in Basel, and this should come as no surprise. At the council he was exposed to all the great religious issues of the day, and he enjoyed the opportunity and authority to address those issues. Especially during the early years when Nider was there, the Council of Basel became in many ways the center of the entire Western Christian world. As he wrote, he saw witchcraft not as an isolated horror (which at the time, in fact, it very much still was) but as a horrible aspect of that larger world.

Nider's accounts offer several important insights into how clerical authorities may have understood witchcraft in the early fifteenth century. For such men, at the heart of this new crime lay the involvement of witches with demons and their reliance on demonic power to perform harmful sorcery. Nider explicitly saw witchcraft as essentially identical in its basic operations to necromancy, the complex and ritualistic invocation of demons practiced by learned magicians in the later Middle Ages. An attentive reading of his accounts, however, confirms that accusations of witchcraft typically derived from a very different sort of magic commonly practiced by a wide variety of people at all levels of medieval society, for his stories of the "witch" Staedelin contain no reference to secret cults, nocturnal conventicles, or apostasy. Staedelin engaged in common *maleficium*, which often aimed to produce harm and perhaps was sometimes even self-consciously demonic, but never involved deep familiarity with demons, and certainly not complete subjugation to them or to Satan. Scholars have long recognized this essential dichotomy in witchcraft.[9] In his *Formicarius* and other writings, Nider clearly conflated elements of these two separate magical systems. Moreover, he resolutely refused to recognize any difference or distinction between them. Thus these sources illustrate how clerical authorities, driven by their need to understand common magical practices within a system that conformed to their established notions of how demonic magic functioned, elaborated the basic crime of *maleficium* into the vast diabolical conspiracy of witchcraft.

Yet Nider's accounts of sorcery and witchcraft, when taken in isolation, do not fully explain why he was drawn to these issues. Every aspect of the witch stereotype had existed independently for centuries without generating the sort of notions that so quickly crystallized only in the early 1400s; and even after the idea of witchcraft had fully developed, some authorities, including clerics, refused to accept the satanic witch as a reality. The key to understanding why Nider was drawn to this idea, and thus perhaps why others were as well, lies in his writings on related issues. Much evidence exists to demonstrate that many of the earliest witch trials in the fifteenth century developed out of trials for heresy or were in some way spawned by the persecution of heretics, mostly Waldensians, in lands around the western Alps. The very word for Waldensians in these regions, *vaudois*, became a name for witches. That fact tells us relatively little, however, as the word also served as a general term of opprobrium applied to other heretics, sorcerers, prostitutes, thieves, and any sort of immoral riff-raff.[10] Still, one might easily infer that profound concern over witchcraft would accompany and perhaps even result from profound concern over heresy. Nider demonstrates that this was not always the case. Surviving evidence suggests that he participated in an inquisition into heresy only once in his life, in the interrogation of a Free Spirit in Regensburg. He never wrote at all about the Waldensians, the heretics most closely associated with witchcraft. Despite his extensive involvement with the most successful and threatening variety of heretics in the early fifteenth century, the Hussites of Bohemia, he exhibited relatively little interest in them. He actually wrote much more about the heresy of the Free Spirit, which was on the wane in his day.[11] While he was convinced that such heretics still existed in threatening numbers, here too his concern seems muted, especially in light of his profound support and praise for beguines, whom other clerical authorities so often accused of the heresy of the Free Spirit, among other errors.

Of all the heresies of the late Middle Ages, that of the Free Spirit would probably have been the most "logical" choice to become associated with witchcraft. These heretics existed, supposedly, in a vast network of secret cells spread all over Europe, and they were commonly accused of nocturnal gatherings, orgies, and devil worship. Hussites, too, were occasionally slandered with such standard canards as orgiastic gatherings and nude rites.[12] Nevertheless, clerical authorities did not regularly accuse the Hussites of witchcraft. Nor did they typically implicate heretics of the Free Spirit in this new crime, or Jews, although many standard clerical anti-Jewish calumnies were transferred to witches. Ironically, the Waldensians of the Alps were probably the heretics least suited for close association with witchcraft. Surviving in small groups in relatively remote areas, they clearly presented no threat to the institutions of the church or to their orthodox neighbors. Authorities did try to paint them with the standard antiheretical brush, accusing them of nocturnal gatherings, orgies, and other immoral acts, but such accusations do not seem to have been widely accepted. Still, in the earliest witch trials, Waldensians and those associated with *vauderie* stood at great risk.[13] Nider helps to clarify the relationship between heresy and witchcraft. Certainly witchcraft was a heresy, and becoming a witch entailed rejecting the true faith and engaging in acts that for clerical authorities typified heretical behavior — nocturnal gatherings, orgies, desecration of the cross, and so forth. Yet for all that it incorporated elements of heresy, witchcraft was a theoretically distinct crime and witches were not simply interchangeable with other types of heretics. They represented a separate form of aberration and they entered into a different sort of association with the devil, rooted in traditions of demonic magic, not the beliefs or practices of earlier heretical groups, real or imagined. Thus concern over other heresies did not necessarily translate into concern over witchcraft, or vice versa. There is no real difficulty, then, in explaining why any and all charges of heresy did not automatically begin to carry presumptions of witchcraft in the early fifteenth century. The close association of Waldensians with witches appears to have been unique to the Alpine region, and must have arisen from specific local conditions. For understanding the origins of the earliest witch trials, these factors are crucial. For understanding the more general early development and diffusion of the idea of witchcraft, however, I see the supposed connection to heresy as something of a red herring.

If fear of heresy did not contribute to the rapid development and spread of the idea of witchcraft, what other aspects of the religious world in the early fifteenth century might have played a role? Several scholars have pointed to the widespread desire for reform in the late Middle Ages, emerging especially from the great reforming councils of Constance and Basel. Yet they have rarely pressed this connection very far. In general, they have tended to see witchcraft, like heresy, simply as a deformation that reformers would naturally have wanted to eliminate. This was only part of the story, however. When we look more deeply into how Nider understood the idea of reform, we see that he was not concerned simply with the elimination of abuse and error and the return to an earlier, pristine state. At the root of his reformist convictions and strategies lay the desire to effect a positive moral and spiritual regeneration within individual believers. He saw institutional reforms within the church, mainly in the religious orders, as a means to this end, as the reformed religious life most perfectly facilitated the individual soul's ascent toward God and could serve as an ideal model for all other faithful Christians to follow. He also sought to impart his message of repentance and moral rejuvenation directly to the laity through the medium of sermons. An experienced and effective popular preacher himself, he was clearly impressed by the moralistic, reformist message carried in the sermons of such men as the Dominican Vincent Ferrer and the Franciscan Bernardino of Siena. Through the stories he collected in his *Formicarius*, intended mainly to serve as exempla for use in popular preaching, he delivered the same sort of message. In this way his concern for reform extended to the entire Christian world, and was in turn affected and shaped by his perceptions of the moral state of that world.

In general, we must be careful about relying on reformers or reformist writings for an accurate picture of late medieval religiosity. These men tended naturally to accentuate the negative in their efforts to effect change.[14] Yet Nider was surprisingly even-handed in his judgments and occasionally even optimistic about the state of his world. He saw much virtue still among clerics and within the institutions of the church, and he recognized a widespread and vibrant lay religiosity. His particular points of emphasis, however, are revealing and instructive. He was obsessed with chastity, especially female chastity and virginity, and the effect they had on women's morality and spirituality. These concerns clearly played a key role in shaping his thought when he sought to understand and explain why more women than men appeared to be witches. More basically, however, he was deeply concerned about what he perceived as a very real and very threatening demonic presence in the world, and particularly about demonic opposition to all efforts at reform. This preoccupation fed powerfully into his interest in witchcraft and his willingness to accept and develop that new concept.

Nider's interest in witchcraft was ultimately rooted in his desire for reform. He did not, however, see in witchcraft merely another deformation among many that needed to be eliminated. In fact, he had little interest in hunting and executing witches. Rather he sought to use tales of demonic witches, just as moralizing clerical authors had for centuries used accounts of direct demonic malevolence, to warn the faithful against the dangers of impiety and to motivate them to deeper devotion, to a more profound acceptance of the principles of the faith, and to more frequent and committed participation in ecclesiastical rites and ceremonies. He was also concerned to address some of the problems of belief associated with witchcraft. He warned the laity not to turn to the power of witches for aid, relief, or comfort. Such remedies might occasionally heal the body, but they always imperiled the soul. He also sought to clarify the often murky boundary between illicit witchcraft and superstition on the one hand and allowable spells, blessings, and charms on the other. While the former were entirely forbidden, the faithful could quite legitimately employ the latter to defend themselves against the devil.

Thus Nider was drawn to the idea of witchcraft, accepted it, and developed and employed it in the ways he did because of his reformist concerns. Had he simply invented a figure to embody all of his major concerns, he could scarcely have improved upon the witch. Yet the fact remains that Nider did not invent the witch single-handedly, nor was his approach to witchcraft the only one that was taken in the fifteenth century. Many inquisitors as well as secular judges focused far more directly on how to eradicate these servants of Satan, why they needed to be eradicated, and how to justify such action legally. The lay French judge Claude Tholosan, for one, wrote a treatise defending full secular jurisdiction over the crime of witchcraft on the basis of trials he had conducted in Dauphiné in the 1430s, and the anonymous author of the *Errores Gazariorum,* perhaps the most lurid description of witchcraft written in the early fifteenth century, was almost certainly an inquisitor. Of course, the most famous authority obsessed primarily with the eradication of witchcraft appeared in the second half of the century, the Dominican inquisitor Heinrich Kramer (Institoris), author of the infamous witch-hunting manual *Malleus maleficarum.* But concern over witchcraft rooted in deeper concerns for moral reform was surely not unique to Nider. The rise of witchcraft and the ensuing witch-hunts occurred at exactly the same time as ideas of reform and renewal of all types surged to the forefront of the European consciousness. Certainly after the advent of the Reformation in the early sixteenth century, reformers both Protestant and Catholic stressed those very elements that were central to Nider's concern over witchcraft—fear of the devil and demonic power active in the world, and personal piety as a principal defense.[15] That preoccupation with witchcraft arose more from internalized moral and religious concerns than from a simple desire to eradicate an external deformity might help explain why, throughout the

turbulent religious conflicts in the wake of the Reformation, both Catholics and
Protestants hurled invective at each other but rarely used charges of witchcraft
to eliminate opposing religious groups under their power. Rather, people tended
to accuse fellow members of their own religious confession of being witches.[16]
As Nider helps to demonstrate, the so-called witch craze of Western Europe
was not coincidental to this long age of reform but was in fact an integral aspect
of it.

Now that the specter of the Reformation in the sixteenth century has been
raised, a few concluding words on the fifteenth century and its place in European history, particularly religious history, are required. Scholars have long since
corrected the overly simplistic view that the late Middle Ages were a period of
unmitigated intellectual, cultural, and spiritual decadence and decline, leading
more or less inevitably to the radical ruptures of the Renaissance and Reformation, which jointly marked the beginning of a new era in European history.[17]
Nevertheless, historians could scarcely ignore the fact that profound changes
took place in the course of the fifteenth and sixteenth centuries, perhaps none
more dramatic than the dissolution of the universalism of Western Christianity
into the confessionalism of Catholic and Protestant and all their subdivisions.
Rather than continuing to posit and defend a single revolutionary moment of
change, scholars began to stress gradual shifts and complex interrelationships
between the old and the new. Yet still the net result was analysis that focused
on a transition from one historical era to another. This being the case, while for
several decades historians have in the main avoided drawing a sharp boundary
through this period of transition, they have nevertheless continued to regard the
process of transition from the perspective of either the preceding or the subse-
quent era. Thus the question whether the fifteenth century belongs more properly to the Middle Ages or to the early modern period has remained one of the
largest overarching problems in the historiography of this time.[18]

In respect to religious history, the issue has typically focused on whether one
regards the late medieval period fundamentally as a continuation of the religious
forms and traditions of the High Middle Ages or as a coherent progression of
developments—a steady decline of papal power, increasing desire on the part
of the laity for direct participation in religious and spiritual activities, and
the growing desire for institutional and spiritual reform generally—all of which
culminated in the Protestant Reformation.[19] Both of these views have merit
and both have yielded valuable insights, yet ultimately neither approaches the
fifteenth century on its own terms. Rather this period is regarded either as the
coda to one era or as the precursor to another, and events and developments
within it are almost inevitably assigned meaning and importance only as they

relate to these larger epochs. The problem, of course, is that viewing a period from an outside perspective, while in some cases helpful, also risks obscuring insight into the complex circumstances and confluence of contemporary factors that helped to produce specific developments and events. The issue of witchcraft may be taken as a case in point. Historians of the Middle Ages who have addressed the rise of witchcraft have tended to see this development as the end result of certain long-standing medieval traditions, such as the demonization of heresy, the hereticization and condemnation of magic and sorcery, and the increasing Christianization of the European peasantry, or as a typical manifestation of the persecuting mentality of the medieval clerical elites.[20] Historians of the great witch-hunts of the sixteenth and seventeenth centuries, for their part, generally see the explanation for these terrible events in the economic, social, and cultural conditions of that time, and they rarely inquire into the initial development of the idea of witchcraft in the years before the *Malleus maleficarum*. In general studies of either the late medieval or early modern period, the rise of witchcraft is often glossed over almost completely.

None of these approaches has proved capable of fully unraveling the origins of the idea of witchcraft or of the witch-hunts that it spawned. With scholarship now focusing on the highly complex and nuanced transitions occurring in the later fourteenth and especially fifteenth centuries, this period no longer appears to have been an era of stultifying decadence and decay, but rather one of tremendous energy and vibrant activity. It was also, however, a period of crisis, when numerous received cultural paradigms and social structures were rapidly renegotiated and reconstructed in an attempt to meet the needs of a changing world. As a result, this century has appeared to many scholars to be terribly fragmented, and the rise of witchcraft in particular is often held up as an example of the incoherence and potential irrationality of the period.[21] Yet certain continuities ran through the fifteenth century and bound together various of its seemingly diverse aspects. Focusing particularly on witchcraft and the related issues of heresy and reform, I have tried to show what some of these continuities of concern may have been. I have taken the fifteenth century seriously on its own terms, not as the culmination of one era or as the prelude to another. Likewise I have taken witchcraft seriously, not as an aberration but as an important aspect of the period in which it developed. I have looked back to earlier medieval magical traditions when it seemed appropriate to do so, and I have of course looked forward to the terrible conflagrations to come, but for the most part I have tried to link the emerging idea of the witch laterally to other major religious issues and concerns in the early fifteenth century. That is the context in which most contemporaries would have understood this new phenomenon. That was certainly how Johannes Nider accepted the idea of witchcraft into his world.

APPENDIX I:
CHRONOLOGY OF NIDER'S LIFE AND
DATABLE WORKS

c. 1380–85	Born in Isny, in southern Swabia.
1402 (c. April)	Enters Dominican order at Colmar.
1404–5	Probably travels as *socius* of Johannes Mulberg.
c. 1410	Probably completes his initial studies in liberal arts.
before 1413	Enters University of Cologne to study theology.
1415–18	Attends Council of Constance.
1418–22	Probably travels to reformed Dominican priories in Italy.
1422 (November)	Petitions for admittance to University of Vienna.
1425 (June)	Receives degree in theology.
1426 (June)	Asks to be relieved of university duties; probably departs for Nuremberg soon thereafter.
c. 1427–29	Prior in Nuremberg.
1427–28	*Die 24 goldenen Harfen.*[1]
1428	Reforms Dominican convent of St. Catherine in Nuremberg.
1429 (April)	Arrives in Basel as prior to begin reform there.
1429–34/35	Prior in Basel.
1430	*De lepra morali.*[2]
1430–31	*Contra heresim Hussitarum.*[3]
1431 (July 23)	Council of Basel officially opens.
1431 (summer/autumn)	*De reformatione status cenobitici.*
1431 (November)	Dispatched to negotiate with Hussites.
1432 (April–May)	Negotiations with Hussites in Cheb (Eger).
1433 (January–April)	Negotiations with Hussites at Dominican priory, Basel.
1433–34	*De paupertate perfecta secularium* and *De secularium religionibus.*
1434 (May)	Appointed lecturer at University of Vienna by Dominican chapter general.
1434 (July)	Reforms Dominican priory in Vienna.

1434 (after July)	*De abstinencia esus carnium.*
1434 (autumn)	Sent with delegation from Council of Basel to Regensburg for negotiations with Hussites.
1434 (November)	Returns to Basel and reports to council; probably departs for Vienna soon thereafter.
1436 (April)	Elected dean of theological faculty in Vienna.
1436	Reforms Dominican priory in Tulln, Austria.
1436–38	*Formicarius.*
1438	*Preceptorium divine legis.*
1438 (Pentecost)	Visits Basel and preaches in the area.
1438 (summer)	Reforms Dominican convent of St. Catherine in Colmar.
1438 (August 13)	Dies in Nuremberg.

APPENDIX II:
DATING OF NIDER'S MAJOR
WORKS USED IN THIS STUDY

Contra heresim Hussitarum: spring 1430–fall 1431

Contra heresim Hussitarum exists in only two known manuscript copies: Basel, ÖBU, E I 9, fols. 386r–453v, and Eichstätt, Universitätsbibliothek, Cod. st. 469, fols. 4r–76r. Both refer to Nider as the "prior of Nuremberg" in their opening rubrics, but internal evidence indicates that he must have written the treatise after he had already arrived in Basel.

On fol. 404r Nider discusses several occasions on which the Hussites have been allowed to express their views before Catholic authorities. One such occasion was a debate held in Hungary in the presence of the "King of the Romans," at which learned doctors from both the University of Vienna and the University of Paris confronted the Hussites. Nider could have been referring only to the great debate between Hussite and Catholic theologians held by the emperor Sigismund in Bratislava in April 1429.[1] He then mentions a debate that was to be held in Nuremberg, at which the Hussites were to have spoken in an open hearing "before all the people." To be able to express their positions openly before large audiences was always a Hussite goal, but only once did they come close to forcing this condition on Catholic authorities. After a highly successful military campaign into German lands in early 1430, the Hussites were able to compel Friedrich of Saxony and the city of Nuremberg to accept their conditions for peace, including their demand that on April 23 of that year they be allowed to explain their positions publicly before the laity in Nuremberg. As the time for the debate approached, Friedrich reneged on the deal, claiming he could not arrange a guarantee of safe conduct for the Hussites into his territory. Still, this was the only occasion on which the heretics came so close to their goal of a truly public debate, and so must be the event to which Nider was referring.[2]

Given these facts, Nider must have written *Contra heresim Hussitarum* sometime after the spring of 1430, more than a year into his priorship in Basel. It also seems fairly certain that he wrote before the Council of Basel's own efforts to negotiate with the Hussites got under way, since he makes no mention of them in this treatise. The council officially decided to negotiate with the Bohemians in late September 1431.

De abstinencia esus carnium: mid- to late 1434

De abstinencia esus carnium seems clearly to have been written at and for the Council of Basel.[3] Nider discusses the observance of abstinence in Greek monastic orders, about which he learned, he says, from delegates of the Byzantine emperor sent to the Council of Basel. This delegation arrived in Basel in midsummer 1434. Nider probably departed Basel by the end of 1434, and so must have completed the work during that time.

De paupertate perfecta secularium and *De secularium religionibus:* c. 1433–34

All that is known for certain regarding the dating of these two treatises is that Nider wrote *De paupertate perfecta secularium* sometime before *De secularium religionibus,* since in *De secularium religionibus* (fol. 2r) he refers to the earlier *De paupertate perfecta secularium.* Also in the later *De secularium religionibus* he mentions a work on poverty by Johannes of Dambach, which in most manuscripts is followed by a date of 1434, thereby seeming to indicate that Nider must have written his treatise no earlier than that year. Dambach lived in the mid-fourteenth century, however, and in a single manuscript that I consulted this date was given as 1334. It is not impossible, therefore, that the date of 1434 in other manuscripts is due to scribal error.[4]

Nevertheless, it remains likely that Nider wrote this work at Basel in the mid-1430s. Debate about lay religiosity, and especially about lay people living in voluntary poverty, was widespread at the council. As early as 1433 an anonymous reform tract called for "lollards and beguines" to stop receiving alms and to support themselves through their own labors. This debate only became more spirited when conflict between the secular and mendicant clergy at the council broke out in the late spring of 1434. Since the "secular religious" were often associated with the mendicant orders as tertiaries, attacks on beguines often served as a means to attack the mendicant orders indirectly. By 1435 the Spanish cleric Andreas of Escobar was calling for a ban on beguines altogether.[5]

Nider was away from the council negotiating with the Hussites until the summer of 1432. Upon returning to Basel, he probably became involved in the debate about lay poverty, most likely producing *De paupertate perfecta secularium* in 1433 or early 1434. Then, as secular–mendicant conflict escalated and attacks on beguines became more strident, he produced the more general defense of the lay religious, *De secularium religionibus,* in 1434 before leaving Basel for Vienna.

De reformatione status cenobitici: mid- to late 1431 (possibly early 1432)

In the prologue (fol. 186v) Nider indicates that he is writing at the request of the master general of his order, Barthélemy Texier. He also notes that he is currently engaged in an embassy from the Council of Basel to the emperor, which is occupying much of his time. Nevertheless, he resolves to begin working on the desired treatise in whatever free time he has. The embassy to which he refers must have been that headed by Johannes of Ragusa, which met with the emperor Sigismund in Nuremberg in May 1431.[6] Thus Nider must have begun writing *De reformatione status cenobitici* in mid-1431. How long he took to complete this lengthy treatise while he was occupied with so many other tasks is uncertain.

Formicarius: late 1436–early 1438

Nider wrote the *Formicarius* mainly in 1437, possibly beginning in late 1436 and finishing in early 1438, while at the University of Vienna. In the first book (1.7, pp. 54 and 55) he twice mentions that the Council of Basel, which convened in June 1431, has been meeting for six years, thus giving a date of 1437. In the third book (3.3, p. 194) he writes that scarcely nine years have passed since he reformed the Dominican convent of St. Catherine in Nuremberg; he accomplished that task in the late autumn of 1428. Finally, in the fifth and last book (5.2, p. 344) he writes again of the reform of St. Catherine's in Nuremberg, here describing it as having occurred scarcely ten years before, indicating that the entire work took at least a year to write and was finished in early 1438.[7]

Preceptorium divine legis: 1438

Preceptorium divine legis must have been written at the same time as or slightly later than the last book of the *Formicarius,* as Nider refers to his accounts of witchcraft in that earlier work here (1.11.cc).

Appendix III:
Manuscript Copies of Nider's Treatises

Most manuscript copies of Nider's works are listed in Thomas Kaeppeli's monumental *Scriptores Ordinis Praedicatorum*.[1] I list here additional manuscript copies of the major treatises used in this book not listed by Kaeppeli, along with some corrections to Kaeppeli's listings. Information is based on the catalogs of the respective collections, except where noted.

De paupertate perfecta secularium
   Munich, Bayerische Staatsbibliothek, Clm. 18195, fols. 243r–259v.
   Nuremberg, Germanisches Nationalmuseum, Hs. 101 221, fol. 266v
      (excerpt).
De reformatione status cenobitici
   Chicago, Newberry Library, Case MS 134, fols. 1r–103r.
   Cologne, Diözesan- und Dombibliothek, Cod. 1067, fols. 1r–152v.
De secularium religionibus
   Emmerich, Stadtarchiv, 13, fols. 20r–23v (excerpts from chaps. 1 and 4).[2]
   Melk, Stiftsbibliothek, Cod. mell. 1833, fols. 161r–167r (Johannes von
      Speyer, *Excerpta ex tractatu magistri Ioannis Nider de eremetis et ana-
      choretis = De secularium,* chaps. 11 and 12).
Formicarius
   Munich, Bayerische Staatsbibliothek, Cgm. 809, fol. 2v (excerpt).
Preceptorium divine legis
   Ansbach, Staatliche Bibliothek (Schloßbibliothek), Ms. lat. 24, fols. 1r–240r.
   Fritzlar, Dombibliothek, Ms. 18, fols. 1r–247r.
   Klosterneuburg, Stiftsbibliothek, Ms. 843, fols. 235r–351v.
   Melk, Stiftsbibliothek, Cod. mell. 1916, fols. 254r–262v (excerpt).
   Munich, Bayerische Staatsbibliothek, Clm. 28301, fol. 262v (excerpt).
   Munich, Bayerische Staatsbibliothek, Clm. 28564, fols. 2v–244r.
   Munich, Universitätsbibliothek, 8° Cod. ms. 79, fols. 166r–167r (excerpt).

Corrections to Kaeppeli listings

No. 2540, *Preceptorium divine legis:* Freiburg in Brg., Univ. Bibl., 673, no
folio numbers listed. Correction: This is not a complete copy, only a brief
excerpt running fols. 65r–69r.

No. 2541, *De reformatione status cenobitici:* München, Staatsbibl., Clm.
7539, fols. 123v–124v. Correction: The treatise runs fols. 55r–124v.

NOTES

Introduction: Witchcraft, Heresy, and Reform in the Fifteenth Century

1. *Errores Gazariorum;* Latin text in *L'imaginaire du sabbat,* 278–87, or, in an inferior edition, in Joseph Hansen, *Quellen und Untersuchungen zur Geschichte des Hexenwahns und der Hexenverfolgung im Mittelalter* (1901; reprint Hildesheim, 1963), 118–22. A partial English translation is found in Alan Kors and Edward Peters, eds., *Witchcraft in Europe, 400–1700: A Documentary History,* 2nd ed. (Philadelphia, 2001), 160–62.

2. Best on these sources is *L'imaginaire du sabbat.*

3. Stuart Clark, *Thinking with Demons: The Idea of Witchcraft in Early Modern Europe* (Oxford, 1997), viii; Erich Meuthen, *Das 15. Jahrhundert,* 3rd ed. (Munich, 1996), 168–69.

4. On manuscript and early printed editions of the *Formicarius,* see Werner Tschacher, *Der Formicarius des Johannes Nider von 1437/38: Studien zu den Anfängen der europäischen Hexenverfolgungen im Spätmittelalter* (Aachen, 2000), 83–124. Reference to Nider is in Heinrich Kramer, *Malleus maleficarum* 2.1.2, trans. Montague Summers (1928; reprint New York, 1971), 100.

5. Carlo Ginzburg, among others, argues strongly against viewing witchcraft solely as a clerical construct. See esp. his *Ecstasies: Deciphering the Witches' Sabbath,* trans. Raymond Rosenthal (New York, 1991). Robin Briggs, *Witches and Neighbors: The Social and Cultural Context of European Witchcraft* (New York, 1996), argues against placing too much emphasis on official persecution.

6. See Françoise Bonney, "Autour de Jean Gerson: Opinions de théologiens sur les superstitions et la sorcellerie au début du XVᵉ siècle," *Le Moyen Age* 77 (1971): 85–98, or more recently Edward Peters, "The Medieval Church and State on Superstition, Magic, and Witchcraft: From Augustine to the Sixteenth Century," in *Witchcraft and Magic in Europe: The Middle Ages,* ed. Bengt Ankarloo and Stuart Clark (Philadelphia, 2002). 173–245, esp. 228–31. I thank Professor Peters for providing me with a copy of this work before its publication. I deal with the relation between superstition and witchcraft more fully in Chapter 6.

7. My approach is to some extent informed by Stuart Clark's magisterial *Thinking with Demons* (as n. 3 above). The present study is more limited in scope than Clark's, but since Clark himself admits to giving little attention to the origins of the ideas he examines (ibid., x), it may perhaps be seen as complementary.

8. "Ordinis zealtor fuit maximus et observancie propagator," from Johannes of Mainz, *Vite fratrum predicatorum conventus Basileensis et de reformatione eiusdem conventus,* Basel, ÖBU, MS A XI 42, fol. 107v. "Also hat maister Iohannes Nider geton, also hat er gelert und gehassen und verboten und also hat er selb gelebt," from Johannes Meyer, *Buch der Reformacio Predigerordens,* ed. Benedictus Maria Reichert, QF, vols. 2–3 (Leipzig, 1908–9), 3:26.

9. On this struggle, best is Joachim Stieber, *Pope Eugenius IV, the Council of Basel, and the Secular and Ecclesiastical Authorities in the Empire: The Conflict over Supreme Authority and Power in the Church* (Leiden, 1978).

10. On the role of the Dominican order and the Dominican priory at the Council of Basel, see Franz Egger, *Beiträge zur Geschichte des Predigerordens: Die Reform des Basler Konvents, 1429, und die Stellung des Ordens am Basler Konzil, 1431–1448* (Bern, 1991).

11. Jeffrey Burton Russell, *Witchcraft in the Middle Ages* (Ithaca, N.Y., 1972), 234; E. William Monter, *Witchcraft in France and Switzerland: The Borderlands during the Reformation* (Ithaca,

N.Y., 1976), 21–22; Andreas Blauert, *Frühe Hexenverfolgungen: Ketzer-, Zauberei- und Hexenprozesse des 15. Jahrhunderts* (Hamburg, 1989), 111; idem, "Die Erforschung der Anfänge der europäischen Hexenverfolgungen," in *Ketzer, Zauberer, Hexen: Die Anfänge der europäischen Hexenverfolgungen*, ed. Andreas Blauert (Frankfurt a/M, 1990), 11–42, at 19–20; Martine Ostorero, *Folâtrer avec les démons: Sabbat et chasse aux sorciers à Vevey (1448)* (Lausanne, 1995), 27–28; *L'imaginaire du sabbat*, 13; Tschacher, *Der Formicarius*, 329–33.

12. Schieler, *Magister Johannes Nider aus dem Orden der Prediger-Brüder* (Mainz, 1885). More recently see Margit Brand, *Studien zu Johannes Niders deutschen Schriften* (Rome, 1998), and Tschacher, *Der Formicarius*. Brand's fine study is limited to Nider's writings in German, which represent only a fraction of his total work. Tschacher's book is the most extensive and best study of Nider to date, but it still focuses primarily on witchcraft. Between them, Brand and Tschacher summarize most other recent scholarship.

13. Discussion of Nider in relation to Free Spirits is found in Robert E. Lerner, *The Heresy of the Free Spirit in the Later Middle Ages*, rev. ed. (Notre Dame, Ind., 1991), 174–76. Mention of Nider's treatises is in Alexander Patschovsky, "Beginen, Begarden und Terziaren im 14. und 15. Jahrhundert: Das Beispiel des Basler Beginenstreits (1400/04–1411)," in *Festschrift für Eduard Hlawitschka zum 65. Geburtstag*, ed. Karl Rudolf Schnith and Roland Pauler (Munich, 1993), 403–18, at 407. Only one other study of late medieval beguines gives even passing attention to these treatises: Jean-Claude Schmitt, *Mort d'une hérésie: L'Eglise et les clercs face aux béguines et aux béghards du Rhin supérieure du XIVe et XVe siècle* (Paris, 1978), 161–63. A fine, detailed study of one of these treatises is John Van Engen, "Friar Johannes Nyder on Laypeople Living as Religious in the World," in *Vita Religiosa im Mittelalter: Festschrift für Kaspar Elm zum 70. Geburtstag*, ed. Franz J. Felten and Nikolas Jaspert (Berlin, 1999), 583–615.

14. Ginzburg, *Ecstasies*, 69. Detailed analysis has since been provided by Chène in *L'imaginaire du sabbat*, 101–265, and Tschacher, *Der Formicarius*, esp. 83–243. Tschacher also provides an excellent survey of Nider's place in earlier scholarship on witchcraft (11–21).

15. Nider produced fourteen major works on theological and pastoral issues, along with two large sermon collections and various uncollected sermons and letters. His most popular treatises exist in scores of manuscript copies, and ten of his works were later printed in more than forty early editions. See Thomas Kaeppeli, *Scriptores Ordinis Praedicatorum medii aevi*, 4 vols. (Rome, 1970–93), 2:500–515 and 4:164–65; more detailed discussion in Tschacher, *Der Formicarius*, 222–43.

16. Writing in the mid–nineteenth century, for example, the ever rational and enlightened Michelet termed Nider "the prince of fools, a genuine Teutonic dullard." See Jules Michelet, *Satanism and Witchcraft: The Classic Study of Medieval Superstition*, trans. A. R. Allinson (New York, 1992), 323.

17. Richard Kieckhefer, *Magic in the Middle Ages* (Cambridge, 1989), 199–200; Blauert, *Frühe Hexenverfolgungen*, 120.

18. See Robin Briggs, "'Many Reasons Why': Witchcraft and the Problem of Multiple Explanation," in *Witchcraft in Early Modern Europe: Studies in Culture and Belief*, ed. Jonathan Barry, Marianne Hester, and Gareth Roberts (Cambridge, 1996), 49–63.

19. Johan Huizinga, *The Autumn of the Middle Ages*, trans. Rodney J. Payton and Ulrich Mammitzsch (Chicago, 1996), 286–87.

20. On historiographical developments, see the introduction to *Handbook of European History, 1400–1600: Late Middle Ages, Renaissance, and Reformation*, ed. Thomas A. Brady Jr., Heiko A. Oberman, and James D. Tracy, 2 vols. (Leiden, 1994–95), 1:xiii–xxiv; also Meuthen, *Das 15. Jahrhundert* (as n. 3 above), 113–20.

21. Meuthen, *Das 15. Jahrhundert*, 2.

22. For an overview of the various ecclesiastical crises in this period, see John Van Engen, "The Church in the Fifteenth Century," in Brady et al., *Handbook of European History* (as n. 20 above), 1:305–30, along with additional literature cited there.

1. The Life Of Johannes Nider

1. *MC*, 1:91–92.

2. Johannes of Mainz, *Vita fratrum predicatorum conventus Basileensis et de reformatione eiusdem conventus*, Basel, ÖBU, MS A XI 42, fols. 97r–119r; Johannes Meyer, *Liber de viris illustribus Ordinis Praedicatorum*, ed. Paulus von Loë, QF, vol. 12 (Leipzig, 1918); Meyer, *Buch der Reformacio Predigerordens*, ed. Benedictus Maria Reichert, QF, vols. 2–3 (Leipzig, 1908–9). On these sources, especially Johannes of Mainz, see Franz Egger, *Beiträge zur Geschichte des Predigerordens: Die Reform des Basler Konvents, 1429, und die Stellung des Ordens am Basler Konzil, 1431–1448* (Bern, 1991), 25–62.

3. *Formicarius* 5.4, p. 353.

4. *Formicarius* 3.7, pp. 226–28. See also Robert E. Lerner, *The Heresy of the Free Spirit in the Later Middle Ages*, rev. ed. (Notre Dame, Ind., 1991), 175–76.

5. Biographical information is also given by Chène in *L'imaginaire du sabbat*, 101–5, and by Margit Brand, *Studien zu Johannes Niders deutschen Schriften* (Rome, 1998), 11–31. The best and most detailed account is now Werner Tschacher, *Der Formicarius des Johannes Nider von 1437/38: Studien zu den Anfängen der europäischen Hexenverfolgungen im Spätmittelalter* (Aachen, 2000), 31–80.

6. William A. Hinnebusch, *The History of the Dominican Order*, 2 vols. (New York, 1965–73), 1:283. In practice this restriction proved difficult to maintain, and in 1323 the order dropped even the official requirement that novices be eighteen years of age. As the Dominican reform movement was dedicated to a strict observance of the rule and early ordinances of the order, however, a minimum age of eighteen may well again have been the norm in observant houses.

7. Johannes of Mainz writes of Nider, "hinc iactabat eciam se totiens pauperis sutoris filium ex Swevia oriundum esse" (*Vita fratrum*, fol. 107r). Nider himself mentions his youth only once, in *Formicarius* 2.6, pp. 131–32, when he tells of returning to Isny briefly to visit his mother after graduating from the University of Vienna.

8. Kaspar Schieler, *Magister Johannes Nider aus dem Orden der Prediger-Brüder* (Mainz, 1885), 3; Tschacher, *Der Formicarius*, 32; Brand, *Johannes Niders deutschen Schriften*, 13.

9. On these movements in general, see Dieter Mertens, "Monastische Reformbewegungen des 15. Jahrhunderts: Ideen—Ziele—Resultate," in *Reform von Kirche und Reich zur Zeit der Konzilien von Konstanz (1414–1418) und Basel (1431–1449)*, ed. Ivan Hlaváček and Alexander Patschovsky (Constance, 1996). On the mendicant orders, see Bernhard Neidiger, "Die Observanzbewegungen der Bettelorden in Südwestdeutschland," *Rottenburger Jahrbuch für Kirchengeschichte* 11 (1992): 175–96. On the Dominican reform in Germany, see Eugen Hillenbrand, "Die Observantenbewegung in der deutschen Ordensprovinz der Dominikaner," in *Reformbemühungen und Observanzbestrebungen im spätmittelalterlichen Ordenswesen*, ed. Kaspar Elm (Berlin, 1989), 219–71; also Sabine von Heusinger, *Johannes Mulberg († 1414): Ein Leben im Spannungsfeld von Dominikanerobservanz und Beginenstreit* (Berlin, 2000), 11–38. Gabriel M. Löhr, *Die Teutonia im 15. Jahrhundert: Studien und Texte vornehmlich zur Geschichte ihrer Reform*, QF, vol. 19 (Leipzig, 1924), also remains essential.

10. Hillenbrand, "Observantenbewegung," 226–27.

11. On Nider's entry, see Löhr, *Teutonia*, 7 n. 4. A list of observant Dominican houses, along with the dates of reform, is given in the foreword to Meyer, *Buch der Reformacio Predigerordens*, 3:ii–vi; and in the appendix to Hillenbrand, "Observantenbewegung," 271.

12. In *Formicarius* 1.6, p. 49, Nider praised Bishop Eckhard as one of the good prelates of Germany, and then added, "ad quem [Eckhard] eandum ob causam a conventu meo nativo ... missus sum per quator dioceses, ut sine macula pravitatis simoniace confirmationis et ordinis sacramenta susciperem."

13. *Formicarius* 2.1, pp. 99–100. Best on Mulberg is Heusinger, *Johannes Mulberg*, as n. 9 above.

14. Hermann Keussen, ed., *Die Matrikel der Universität Köln, 1389–1559,* 3 vols. (Bonn, 1928–31), 3:11. See also Isnard Wilhelm Frank, *Hausstudium und Universitätsstudium der Wiener Dominikaner bis 1500,* Archiv für österreichische Geschichte, vol. 127 (Vienna, 1968), 203.

15. For an overview of the Dominican educational system, see Hinnebusch, *History,* 2:19–98. On the possible course of Nider's education, see Tschacher, *Der Formicarius,* 37–38.

16. "In tempore quo artes primum in universitate Wienensi audivi": *Formicarius* 4.11, pp. 322–23.

17. On his matriculation in 1422, see *Die Matrikel der Universität Wien,* 6 vols. (Graz, 1956–), 1:137. That he was not well known to the faculty ("non erat multum notus") is found in Paul Uiblein, ed., *Die Akten der Theologischen Fakultät der Universität Wien,* 2 vols. (Vienna, 1978), 1:47. See also Frank, *Hausstudium,* 203. The Dominican Franz of Retz, who eventually served as Nider's master in Vienna, had been teaching there since 1388, and would surely have remembered Nider had he been in Vienna previously. See also the position of Tschacher, *Der Formicarius,* 40–41.

18. *Formicarius* 1.3, p. 23; 1.8, p. 60; 2.7, p. 139; 4.2, p. 266; 5.11, p. 413.

19. As stated in Tschacher, *Der Formicarius,* 38–39: "Man wird auch nicht sehr fehlgehen, Niders Kölner Studienzeit in die Jahre zwischen 1410 und 1413 zu datieren."

20. Nider mentions his presence at the council in *Formicarius* 1.7, p. 53; 3.1, p. 181; 3.2, p. 190; and 3.9, p. 238, but without providing any means for exact dating.

21. *Formicarius* 3.9, p. 238.

22. "Quantum memoro, de reformatione multum tractabatur ... et letatus sum pro tunc in his que dicta sunt mihi ... sed frustrati sumus a desiderio nostro": *Formicarius* 1.7, p. 53.

23. *Formicarius* 1.9, p. 67.

24. See the cautious and reliable account in Tschacher, *Der Formicarius,* 45–46. An overview of the Dominican reform in Italy can be found in R. Creytens and A. d'Amato, "Les actes capitulaires de la congregation Dominicaine de Lombardie (1482–1531)," *Archivum Fratrum Praedicatorum* 31 (1961): 213–306, at 214–29.

25. Records of Nider's admission and later studies are found in Uiblein, *Akten,* 1:47–48 and 51. On his studies in Vienna, see Frank, *Hausstudium,* 202–5, and Tschacher, *Der Formicarius,* 47–49. Nider briefly mentioned his master, Franz of Retz, in *Formicarius* 4.7, pp. 298–300.

26. Term coined in Berndt Hamm, "Frömmigkeit als Gegenstand theologiegeschichtlicher Forschung: Methodisch-historische Überlegungen am Beispiel von Spätmittelalter und Reformation," *Zeitschrift für Theologie und Kirche* 74 (1977): 464–97, esp. 479. See also Berndt Hamm, "Von der spätmittelalterlichen reformatio zur Reformation: Der Prozeß normativer Zentrierung von Religion und Gesellschaft in Deutschland," *Archiv für Reformationsgeschichte* 84 (1993): 7–82, esp. 18–24.

27. Neidiger, "Observanzbewegungen," 182.

28. Tschacher, *Der Formicarius,* 216–20 and 279–82.

29. There has long been some debate about whether Nider received his degree in 1425 or 1426. To my mind, however, this debate has now been resolved. See the persuasive arguments and evidence in Tschacher, *Der Formicarius,* 49–50.

30. Nider's petition is recorded in Uiblein, *Akten,* 1:57. In *Formicarius* 4.7, p. 300, Nider states he administered last rites to his former master, Franz of Retz, who died on September 8, 1427. So he either had returned to Vienna or had not yet left the city by that date.

31. Uiblein, *Akten,* 2:450 n. 384; Frank, *Hausstudium,* 204; Hillenbrand, "Observantenbewegung," 249–50; Brand, *Johannes Niders deutschen Schriften,* 19. The title of vicar designated a loosely defined office created by the master general essentially to function as his direct representative in a given situation or area.

32. See Löhr, *Teutonia,* 15; Brand, *Johannes Niders deutschen Schriften,* 21; Tschacher, *Der Formicarius,* 52.

33. Texier was a strong supporter of reform. See R. P. Mortier, *Histoire des Maîtres Généraux de l'Ordre des Frères Prêcheurs,* 8 vols. (Paris, 1903–20), 4:415. Nider praised Texier, along with Nicolas Notel, the provincial of Teutonia, in *Formicarius* 1.7, p. 56. See also Hillenbrand, "Observantenbewegung," 233.

34. "Cui reformationi una voce omnes sorores reclamabant": *Formicarius* 3.3, pp. 194–95.

35. *Formicarius* 3.3, p. 195. Nider also briefly mentions the great difficulties the reformers faced in Nuremberg in *Formicarius* 5.2, pp. 344–45.

36. Theodor von Kern, "Die Reformation des Katharinenklosters zu Nürnberg im Jahre 1428," *Jahrbuch des historischen Vereins in Mittelfranken* 31 (1863): 1–20, esp. 3–6.

37. Essential on such points is the work of Bernhard Neidiger. See esp. his *Mendikanten zwischen Ordensideal und städtischer Realität: Untersuchungen zum wirtschaftlichen Verhalten der Bettelorden in Basel* (Berlin, 1981) and "Stadtregiment und Klosterreform in Basel," in *Reformbemühungen* (as n. 9), 539–67. The only good analysis of mendicant–town relations in English deals with an earlier period but is still valuable: John B. Freed, *The Friars and German Society in the Thirteenth Century* (Cambridge, Mass., 1977), 79–105.

38. Martina Wehrli-Johns, *Geschichte des Zürcher Predigerkonvents (1230–1524): Mendikanten zwischen Kirche, Adel und Stadt* (Zurich, 1980), 182–83.

39. Thomas Kaeppeli, ed., *Registrum litterarum fratris Raymundi de Vineis Capuani*, MOPH, vol. 19 (Rome, 1937), 160.

40. Johannes Kist, "Klosterreform im spätmittelalterlichen Nürnberg," *Zeitschrift für bayerische Kirchengeschichte* 32 (1963): 31–45, at 35.

41. Mertens, "Monastische Reformbewegungen," 157–58, notes that most of the later chronicles and monastic accounts of the fifteenth century were written by reformers. Thus we have only the stories of the ultimate victors lauding their own past heroes, and these must be used with care.

42. *Formicarius* 4.6, p. 290.

43. Mortier, *Histoire des Maîtres Généraux*, 4:228, follows this line of reasoning. Schieler, *Magister Johannes Nider*, 68 and 141, is not explicit about his reasons, but he places Nider's appointment as vicar in 1428. For a full discussion of the debate, see Tschacher, *Der Formicarius*, 51, esp. n. 96.

44. See Emil A. Erdin, *Das Kloster der Reuerinnen Sancta Maria Magdalena an den Steinen zu Basel: Von den Anfängen bis zur Reformation (ca. 1230–1529)* (Fribourg, 1956), 49–59.

45. Johannes of Mainz, "Vita fratrum," fol. 98r; Meyer, *Buch der Reformacio Predigerordens*, 3:70. See discussion in Egger, *Geschichte des Predigerordens*, 63; Neidiger, "Observanzbewegungen," 184–85; Neidiger, "Stadtregiment," 543–44.

46. Löhr, *Teutonia*, 53–54.

47. Meyer, *Buch der Reformacio Predigerordens*, 3:70, states that "die bruder, die wider die gaistlichait warent, und och die swöstern des closters zu Clingental, schweren widerstand daten, und die layen yren fründen." Further details in Egger, *Geschichte des Predigerordens*, 65.

48. Egger, *Geschichte des Predigerordens*, 66. The typical process of reform is described in Löhr, *Teutonia*, 2–5.

49. Complete list of directives edited in Löhr, *Teutonia*, 54–63.

50. Hillenbrand, "Observantenbewegung," 236; Renée Weis-Müller, *Die Reform des Klosters Klingental und ihr Personenkreis* (Basel, 1956), 15–16.

51. Hillenbrand, "Observantenbewegung," 236; Egger, *Geschichte des Predigerordens*, 66–67.

52. See MC, 2:126–28; CB, 2:41 and 46–47. Also Johannes Helmrath, *Das Basler Konzil: Forschungsstand und Probleme* (Cologne, 1987), 23–24, and Joachim W. Stieber, *Pope Eugenius IV, the Council of Basel, and the Secular and Ecclesiastical Authorities in the Empire: The Conflict over Supreme Authority and Power in the Church* (Leiden, 1978), 17–18. Still the most complete treatment of Basel's organization and operation is Paul Lazarus, *Das Basler Konzil: Seine Berufung und Leitung, seine Gliederung und seine Behördenorganisation* (1912; reprint Vaduz, 1965).

53. On Nider's membership, see CB, 2:304.

54. Lazarus, *Basler Konzil*, 123, 127–28, 147–49, 182–83.

55. On the role of the Dominicans in the negotiations with the Hussites, the best account is Egger, *Geschichte des Predigerordens*, 135–66. See also Helmrath, *Basler Konzil*, 353–72, and E. F. Jacob, "The Bohemians at the Council of Basel, 1433," in *Prague Essays*, ed. R. W. Seton-Watson (Oxford, 1949), 81–123. For more on Nider's role, see below. On Sigismund's stays in the Dominican

priory, see Egger, *Geschichte des Predigerordens,* 204. On the emperor's activity in Basel in general, see Jörg K. Hoensch, *Kaiser Sigismund: Herrscher an der Schwelle zur Neuzeit, 1368–1437* (Munich, 1996), 405–28.

56. *MC,* 1:68–70.

57. On his appointment, see Lazarus, *Basler Konzil,* 21–22. On his activity in general, see Gerald Christianson, *Cesarini: The Conciliar Cardinal, the Basel Years, 1431–1438* (St. Ottilien, 1979).

58. On this exchange see *MC,* 1:68. As early as March 4, the French abbot Alexander of Vézelay, who had arrived in Basel in late February, was urging the leaders of the town clergy that the council should begin as soon as possible, and a few days later, on March 11, a delegation from the University of Paris arrived with much the same message. Nider was present to hear both speeches. See *MC,* 1:68–70.

59. *De reformatione,* prologue, fol. 186v. On this mission, see Egger, *Geschichte des Predigerordens,* 98–99. Nider, who perhaps went as a personal assistant to Ragusa, is not listed among the three official members of the delegation. *MC,* 1:77.

60. *MC,* 2:17–18; *CB,* 2:8.

61. *MC,* 1:89–90. On this otherwise "insignificant, if not ridiculous, little war," see Richard Vaughan, *Philip the Good: The Apogee of Burgundy* (New York, 1970), 64–65.

62. *MC,* 1:112–13

63. *MC,* 1:125. The others were Johannes of Ragusa, Jacobus Mercerius, Raymund of Tilio, Johannes of Montenegro, Juan of Torquemada, and Guido Flamochetti.

64. *MC,* 2:35; *CB,* 2:18 and 5:8.

65. *MC,* 1:138–39.

66. Stieber, *Pope Eugenius,* 12–15. See also Loy Bilderback, "Eugene IV and the First Dissolution of the Council of Basle," *Church History* 36 (1967): 243–53.

67. These letters have been preserved in Johannes of Ragusa's *Tractatus quomodo Bohemi reducti sunt ad unitatem ecclesiae,* edited in *MC,* 1:174–86.

68. *MC,* 1:190–99, 206, 208–10, 214–17, 224. Chapter 3 gives a more detailed discussion of Nider's role in this mission.

69. Egger, *Geschichte des Predigerordens,* 141.

70. Aloysius Krchnák, *De vita et operibus Ioannis de Ragusio* (Rome, 1960), 25–26.

71. *CB,* 2:304 and 522.

72. "Magna controversia orta est in sacro concilio inter curatos et religiosos mendicantes," the Benedictine Ulrich Stökel of Tegernsee wrote to his abbot in a letter of May 8, 1434 (*CB,* 1:81–83). On this conflict in general, see R. N. Swanson, "The 'Mendicant Problem' in the Later Middle Ages," in *The Medieval Church: Universities, Heresy, and the Religious Life, Essays in Honour of Gordon Leff,* ed. Peter Biller and Barrie Dobson (Woodbridge, 1999), 217–38, mention of Basel but no detail at 237.

73. *MC,* 2:701–2.

74. On this incident, see Egger, *Geschichte des Predigerordens,* 171–75; Helmrath, *Basler Konzil,* 124–25.

75. Joseph Gill, *Eugenius IV: Pope of Christian Union* (Westminster, Md., 1961), 45.

76. Antony Black, *Council and Commune: The Conciliar Movement and the Fifteenth Century Heritage* (London, 1989), 54–55; idem, "Diplomacy, Doctrine, and the Disintegration of an Idea into Politics," in *Studien zum 15. Jahrhundert: Festschrift für Erich Meuthen,* ed. Johannes Helmrath and Heribert Müller, 2 vols. (Munich, 1994), 1:77–85, here 79–80.

77. For one example, see Joachim W. Stieber, "The 'Hercules of the Eugenians' at the Crossroads: Nicholas of Cusa's Decision for the Pope and against the Council in 1436/1437—Theological, Political, and Social Aspects," in *Nicholas of Cusa in Search of God and Wisdom: Essays in Honor of Morimichi Wanatabe by the American Cusanus Society,* ed. Gerald Christianson and Thomas M. Izbicki (Leiden, 1991), 221–55, here 230–31.

78. For propositions put before the council from 1433 to 1436 calling for curtailment of the mendicants' privileges, see *CB,* 1:81–83, 226–27, 409–10, 4:150, 8:105–8. See also Egger,

Geschichte des Predigerordens, 186–89, and Thomas M. Izbicki, "The Council of Ferrara-Florence and Dominican Papalism," in *Christian Unity: The Council of Ferrara-Florence, 1438/9–1989,* ed. Giuseppe Alberigo (Louvain, 1991), 429–43.

79. Some observers have considered Nider an extreme papalist on little more evidence, it would seem, than the habit he shared with other Dominican theorists of papal power. Black, *Council and Commune,* 33, writes: "The Dominicans provided the outstanding champions of the papacy at this time: Torquemada, Kalteisen, Montenigro, Nieder [*sic*], Hüntpichler." Unfortunately, this incorrect association is repeated verbatim in the standard survey of the Council of Basel, Helmrath, *Basler Konzil,* 126: "Die 'outstanding champions of the papacy' waren: Torquemada, Montenigro, Kalteisen, Nider." In fact, Nider never wrote explicitly about papalism, conciliarism, or other ecclesiological issues. His reformist writings reveal, however, that if anything, he leaned toward the conciliarist side. See Michael D. Bailey, "Abstinence and Reform at the Council of Basel: Johannes Nider's *De abstinencia esus carnium,*" *Mediaeval Studies* 59 (1997): 225–60, esp. 241–42; also Chapter 4 below.

80. Egger, *Geschichte des Predigerordens,* 191–93.

81. Tschacher, *Der Formicarius,* 68.

82. Frank, *Hausstudium,* 215; Tschacher, *Der Formicarius,* 68. On Nider's expressed desire to return to Vienna, see Uiblein, *Akten,* 1:57.

83. *MC,* 2:675 and 769.

84. Uiblein, *Akten,* 1:115. See also Frank, *Hausstudium,* 215.

85. Johannes of Mainz, *Vite fratrum,* fol. 108v.

86. Joseph Aschbach, *Geschichte der Wiener Universität im ersten Jahrhunderte ihres Bestehens* (Vienna, 1865), 589.

87. "'Gelobs tu, daz des sy Christus der behalte der wellt?' Do sprach er: 'Ich glob es.' Und zu hand do er dis wort gesprochen hatt, do verschied er und entschlieff in dem herrn": Meyer, *Buch der Reformacio Predigerordens,* 3:31.

88. Meyer, *Buch der Reformacio Predigerordens,* 3:27, seems to have been the first to comment on the breadth and quality of Nider's writings even while he was so busy with other activities.

89. See Introduction, n. 11.

90. *Formicarius* 5.3, p. 349.

91. *Formicarius* 5.8, p. 387.

2. Witchcraft in the Writings of Johannes Nider

1. On the problem of terminology, see Jean-Patrice Boudet, "La genèse médiéval de la chasse aux sorcières: Jalons en veu d'une relecture," in *Le mal et le diable: Leur figures à la fin du Moyen Age,* ed. Nathalie Nabert (Paris, 1996), 35–52, at 36. Unfortunately, Boudet's own definition of witchcraft simply as "oral" and "popular" magic, as opposed to learned demonic magic, is problematic for the late Middle Ages. Jeffrey Burton Russell, *Witchcraft in the Middle Ages* (Ithaca, N.Y., 1972), 13–19, provides a good discussion of the issue, although I disagree with his conclusion that "European witchcraft is best considered a form of heresy" (19).

2. Richard Kieckhefer, *Magic in the Middle Ages* (Cambridge, 1989), 37; Julio Caro Baroja, *The World of the Witches,* trans. O. N. V. Glendinning (Chicago, 1964), 18–19; Richard Gordon, "Imagining Greek and Roman Magic," in *Witchcraft and Magic in Europe: Ancient Greece and Rome,* ed. Bengt Ankarloo and Stuart Clark (Philadelphia, 1999), 159–275, at 244–66.

3. The inquisitor Nicolau Eymeric had worked out the necessity of idolatry in performing demonic magic in the mid-1370s in his *Tractatus contra demonum inuocatores* and *Directorium inquistorum.* More on Eymeric below. Pierrette Paravy has noted the primacy of apostasy in the early treatise on witchcraft *Ut magorum et maleficiorum errores manifesti ignorantibus fiant,* written c. 1436 by the French secular judge Claude Tholosan. See her "A propos de la genèse médiévale des chasses aux sorcières: Le traité de Claude Tholosan, juge dauphinois (vers 1436)," *Mélanges de l'Ecole française de Rome* 91 (1979): 333–79, at 342–43, or *L'imaginaire du sabbat,* 425–26. I

see apostasy figuring centrally in all the major treatises on witchcraft from the 1430s. See my article "The Medieval Concept of the Witches' Sabbath," *Exemplaria* 8 (1996): 419–39. On the development of the conspiracy theory of witchcraft, see Werner Tschacher, "Vom Feindbild zur Verschwörungstheorie: Das Hexenstereotyp," in *Verschwörungstheorien: Anthropologische Konstanten—historische Varianten,* ed. Ute Caumanns and Mathias Niendorf (Osnabrück, 2000), 49–74.

4. The term "sabbath" or "sabbat" came to be used only in the second half of the fifteenth century. Earlier these gatherings were generally termed "synagogues." See Agostino Paravicini Bagliani, Kathrin Utz Tremp, and Martine Ostorero, "Le sabbat dans les Alps: Les prémices médiévales de la chasse aux sorcières," in *Sciences: Raison et déraisons* (Lausanne, 1994), 67–89, at 70. For characteristics of sabbaths, see Bailey, "Witches' Sabbath," esp. 438–39. A number of important essays are found in *Le sabbat des sorciers (XVᵉ–XVIIᵉ siècles),* ed. Nicole Jacques-Chaquin and Maxime Préaud (Grenoble, 1993).

5. Much scholarship has focused on the origins of witchcraft at this time and in these lands. Most recently see the excellent survey in Werner Tschacher, *Der Formicarius des Johannes Nider von 1437/38: Studien zu den Anfängen der europäischen Hexenverfolgungen im Spätmittelalter* (Aachen, 2000), 293–340. Also Andreas Blauert, *Frühe Hexenverfolgungen: Ketzer-, Zauberei- und Hexenprozesse des 15. Jahrhunderts* (Hamburg, 1989); Arno Borst, "The Origins of the Witch-Craze in the Alps," in idem, *Medieval Worlds: Barbarians, Heretics, and Artists in the Middle Ages,* trans. Eric Hansen (Chicago, 1992), 101–22; Pierrette Paravy, *De la Chrétienté romaine à la Réforme en Dauphiné: Evêques, fidèles et déviants (vers 1340–vers 1530),* 2 vols. (Rome, 1993), 2:771–905; Martine Ostorero, *Folâtrer avec les démons: Sabbat et chasse aux sorciers à Vevey (1448)* (Lausanne, 1995). On early treatises and accounts of witchcraft, see *L'imaginaire du sabbat.*

6. On the reality vs. the idea of witchcraft and the difficulty of separating them, see Brian P. Levack, *The Witch-Hunt in Early Modern Europe,* 2nd ed. (London, 1995), 11–20, and the important observations in Stuart Clark, *Thinking with Demons: The Idea of Witchcraft in Early Modern Europe* (Oxford, 1997), 5–8. The most important local study, in respect to Nider's accounts, is the discussion of social, economic, and political factors underlying early witch trials in the Simme valley of the western Alps in Borst, "Origins of the Witch-Craze." See also the series of studies undertaken by scholars at the University of Lausanne: Ostorero, *Folâtrer avec les démons;* Eva Maier, *Trente ans avec le diable: Une nouvelle chasse aux sorciers sur la Riviera lémanique (1477–1485)* (Lausanne, 1996); Sandrine Strobino, *Françoise sauvée des flammes? Une Valaisanne accusée de sorcellerie au XVᵉ siècle* (Lausanne, 1996); Laurence Pfister, *L'enfer sur terre: Sorcellerie à Dommartin (1498)* (Lausanne, 1997); and Georg Modestin, *Le diable chez l'évêque: Chasse aux sorciers dans le diocese de Lausanne (vers 1460)* (Lausanne, 1999).

7. See Edward Peters, "The Medieval Church and State on Superstition, Magic, and Witchcraft: From Augustine to the Sixteenth Century," in *Witchcraft and Magic in Europe: The Middle Ages,* ed. Bengt Ankarloo and Stuart Clark (Philadelphia, 2002), 173–245.

8. See Kieckhefer, *Magic,* 37–40; Edward Peters, *The Magician, the Witch, and the Law* (Philadelphia, 1978), 5–11; Valerie J. Flint, *The Rise of Magic in Early Medieval Europe* (Princeton, 1991), 101–8 and 145–53. On the development of Christian conceptions of demonic magic in the patristic era, see Peter Brown, "Sorcery, Demons, and the Rise of Christianity: From Late Antiquity into the Middle Ages," in *Witchcraft Confessions and Accusations,* ed. Mary Douglas (London, 1970), 17–45, reprinted in Peter Brown, *Religion and Society in the Age of St. Augustine* (London, 1972), 119–46; also Valerie J. Flint, "The Demonisation of Magic and Sorcery in Late Antiquity: Christian Redefinitions of Pagan Religions," in *Witchcraft and Magic in Europe* (as n. 2), 277–348, esp. 315–48.

9. Heinrich Kramer, *Malleus maleficarum* 1.1, trans. Montague Summers (1928; reprint New York, 1971), 1. On papal bulls dealing with sorcery and witchcraft, see Joseph Hansen, *Quellen und Untersuchungen zur Geschichte des Hexenwahns und der Hexenverfolgung im Mittelalter* (1901; reprint Hildesheim, 1963), 1–37; also Henry Charles Lea, *Materials toward a History of Witchcraft,* ed. Arthur C. Howland, 3 vols. (Philadelphia, 1939), 1:220–29.

10. I have explored these issues more generally in my article "From Sorcery to Witchcraft: Clerical Conceptions of Magic in the Later Middle Ages," *Speculum* 76 (2001): 960–90.

11. For example, Russell, *Witchcraft,* argues that witchcraft was primarily a form of heresy. Peters, in *Magician* and more recently in "Medieval Church and State," sees witchcraft as rooted in earlier condemnations of magic. Richard Kieckhefer, *European Witch Trials: Their Foundations in Popular and Learned Culture, 1300–1500* (Berkeley, 1976), explores how elite concern over diabolism shaped the emerging idea of witchcraft. Carlo Ginzburg, *Ecstasies: Deciphering the Witches' Sabbath,* trans. Raymond Rosenthal (New York, 1991), argues that witchcraft originated in vestiges of archaic shamanism such as ideas of night flight and animal transformation. Norman Cohn, *Europe's Inner Demons: The Demonization of Christians in Medieval Christendom,* rev. ed. (London, 1993), gives at least some attention to all these factors, but emphasizes earlier concerns over sorcery and diabolism. I largely follow the arguments of Cohn, Kieckhefer, and Peters.

12. Most extensively Ginzburg, *Ecstasies,* esp. 1–11. Also, in a different vein, Robin Briggs, *Witches and Neighbors: The Social and Cultural Context of European Witchcraft* (New York, 1996), esp. 3–7.

13. See also my position in "Witches' Sabbath," esp. 421–22 and 425–26.

14. On early medieval responses to *maleficium,* see Russell, *Witchcraft,* 71–73; Cohn, *Europe's Inner Demons,* 211–14; Kieckhefer, *Magic,* 177–80. Especially on legal codes, see Peters, *Magician,* 14–15 and 71–78, and *idem,* of his "Medieval Church and State," 187–206.

15. See n. 8 above.

16. See esp. Brown, "Sorcery," 132–38.

17. Latin text in Hansen, *Quellen,* 38–39. English translation and commentary in Alan Kors and Edward Peters, eds., *Witchcraft in Europe, 400–1700: A Documentary History,* 2nd ed. (Philadelphia, 2001), 60–63. Here and below, while translations are my own except where specifically noted, I cite Kors and Peters as a reliable and convenient source.

18. On later developments and interpretations of the canon *Episcopi* in relation to witchcraft, see Werner Tschacher, "Der Flug durch die Luft zwischen Illusionstheorie und Realitätsbeweis: Studien zum sog. Kanon Episcopi und zum Hexenflug," *Zeitschrift der Savigny-Stiftung für Rechtsgeschichte* 116, Kan. Abt. 85 (1999): 225–76; and Walter Stephens, *Demon Lovers: Witchcraft, Sex, and the Crisis of Belief* (Chicago, 2002), 125–44.

19. R. I. Moore, *The Formation of a Persecuting Society: Power and Deviance in Western Europe, 950–1250* (Oxford, 1987). Although Moore deals with the rise of persecution several centuries before the rise of witchcraft, he does link the later witch-hunts to patterns he sees emerging in this period (146–47).

20. English translation from Walter L. Wakefield and Austin P. Evans, eds., *Heresies of the High Middle Ages* (New York, 1969), 78–79. Compare esp. with the *Errores Gazariorum,* quoted at the beginning of this book.

21. Most famously, the inquisitor Konrad of Marburg, who was in fact an episcopal appointee, although the appointment was later sanctioned by the pope, claimed to have found a sect in the Rhineland that worshiped a demon in the form of a pallid man. This idea then found its way into Gregory IX's bull *Vox in Rama,* issued in 1233. See Russell, *Witchcraft,* 159–61; Cohn, *Europe's Inner Demons,* 48–49. On Konrad's extremism, see Richard Kieckhefer, *Repression of Heresy in Medieval Germany* (Philadelphia, 1979), 14–15.

22. Hansen, *Quellen,* 1; Kors and Peters, *Witchcraft,* 117–18.

23. See Russell, *Witchcraft,* 169–73; Peters, *Magician,* 129–33; and Anneliese Maier, "Eine Verfügung Johannes XXII. über die Zuständigkeit der Inquisition für Zaubereiprozesse," *Archivum Fratrum Praedicatorum* 22 (1952): 226–46, reprinted in Maier, *Ausgehendes Mittelalter: Gesamelte Aufsätze zur Geistesgeschichte des 14. Jahrhunderts,* 3 vols. (Rome, 1964–77), 2:59–80.

24. Hansen, *Quellen,* 4–5; Kors and Peters, *Witchcraft,* 119.

25. Hansen, *Quellen,* 5–6; Kors and Peters, *Witchcraft,* 119–20.

26. "Si quis demones invocaverit vel eorum auxilium postulaverit ... excommunicatus est ipso facto per constituciones Iohannis 22 Super illius speculam": Nider, *Manuale confessorum* 1.6, Munich, Bayerische Staatsbibliothek, MS Clm. 9804, p. 385.

27. Bernard Gui, *Practica inquisitionis heretice pravitatis,* ed. C. Douais (Paris, 1886). The

section on sorcerers and diviners is 5.6.1–2, pp. 292–93. Other sections dealing with magical practices are 3.40–43, pp. 150–59, and 5.7.12, p. 301. Parts of these sections have been edited in Hansen, *Quellen*, 47–55. An English translation of one section (5.6.1–2) appears in Wakefield and Evans, *Heresies of the High Middle Ages*, 444–45. For a more extended discussion, see Bailey, "From Sorcery to Witchcraft," 967–71.

28. Nicolau Eymeric, *Directorium inquisitorum* 2.42–43, ed. F. Peña (Rome, 1587), pp. 335–43. Selected translations from these sections in Kors and Peters, *Witchcraft*, 122–27. For additional analysis of this treatise and Eymeric's earlier *Tractatus contra demonum inuocatores*, see Bailey, "From Sorcery to Witchcraft," 971–76.

29. Technically, *necromantia* meant divination via the spirits of the dead, but was used interchangeably with *nigromantia*, meaning black magic more generally. See Richard Kieckhefer, *Forbidden Rites: A Necromancer's Manual of the Fifteenth Century* (University Park, Pa., 1998), 4 and 19 n. 14. For Nider's use of this term, see n. 43 below.

30. Kieckhefer, *Magic*, 153–56. See also Kieckhefer, *Forbidden Rites*, 4. Cohn, *Europe's Inner Demons*, 102–17, deals somewhat with this clerical subculture of magic, as does Peters, *Magician*, esp. 85–91.

31. Eymeric, *Directorium* 2.43.1, p. 338. Hemmerlin discussed such texts in his *Tractatus exorcismorum seu adiurationum* and *De credulitate demonibus adhibenda*, printed together in Hemmerlin, *Varie oblectationis opuscula et tractatus* (Strassburg, after 1497), fols. 107r–116v, at fols. 109r and 113r, respectively.

32. *Formicarius* 5.4, p. 353. More on this man below. See also Kieckhefer, *Magic*, 156; Tschacher, *Der Formicarius*, 173.

33. The best chronological survey remains Kieckhefer, *European Witch Trials*, 10–26, and his "Calendar of Witch Trials," ibid., 106–47. See also Blauert, *Frühe Hexenverfolgungen*, 17–24.

34. Kieckhefer, *European Witch Trials*, 10, notes that in the years 1300–1330, two-thirds of all sorcery trials were "political"; that is, taking place at various secular and ecclesiastical courts. On fear of sorcery at courts, see William R. Jones, "The Political Uses of Sorcery in Medieval Europe," *Historian* 34 (1972), 670–87; H. A. Kelly, "English Kings and the Fear of Sorcery," *Mediaeval Studies* 39 (1977): 206–38; Peters, *Magician*, 112–25, and "Medieval Church and State," 218–22. On sorcery and astrology in general at late medieval courts, see esp. Hilary Carey, *Courting Disaster: Astrology at the English Court and University in the Later Middle Ages* (New York, 1992), esp. 25–36, and Jan Veenstra, *Magic and Divination at the Courts of Burgundy and France: Text and Context of Laurens Pignon's "Contre le devineurs" (1411)* (Leiden, 1998), 59–89 and 127–34.

35. Hansen, *Quellen*, 17–18; Kors and Peters, *Witchcraft*, 154–55.

36. On authorities' determination to understand all magic within a (to them) logical and coherent system, see Kieckhefer, *European Witch Trials*, esp. 73–92; also Richard Kieckhefer, "The Specific Rationality of Medieval Magic," *American Historical Review* 99 (1994): 813–36.

37. Kieckhefer, *Forbidden Rites*, esp. 14–17. See also Cohn, *Europe's Inner Demons*, 110–11; Kieckhefer, *Magic*, 167–68.

38. *Preceptorium* 1.11.ee.

39. In *Formicarius* 5.2, pp. 342–43, Nider recounted a story of a maiden who was tormented by a demon and whom clerical exorcism was not able to free. He then listed various reasons why an exorcism might fail.

40. *Formicarius* 1.4, pp. 33–35.

41. Nider mentions that he consulted with this man about witchcraft in *Formicarius* 5.3, p. 349, and discusses his life as a necromancer in *Formicarius* 5.4, p. 353.

42. Kieckhefer, *European Witch Trials*, esp. 27–46. Also Paravy, *De la Chrétienté romaine à la Réforme*, 2:831–40.

43. "PIG. Quia de necromanticis mentionem fecisti, quaero anne differentia eorum sit a maleficis? Et si sic, quae eorum sint opera? THEOL. Necromantici proprie hi dicuntur, qui de terra superstitiosis ritibus mortuos se posse suscitare ad loquendum occulta ostentant. . . . Ex accommodatione tamen usus, necromantici dicuntur qui per pacta demonum per fidem caeremoniis futura predicunt,

aut occulta revelatione demonum aliqua manifestant, aut qui maleficiis proximos laedunt, et a dae-monibus saepe laeduntur": *Formicarius* 5.4, pp. 352–53.

44. "Neque eo quo nocere dicuntur tempore actionem vel passionem per se immediate inferunt, sed per verba, ritus, vel facta quasi per pacta inita cum daemonibus laedere dicuntur": *Formicarius* 5.3, p. 348.

45. "De hoc etiam infra dicetur non autem faciunt ista immediate maleficorum opera actione propria et immediata, sed talia fiunt per demones qui visis maleficiis immediate ex pacto dudum cum maleficis a principio mundi et tempore veteris idolatrie habito sciunt qualem effectum debent ad intentionem maleficorum procurare. Ut exempla gratia: Scopa quam malefica intingit aquam, ut pluat, non causat pluviam, sed demon talibus visis qui, si deus permiserit, potestatem habet in omnia corporalia, et in aerem, ventos, et nubes, ut statim talia procuraret et causare valeat. Maga siquidem signum dat per scopam, sed demon illud procurat et agit ut pluat per demonis actionem, cui maga mala fide et opere servit et se tradidit obsequiis illius vel aliis": *Preceptorium* 1.11.v. Nider also makes mention of the necessity of pacts, either explicit or implicit, in forms of divination in his *De lepra morali,* fols. 60v–61r.

46. Tschacher, *Der Formicarius,* 401. On the necessity of pacts for Augustine and Aquinas, see Cohn, *Europe's Inner Demons,* 113–14, and Tschacher, *Der Formicarius,* 250–51. Thomas Linsen-mann, *Die Magie bei Thomas von Aquin* (Berlin, 2000), deals extensively with theories of magic in the works of both Aquinas and Augustine.

47. *Formicarius* 5.3, p. 349. On these men, see *L'imaginaire du sabbat,* 223–32, and Tschacher, *Der Formicarius,* 173–77. On Peter of Bern, Hansen, *Quellen,* 91 n. 2, first identified him as Peter von Greyerz, who served as Bernese bailiff from 1392 to 1406. More recently, Catherine Chène has identified two other possible men, Peter Wendschatz, who served as bailiff from 1407 to 1410, and Peter von Ey or Eyg, who served from 1413 to 1417. See *L'imaginaire du sabbat,* 224.

48. See Blauert, *Frühe Hexenverfolgungen,* 57–59. Blauert presents a similar argument for redat-ing the account of witchcraft in Valais given in the report of the Lucerne chronicler Johann Fründ (67–68), which I had earlier accepted in my article "Witches' Sabbath," 423–24. This argument has since been refuted, fairly clearly I think, by Kathrine Utz Tremp and Chantal Ammann-Doubliez in *L'imaginaire du sabbat,* 26 and 63–93. Regarding Nider, however, Chène supports Blauert's conclu-sions (*L'imaginaire du sabbat,* 248).

49. "Fuit insuper fama communis, dicto Petro iudice mihi referente, quod in terra Bernensium tredecim infantes devorati essent intra pauca tempora a malficis, quamobrem etiam publica iustitia satis dure exarsit in tales parricidas. Cum autem Petrus quaesivisset a quadam capta malefica, per quem modum infantes comederent, illa respondit: Modus iste est, nam infantibus nondum baptisatis insidiamur, vel etiam baptisatis, praesertim si signo crucis non muniuntur et orationibus, hos in cunabulis vel ad latera iacentes parentum caeremoniis nostris occidimus, quos postquam putantur oppresi esse, vel aliunde mortui, de tumulis clam furto recipimus, in caldari decoquimus, quousque evulsis ossibus tota pene caro efficiatur sorbilis et potabilis. De solidiori huius materia unguentum facimus nostris voluntatibus et artibus ac transmutationibus accommodum. De liquidiori vero humore flascam aut utrem replemus, de quo is qui potatus fuerit, additis paucis caeremoniis, statim conscius efficitur et magister nostrae sectae": *Formicarius* 5.3, p. 351. On infant cannibalism and witchcraft, see Richard Kieckhefer, "Avenging the Blood of Children: Anxiety over Child Victims and the Origins of the European Witch Trials," in *The Devil, Heresy and Witchcraft in the Middle Ages: Essays in Honor of Jeffrey B. Russell,* ed. Alberto Ferreiro (Leiden, 1998), 91–109. Also Paravy, *De la Chrétienté romaine à la Réforme,* 2:832–33.

50. "Modum autem eundem alius iuvenis maleficus captus et incineratus, tandem licet (ut credo) vere poenitens, distinctius referavit … in Bernensium namque iudicio captus dictus iuvenis cum uxore, et ab eadem in distinctam turrim repositus dixit: Si meorum facinorum veniam consequi pos-sem, omnia quae de maleficiis scio, libens patefacerem…. Ordo, inquit, talis est, quo etiam seduc-tus sum. Oportet primo, dominica die, antequam aqua benedicta consecratur, ecclesiam introire mox futurum discipulum cum magistris, et ibidem abnegare coram eis Christum, eius fidem, baptisma et uniuersalem ecclesiam. Diende homagium praestare magisterulo, id est, parvo magistro,

ita enim daemonem et non aliter vocant, postremo de utre bibit supradicto, quo facto statim se in interioribus sentit imagines nostrae artis concipere, et retinere ac principales ritus huius sectae. In hunc modum seductus sum": *Formicarius* 5.3, pp. 351–52.

51. Kieckhefer, *European Witch Trials*, 20.

52. "Deinde antefato inquisitore mihi referente hoc anno percepi quod in Lausanensi ducatu quidam malefici proprios natos infantes coxerant et comederant. Modus autem discendi talem artem fuit, ut dixit, quod malefici in certam concionem venerunt et opere eorum visibiliter daemonum in assumpta imagine viderunt hominis, cui discipulus necessario dare habebat fidem de abnegando Christianismo, de Eucharistia nunquam adoranda, et de calcando super crucem ubi latenter valeret": *Formicarius* 5.3, pp. 350–51. Note that there is, in fact, no Duchy of Lausanne; rather there are the Diocese of Lausanne and the Duchy of Savoy, which share considerable overlap.

53. Blauert, *Frühe Hexenverfolgungen*, 57–59.

54. *Formicarius* 5.3, p. 350.

55. "Primo verbis certis in campo principem omnium demoniorum imploramus, ut de suis mittat aliquem, [qui] a nobis designatum percutiat, deinde veniente certo daemone in campo [viz. compito] aliquo viarum pullum nigrum immolamus, eundem in altum projiciendo ad aera, quo daemone sumpto, obedit, et statim auram concitat … grandines et fulgara projiciendo": *Formicarius* 5.4, p. 358. For the nonsensical "in campo aliquo viarum," Basel, ÖBU, MS B III 15, fol. 170r, provides "compito," as well as the "qui" in "qui a nobis designatum percutiat."

56. *Formicarius* 5.4, pp. 353–54.

57. "Sciverunt hi duo quando sibi placuit tertiam partem fimi, feni, vel frumenti, aut cuiuscumque rei de vicini agro, nemine vidente, ad proprium agrum deferre; grandines vastissimas, et auras laesivas cum fulminibus procurare; in aspectu parentum infantes propre aquam ambulantes in ipsam, nullo vidente, projicere eos; sterilitatem in hominibus et iumentis efficere; in rebus et corporalibus proximos laedere": *Formicarius* 5.4, p. 354.

58. On the elements of the common tradition of magic, see Kieckhefer, *European Witch Trials*, 48–64, and Paravy, *De la Chrétienté romaine à la Réforme*, 2:830–40 and 855–57.

59. On the economic and social conditions that may have driven Staedelin, see Borst, "Origins of the Witch-Craze" (as n. 5 above).

60. See nn. 49 and 50 above. Use of babies' corpses to produce magical powders was a common element in most early descriptions of witchcraft. See Bailey, "Witches' Sabbath," 438.

61. Much of this literature is summarized in Christa Habiger-Tuczay, *Magie und Magier im Mittelalter* (Munich, 1992), 269–89. Unfortunately, she does not discuss the single most important, albeit problematic, study: Ginzburg, *Ecstasies*. Other valuable studies include Gábor Klaniczay, "Shamanistic Elements in Central European Witchcraft," in idem, *The Uses of Supernatural Power: The Transformation of Popular Religion in Medieval and Early-Modern Europe* (Cambridge, 1990), 129–50; Gustav Henningsen, "'The Ladies from Outside': An Archaic Pattern of the Witches' Sabbath," in *Early Modern Witchcraft: Centres and Peripheries,* ed. Bengt Ankarloo and Gustav Henningsen (Oxford, 1990), 191–215; Wolfgang Behringer, *Shaman of Oberstdorf: Chonrad Stoeckhlin and the Phantoms of the Night,* trans. H. C. Erik Midelfort (Charlottesville, Va., 1998); and Éva Pócs, *Between the Living and the Dead: A Perspective on Witches and Seers in the Early Modern Age,* trans. Szilvia Rédey and Michael Webb (Budapest, 1999). Perhaps the best example of the transformation of shamanistic practices into witchcraft would be that of the Friulian *benandanti,* uncovered by Carlo Ginzburg, *The Night Battles: Witchcraft and Agrarian Cults in the Sixteenth and Seventeenth Centuries,* trans. John and Anne Tedeschi (Baltimore, 1983).

62. Bailey, "Witches' Sabbath," 439.

63. See Introduction, n. 1.

64. Original redating by Paravy, "A propos de la genèse," 333–34, based on a second copy of the tract she discovered in the Vatican Library (MS Vat. Lat. 456, fols. 205v–206r). See also *L'imaginaire du sabbat,* 273–74; Tschacher, *Der Formicarius,* 321–22. It should be noted that the most extended descriptions of flight in the *Errores* are in fact entirely absent from the earlier Vatican copy, and seem to have been added to the slightly later Basel copy (Basel, ÖBU, MS A II 34, fols.

319r–320v) based on testimony about such activities found in trials conducted in Lausanne by the Dominican inquisitor Ulric de Torrenté (*L'imaginaire du sabbat*, 273, 321–23, 328–29). Thus even for the original author of the *Errores*, flight was not fundamental to the witch stereotype.

65. *Formicarius* 2.4, pp. 123–24; repeated briefly in *Preceptorium* 1.10.a. The story obviously echoes the famous tenth-century canon *Episcopi*, although Nider never mentions it in his account. On minor but interesting differences between Nider and the earlier canon, see *L'imaginaire du sabbat*, 215–18.

66. *Formicarius* 2.4, p. 224.

67. See Cohn, *Europe's Inner Demons*, 162–80; Ginzburg, *Ecstasies*, esp. 89–110.

68. "De loco ad locum per aera, ut putabant, transmeare": *Formicarius* 5.4, p. 354.

69. *Formicarius* 5.1, pp. 337–38.

70. *Preceptorium* 1.11.r, also 1.11.h.

71. Levack, *Witch-Hunt*, 133–34.

72. See Edith Ennen, "Zauberinnen und fromme Frauen—Ketzerinnen und Hexen," in *Der Hexenhammer: Entstehung und Umfeld des "Malleus maleficarum" von 1487*, ed. Peter Segl (Cologne, 1988), 7–22; also Sophie Houdard, *Les sciences du diable: Quatre discours sur la sorcellerie (XVᵉ–XVIIᵉ siècle)* (Paris, 1992), 42–47.

73. Susanna Burghartz, "The Equation of Women and Witches: A Case Study of Witchcraft Trials in Lucerne and Lausanne in the Fifteenth and Sixteenth Centuries," in *The German Underworld: Deviants and Outcasts in German History*, ed. Richard J. Evans (London, 1988), 57–74, at 60; Houdard, *Les sciences du diable*, 42. Compare Nider's arguments as presented below with Kramer, *Malleus* 1.6, trans. Summers (as n. 9), pp. 42–44.

74. Clark, *Thinking with Demons*, 112–18. See also Stuart Clark, "The 'Gendering' of Witchcraft in French Demonology: Misogyny or Polarity?" *French History* 5 (1991): 426–37. Similar concerns are raised, from a different angle, in Robin Briggs, "Women as Victims? Witches, Judges and the Community," *French History* 5 (1991): 438–50, esp. 438–40, and Briggs, *Witches and Neighbors*, 259–63.

75. For a brief survey of past approaches, see Burghartz, "Women and Witches," 57–58. For a more detailed review of the literature up to 1995, see Elspeth Whitney, "The Witch 'She'/the Historian 'He': Gender and the Historiography of the European Witch-Hunts," *Journal of Women's History* 7 (1995): 77–101 (although I do not always agree with her assessments). More recently, see Gerhild Scholz Williams, *Defining Dominion: The Discourses of Magic and Witchcraft in Early Modern France and Germany* (Ann Arbor, 1995); Sigrid Brauner, *Fearless Wives and Frightened Shrews: The Construction of the Witch in Early Modern Germany* (Amherst, Mass., 1995); Deborah Willis, *Malevolent Nurture: Witch-Hunting and Maternal Power in Early Modern England* (Ithaca, N.Y., 1995); Elizabeth Reis, *Damned Women: Sinners and Witches in Puritan New England* (Ithaca, N.Y., 1997); Dyan Elliott, *Fallen Bodies: Pollution, Sexuality, and Demonology in the Middle Ages* (Philadelphia, 1999).

76. David Harley, "Historians as Demonologists: The Myth of the Midwife-Witch," *Social History of Medicine* 3 (1990): 1–26, effectively demonstrates that very few midwives were ever tried for witchcraft. See also Briggs, *Witches and Neighbors*, 279–81. Nevertheless both Harley ("Historians as Demonologists," 4–6 and 12–13) and Briggs (*Witches and Neighbors*, 277–79) continue to assert that more marginal kinds of folk healing did figure in accusations of witchcraft, and that such healing was "more often the province of women" (Briggs, 279). For a detailed regional study, see Robin Briggs, "Circling the Devil: Witch-Doctors and Magical Healers in Early Modern Lorraine," in *Languages of Witchcraft: Narrative, Ideology, and Meaning in Early Modern Culture*, ed. Stuart Clark (New York, 2001), 161–78.

77. Briggs, *Witches and Neighbors*, 261.

78. See Claudia Opitz, "Hexenverfolgung als Frauenverfolgung? Versuch einer vorläufiger Bilanz," in *Der Hexenstreit: Frauen in der frühneuzeitlichen Hexenverfolgung*, ed. Claudia Optiz (Freiburg i/Br., 1995), 246–70; also the multifaceted arguments in Briggs, *Witches and Neighbors*, 259–86.

79. I derive these figures from the "Calendar of Witch Trials" in Kieckhefer, *European Witch Trials*, 106–47. My figures differ slightly from those in Burghartz, "Women as Witches," 59–60. For the fifteenth century, see also the figures for trials in Dauphiné in Paravy, *De la Chrétienté romaine à la Réforme*, 2:783.

80. Monica Blöcker, "Frauenzauber—Zauberfrauen," *Zeitschrift für schweizerische Kirchengeschichte* 76 (1982): 1–39.

81. Russell, *Witchcraft*, 261–62.

82. *Formicarius* 5.8, pp. 385–88. Nider referred to the two women in Paris as "magae vel maleficae" (p. 388). Of Joan he wrote, "ipsa fassa est, se habere familiarem dei angelum, qui iudicio literatissimorum virorum iudicatus est esse malignus spiritus ex multis coniecturis et probationibus, per quem spiritum velut magam effectam" (p. 387). That he labeled her *maga* rather than the more standard *malefica* perhaps indicates that he did not consider her primary crime to be the practice of harmful sorcery *(maleficium)* in the sense usually associated with witchcraft. See the insightful point by Tschacher, *Der Formicarius*, 435–36.

83. "PIG. Mirari non sufficio, quomodo fragilis sexus in tantas audeat prosilire praesumptiones. THEOL. Apud simplices tui similes mira sunt ista, sed in prudentum oculis haec rara non sunt": *Formicarius* 5.8, p. 388.

84. "Sunt enim tria in rerum natura, quae si suae conditionis limites excedunt, aut in diminutione, aut in excessu, bonitatis vel malitiae apicem sibi vendicant, lingua videlicet, ecclesiasticus, et femina, quae si bono reguntur spiritu optima, si vero malo pessima fieri consueverunt": *Formicarius* 5.8, p. 388.

85. *Formicarius* 5.8, p. 390.

86. *Preceptorium* 1.11.bb. After carnality, loquacity was the vice for which clerical authorities most frequently criticized women. See Barbara Newman, *From Virile Woman to WomanChrist: Studies in Medieval Religion and Literature* (Philadelphia, 1995), 23.

87. *Formicarius* 5.8, p. 390–91.

88. On Nider specifically, see Tschacher, *Der Formicarius*, 188–99. More generally see Caroline Walker Bynum, *Fragmentation and Redemption: Essays on Gender and the Human Body in Medieval Religion* (New York, 1991), 152 and 156. R. Howard Bloch, *Medieval Misogyny and the Invention of Western Romantic Love* (Chicago, 1991), 65–91, traces the roots of this view of women in earlier literature.

89. I develop this argument in somewhat more detail in my article "From Sorcery to Witchcraft," 985–88.

90. For example, the treatise by the French secular judge Claude Tholosan, *Ut magorum et maleficiorum errores manifesti ignorantibus fiant* (c. 1436), presents a similar understanding of witchcraft, while arguing for secular jurisdiction over the crime. Paravy, "A propos de la genèse," passim, and *De la Chrétienté romaine à la Reformé*, 2:792–803. See now also *L'imaginaire du sabbat*, 417–38. In 1430 Duke Amadeus VIII of Savoy issued his *Statuta sabaudie*, dealing in part with sorcerers and heretics. Here he ordered his secular officials to cooperate with ecclesiastical authorities in the detection and prosecution of such criminals. See *Statuta sabaudie* (Geneva, 1512), fols. 1v–2r.

3. The Threat of Heresy: Hussites, Free Spirits, and Beguines

1. The connection between witchcraft and heresy is most fully developed in Jeffrey Burton Russell, *Witchcraft in the Middle Ages* (Ithaca, N.Y., 1972). See also Jeffrey B. Russell and Marc W. Wyndham, "Witchcraft and the Demonization of Heresy," *Mediaevalia* 2 (1976): 1–21.

2. On heresy and early witch trials, see Andreas Blauert, *Frühe Hexenverfolgungen: Ketzer-, Zauberei- und Hexenprozesse des 15. Jahrhunderts* (Hamburg, 1989), esp. 37–50; Bernard Andenmatten and Kathrin Utz Tremp, "De l'hérésie à sorcellerie: L'inquisiteur Ulric de Torrenté OP (vers 1420–1445) et l'affermissement de l'inquisition en Suisse romande," *Zeitschrift für schweizerische Kirchengeschichte* 86 (1992): 69–119; Kathrin Utz Tremp, "Ist Glaubenssache Frauensache? Zu den

Anfängen der Hexenverfolgung in Freiburg (um 1440)," *Freiburger Geschichtsblätter* 72 (1995): 9–50; Martine Ostorero, *Folâtrer avec les demons: Sabbat et chasse aux sorciers à Vevey (1448)* (Lausanne, 1995), esp. 169–82. The argument about papal inquisitors expanding their concern from heresy to witchcraft is found in Richard Kieckhefer, *Repression of Heresy in Medieval Germany* (Philadelphia, 1979), 107.

3. Kieckhefer, *Repression of Heresy*, 6.

4. The best account is now Malcolm Lambert, *The Cathars* (Oxford, 1998).

5. Kieckhefer, *Repression of Heresy*, 88–90. The scholarly literature on the Hussite movement is vast. The best overview in English is Malcolm Lambert, *Medieval Heresy: Popular Movements from the Gregorian Reform to the Reformation*, 2nd ed. (Oxford, 1992), 284–348. For the intellectual development of the movement up to 1424, see Howard Kaminsky's profound *A History of the Hussite Revolution* (Berkeley, 1967). The standard narrative account until 1424 remains Frederick Heymann, *John Žižka and the Hussite Revolution* (Princeton, 1955). For the history of the movement after 1424, see František M. Bartoš, *The Hussite Revolution 1424–1437*, ed. John M. Klassen (New York, 1986).

6. The standard study is Robert E. Lerner, *The Heresy of the Free Spirit in the Later Middle Ages*, rev. ed. (Notre Dame, Ind., 1991).

7. *Formicarius* 3.5, pp. 214–16; Lerner, *Heresy of the Free Spirit*, 14–15 and 174–75.

8. In English see Ernest W. McDonnell, *The Beguines and Beghards in Medieval Culture, with Special Emphasis on the Belgian Scene* (New Brunswick, N.J., 1954), and more recently Walter Simons, *Cities of Ladies: Beguine Communities in the Medieval Low Countries, 1200–1565* (Philadelphia, 2001). A classic treatment of beguine origins is Herbert Grundmann, *Religious Movements in the Middle Ages: The Historical Links between Heresy, the Mendicant Orders, and the Woman's Religious Movement in the Twelfth and Thirteenth Century, with the Historical Foundations of German Mysticism*, trans. Steven Rowan (Notre Dame, Ind., 1995), 139–86 and 241–45. Andreas Wilts, *Beginen im Bodenseeraum* (Sigmaringen, 1994), although a regional study, offers wide-ranging conclusions and insights. For an overview of all the lay religious, not just beguines, see Kaspar Elm, "*Vita regularis sine regula*: Bedeutung, Rechtsstellung und Selbstverständnis des mittelalterlichen und frühneuzeitlichen Semireligiosentums," in *Häresie und vorzeitige Reformation im Spätmittelalter*, ed. František Šmahel (Munich, 1998), 239–73.

9. On beguines and the Free Spirit, see Lerner, *Heresy of the Free Spirit*, esp. 35–60.

10. For an overview of persecution in German lands, see Kieckhefer, *Repression of Heresy*, 19–51. The best case study is Alexander Patschovsky, "Straßburger Beginenverfolgungen im 14. Jahrhundert," *Deutsches Archiv für Erforschung des Mittelalters* 30 (1974): 56–198. The more general study by Jean-Claude Schmitt, *Mort d'une hérésie: L'Eglise et les clercs face aux beguines et aux béghards du Rhin supérieur du XIVe au XVe siècle* (Paris, 1978), must be used with caution.

11. While Nider's missions as a conciliar envoy to the Hussites are well known, his treatise *Contra heresim Hussitarum* has never been examined by modern scholarship. Likewise, while his *Formicarius* is known as an important fifteenth-century source on the heresy of the Free Spirit (see Lerner, *Heresy of the Free Spirit*, 11–13 and 175–76), his long treatise on the lay religious life, *De secularium religionibus*, has only recently received attention, and his treatise on lay poverty and mendicancy, *De paupertate perfecta secularium*, has never been studied. See n. 68 below.

12. Kieckhefer, *Repression of Heresy*, 87.

13. Kaminsky, *Hussite Revolution*, 1.

14. On Hussite origins in the Bohemian reform movement, see Kaminsky, *Hussite Revolution*, 8; Lambert, *Medieval Heresy*, 285–86. On later developments, including Wyclifite influence, see esp. Lambert, *Medieval Heresy*, 289–96.

15. Discussion of Hus's doctrines is found in Gordon Leff, *Heresy in the Later Middle Ages: The Relationship between Heterodoxy and Dissent, c. 1250–1450*, 2 vols. (New York, 1967), 2:655–85. Studies such as Kaminsky, *Hussite Revolution*, 35–40, and Lambert, *Medieval Heresy*, 307–8, argue that Hus was more a reformer than a heretic. Kaminsky, *Hussite Revolution*, 52, and Leff, *Heresy*, 2:627, both maintain that Hus was condemned at Constance more for his strict religious ideals and

their political subversiveness than for any doctrinal error. Jürgen Miethke, "Die Prozesse in Konstanz gegen Jan Hus und Hieronymus von Prag—ein Konflikt unter Kirchenreformern?" in *Häresie und vorzeitige Reformation* (as n. 8), 147–67, disagrees, arguing that Hus's trial rarely touched on matters of reform and dealt instead with real errors of belief.

16. Nider mentions preaching a crusade at some point early in his career in *Formicarius* 3.9, pp. 237–38. One such crusade was organized in early 1427, mainly at the instigation of Friedrich Hohenzollern of Brandenburg. See Bartoš, *Hussite Revolution,* 25–26. The next major crusade was organized by Cardinal Cesarini in the summer of 1431, when Nider was in Basel.

17. See Appendix II.

18. See Lambert, *Medieval Heresy,* 333; Leff, *Heresy,* 2:689; Kaminsky, *Hussite Revolution,* 369–75; Heymann, *John Žižka,* 148–57.

19. Hussite pamphlets spread as far as the Netherlands, France, and even Spain. Heymann, *John Žižka,* 462.

20. Both manuscript copies (Basel, ÖBU, MS E I 9, fols. 386r–453v, and Eichstätt, Universitätsbibliothek, MS 469, fols. 4r–76r) break off at exactly the same point, between the eleventh and twelfth Hussite arguments in favor of utraquism.

21. The Basel copy of the treatise is found in a manuscript from the personal collection of the Dominican Johannes of Ragusa containing materials relating to the debates with the Hussites.

22. *Contra heresim,* fols. 386r–387r.

23. "Nec omnes idem senciunt, nec uno nomine se vocant, quia alii Taborite, alii Orphani, alii de nova civitate, alii de vetere": *Contra heresim,* fol. 401r–v.

24. *Contra heresim,* fol. 402r.

25. "Non Carthusiensis, non reformatos, nec deformatos in regno suo vivere sinebant": *Formicarius* 3.9, pp. 238–39.

26. *Contra heresim,* fol. 412v. This from Aquinas, *Summa theologiae* 2.2.40.2. See Aquinas, *Opera,* 2:580.

27. *Contra heresim,* fols. 415v–418v. Nider cited Aquinas, *Quodlibet* 4.10 and *In quattuor libros sententiarum* 4.4.3. These passages, however, speak only of martyrdom, not specifically the defense of the *res publica.* See Aquinas, *Opera,* 3:461 and 1:442.

28. Kaminsky, *Hussite Revolution,* 269–74 and 284–88; Lambert, *Medieval Heresy,* 308–9 and 320–22.

29. Werner Krämer, *Konsens und Rezeption: Verfassungsprinzipien der Kirche im Basler Konziliarismus, mit Edition ausgewählter Texte* (Münster, 1980), 69 and 319–20 (on such treatises in general), 90–92 and 188 (on Ragusa), 227–28 (on Segovia). Jürgen Miethke, "Konziliarismus—die neue Doktrin einer neuen Kirchenverfassung," in *Reform von Kirche und Reich zur Zeit der Konzilien von Konstanz (1414–1418) und Basel (1431–1449),* ed. Ivan Hlaváček and Alexander Patschovsky (Constance, 1996), 29–59, at 34, notes that it was the heretics John Wyclif and Jan Hus who wrote the first treatises *de ecclesia* and thereby initiated the entire late medieval debate about the proper form and nature of "the church."

30. "Non tamen negatur quando in causibus multis licitum est et utile disputare cum hereticis": *Contra heresim,* fol. 405r.

31. "Si nulli laico licet publice vel privatim de fide katholica disputare, tamen graduatis in theologia facultate licitum est coram sue facultatis super positis scolastice de fide disputare": *Contra heresim,* fol. 405v.

32. *Contra heresim,* fol. 398v.

33. *Contra heresim,* fols. 396v–400v; "Sed talis unanimitas cordium nunquam esse potest cum hereticis," on fol. 400r.

34. Bartoš, *Hussite Revolution,* 69–70; Gerald Christianson, *Cesarini: The Conciliar Cardinal, the Basel Years, 1431–1438* (St. Ottilien, 1979), 23–24 and 27.

35. For reaction in Basel, see Rudolf Wackernagel, *Geschichte der Stadt Basel,* 3 vols. (Basel, 1907–24), 1:474–75. On the council's fears, see *MC,* 2:112.

36. *MC,* 1:113–14 and 138. On the course of the negotiations, the most extended account in

English is Bartoš, *Hussite Revolution,* 73–111. See also Johannes Helmrath, *Das Basler Konzil: Forschungsstand und Probleme* (Cologne, 1987), 353–72, and E. F. Jacob, "The Bohemians at the Council of Basel," in *Prague Essays,* ed. R. W. Seton-Watson (Oxford, 1949), 81–123. Franz Egger, *Beiträge zur Geschichte des Predigerordens: Die Reform des Basler Konvents 1429 und die Stellung des Ordens am Basler Konzil 1431–1448* (Bern, 1991), 135–66, focuses on the role played by Dominicans in these negotiations.

37. Many of these letters are recorded in Ragusa's *Tractatus quomodo Bohemi reducti sunt ad unitatem ecclesiae,* edited in *MC,* 1:133–286. Some are also found in Mansi, vol. 29. Three (*MC,* 1:139–44 and 185) are given in German translation in Wilhelm Oehl, ed., *Deutsche Mystikerbriefe des Mittelalters 1100–1500* (Munich, 1931), 508–14.

38. *MC,* 1:140–41, quote at 140.

39. Lambert, *Medieval Heresy,* 345; Bartoš, *Hussite Revolution,* 102–10.

40. *MC,* 1:142. Bartoš, *Hussite Revolution,* 107, argues that the council used the delegation it sent to Prague in 1433 to spy out the Hussites and determine whether the moderates could be split from the radicals, but makes no mention of the origins or possible earlier use of this strategy.

41. The relevant correspondence is found in Mansi, 29:644–45; and *MC,* 1:190–91, 206, 208–10.

42. Bartoš, *Hussite Revolution,* 81–82; Heymann, *John Žižka,* 464–65; Josef Maček, *The Hussite Movement in Bohemia,* 2nd ed., trans. Vilém Fried and Ian Milner (1958; reprint New York, 1980), 84–85.

43. *MC,* 1:220.

44. Accounts of Hussites are found mainly in *Formicarius* 3.9–11.

45. *Formicarius* 3.5, pp. 212–13, and 3.7, pp. 226–28.

46. Leff, *Heresy,* 1:315; Kieckhefer, *Repression of Heresy,* 19. See also McDonnell, *Beguines,* 523–38; and esp. Lerner, *Heresy of the Free Spirit,* 46–48 and 78–84.

47. On possible variations between the conciliar and final forms of these decrees, see Jacqueline Tarrant, "The Clementine Decrees on the Beguines: Conciliar and Papal Versions," *Archivum Historiae Pontificae* 12 (1974): 300–308. I am concerned here, however, only with the text of the decrees as issued.

48. *Ad nostrum,* Clem. 5.3.3; Emil Friedberg, ed., *Corpus iuris canonici,* 2 vols. (1879–81; reprint Graz, 1959), 2: col. 1183–84. Its main charges are summarized in Lerner, *Heresy of the Free Spirit,* 82.

49. Lerner, *Heresy of the Free Spirit,* 78–79.

50. *Cum de quibusdam mulieribus,* Clem. 3.11.1; Friedberg, *Corpus iuris canonici,* 2: col. 1169. An English translation, minus the important escape clause (see below), is given in McDonnell, *Beguines,* 524. See also Lerner, *Heresy of the Free Spirit,* 47.

51. "Sane per praedicta prohibere nequaquam intendimus, quin, si fuerint fideles aliquae mulieres, quae promissa continentia vel etiam non promissa, honeste in suis conversantes hospitiis, poenitentiam agere voluerint et virtutum Domino in humilitatis spiritu deservire, hoc eisdem liceat, prout Dominus ipsis inspirabit": Friedberg, *Corpus iuris canonici,* 2: col. 1169.

52. Here I am in agreement with Tarrant, "Clementine Decrees," 304.

53. On the initial and later persecutions in Strassburg, see Patschovsky, "Straßburger Beginenverfolgungen," passim; also Lerner, *Heresy of the Free Spirit,* 85–105. On the persecutions in Basel beginning in 1318, see Brigitte Degler-Spengler, *Die Beginen in Basel* (Basel, 1970), 25–28, and Clément Schmitt, "Le conflict des Franciscans avec le clergé séculaire à Bâle sous l'évêque Gérard de Wippingen (1318–1324)," *Archivum Franciscanum Historicum* 54 (1961): 216–25.

54. "Nonulli tamen profanae multitudinis viri, qui vulgariter Fraticelli, seu fratres de paupere vita, Bizochi sive Beguini vel aliis nominibus nuncupantur": Extrav. Jo. XXII 7.1. Friedberg, *Corpus-Iuris Canonici,* 2: col. 1213–14, quote at col. 1213. The problem arose because of an imprecision in Latin terminology. The distinction between "beguin" and "beguine" is a convention of modern scholarship. Medieval sources used the same word, *beginus,* for both. In fact, the beguins of southern Europe held many heretical views never associated with the beguines of the north, but that did

not prevent confusion and conflation in the Middle Ages. For an overview see David Burr, *The Spiritual Franciscans: From Protest to Persecution in the Century after Saint Francis* (University Park, Pa., 2001), esp. 239–59.

55. Lerner, *Heresy of the Free Spirit*, 48; Leff, *Heresy*, 1:332. The Franciscan first order was for men, the second order for women, and the third or tertiary order for lay people who wanted to live devout lives but did not wish to take full vows.

56. "Beguinas huiusmodi inculpabiles, ut praemittitur, nec suspectas sub prohibitione et abolitione praemisis . . . declaramus et columus non includi": *Ratio recta*, Extrav. comm. 3.9.1; Friedberg, *Corpus iuris canonici*, 2: col. 1279–80.

57. For an overview, see Kieckhefer, *Repression of Heresy*, 22–28. Episcopal actions against beguines in the Rhineland are listed in Eva Gertrude Neumann, *Rheinisches Beginen- und Begardenwesen: Ein Mainzer Beitrag zur religiösen Bewegung am Rhein* (Meisenheim am Glan, 1960), 150–61. Lerner, *Heresy of the Free Spirit*, 125–63, concentrates on the persecution of beguines for the heresy of the Free Spirit in this period.

58. The so-called *Basler Beginenstreit* has received much scholarly attention. See Degler-Spengler, *Beginen in Basel*, 32–39; Alexander Patschovsky, "Beginen, Begarden und Terziaren im 14. und 15. Jahrhundert: Das Beispiel des Basler Beginenstreits (1400/04–1411)," in *Festschrift für Eduard Hlawitschka zum 75. Geburtstag*, ed. Karl Rudolf Schnith and Roland Pauler (Munich, 1993), 403–18; and more recently Sabine von Heusinger, "Beginen am Mittel- und Oberrhein zu Beginn des 15. Jahrhunderts," *Zeitschrift für die Geschichte des Oberrheins* 148 (2000): 67–96, esp. 69–87, and eadem, *Johannes Mulberg OP († 1414): Ein Leben im Spannungsfeld von Dominikaner-observanz und Beginenstreit* (Berlin, 2000), 47–82.

59. "Ex quibus patet quam periculosus videtur status beghardorum et beguinarum": *De secularium religionibus*, fol. 4v.

60. Lerner, *Heresy of the Free Spirit*, 162–63; Kieckhefer, *Repression of Heresy*, 27–28.

61. On conditions around Constance, see Wilts, *Beginen im Bodenseeraum*, 219.

62. In Strassburg in 1374, for example, beguines were attacked for their illicit mendicancy rather than supposed heresy. Patschovsky, "Straßburger Beginenverfolgungen," 79–80. On the issues behind the attack on beguines in Basel, see Heusinger, *Johannes Mulberg*, esp. 50–55.

63. *Formicarius* 3.7, pp. 226–28. See also Lerner, *Heresy of the Free Spirit*, 175–76.

64. *Formicarius* 3.2, p. 192: 3.6, pp. 221–22; and 3.5, pp. 214–16, respectively. On Nikolaus of Basel, see Lerner, *Heresy of the Free Spirit*, 151–53.

65. *Formicarius* 3.5, pp. 212–13; 3.1, pp. 181–82; 3.2, p. 191; and 3.6, pp. 220–21, respectively.

66. *Formicarius* 2.2, pp. 112–13, on the female recluse; 2.6, pp. 133–34, on the canoness; 1.4, pp. 35–36, and 2.11, pp. 167–68, on the number of religious women around Constance and Basel.

67. While the term "beguine" was typically applied to almost any sort of female lay religious, in discussing positive examples, Nider probably wanted to avoid the heretical implications the word often carried. In a separate defense of beghards and beguines, he stated that he applied such terms to nonheretics only because it was common usage: "Necquamquam intelligere volo de istis qui et que dampnati sunt . . . sed quia vulgus eciam alios viros et feminas deo in seculo devote servientes, presertim eos qui sunt extra matrimonium communiter, vocat beginas et beghardos, idcirco ex accom[m]odacione usus eisdem nominibus uti cogor" (*De secularium religionibus*, fol. 6r). He also stressed that his defense of such "beguines" should not be used to exonerate heretics: "Hortor autem ut ex dicendis non laxetur nimia licencia ad defensionem beghardorum vel beginarum, si reperiantur effrenes discoli et scandalosi in suis observanciis" (fol. 1r).

68. On the dating of these treatises, see Appendix II. John Van Engen, "Friar Johannes Nyder on Laypeople Living as Religious in the World," in *Vita Religiosa im Mittelalter: Festschrift für Kaspar Elm zum 70. Geburtstag*, ed. Franz J. Felten and Nikolas Jaspert (Berlin, 1999), 583–615, provides an excellent overview of *De secularium religionibus*. Otherwise, only passing attention has been given in Schmitt, *Mort d'une hérésie*, 161–63, and Patschovsky, "Beginen, Begarden und Terziaren," 407.

69. On William, see Grundmann, *Religious Movements*, 141; McDonnell, *Beguines*, 456–58;

Schmitt, *Mort d'une hérésie*, 56–57. That beguine persecutions throughout the course of the four-teenth century were motivated primarily by secular–mendicant strife is a central argument of Patschovsky, "Straßburger Beginenverfolgungen."

70. On the conflict in Basel, see Degler-Spengler, *Beginen in Basel*, 33; Schmitt, *Mort d'une hérésie*, 128–29; Bernhard Neidiger, *Mendikanten zwischen Ordensideal und städtischer Realität: Untersuchungen zum wirtschaftlichen Verhalten der Bettelorden in Basel* (Berlin, 1981), 126–32; Patschovsky, "Beginen, Begarden und Terziaren," 408; Heusinger, *Johannes Mulberg*, 50–51. On the issue at Constance, see R. N. Swanson, "The 'Mendicant Problem' in the Later Middle Ages," in *The Medieval Church: Universities, Heresy, and the Religious Life, Essays in Honour of Gordon Leff*, ed. Peter Biller and Barrie Dobson (Woodbridge, 1999), 217–38, here 235–36.

71. Mention of the first two treatises is in *CB*, 8:109 and 1:227–28, respectively. On the *Reformation of Kaiser Sigismund*, see Heinrich Koller, ed., *Reformation Kaiser Siegmunds*, Monumenta Germaniae Historica, Staatsschriften des späteren Mittelalters, vol. 6 (Stuttgart, 1964), 216 and 218. On the circulation of Hemmerlin's treatise, see Lerner, *Heresy of the Free Spirit*, 172.

72. "Licet de patrimonio crucifixi vivere sit altario servientibus debitum, nec non aliena stipe sustentari, ordinibus mendicantibus sit a iure concessum, mendicitate tamen se transigere est tam clericis quam laicis validis universaliter illicitum": Mulberg, *Tractatus contra beguinarum*, edited in Heusinger, *Johannes Mulberg*, 135–72, quote at 141. That Mulberg was driven to act against the beguines by his strong reformist impulses has been noted by numerous scholars. See Schmitt, *Mort d'une hérésie*, 155–58; Neidiger, *Mendikanten*, 132; Patschovsky, "Beginen, Begarden und Terziaren," 407. This is a central argument of Heusinger, *Johannes Mulberg*.

73. *De paupertate*, fol. 23v.

74. For secular authorities, this was primarily an economic and social matter. So long as beguines were perceived as performing useful social functions, relations with secular officials were good. The beguines of Bern, for example, largely avoided conflict of the type that struck in Basel in the early 1400s because they cared for the sick and thus were perceived as useful members of the community. See Kathrin Utz Tremp, "Zwischen Ketzerei und Krankenpflege—Die Beginen in der spätmittelal-terlichen Stadt Bern," in *Zwischen Macht und Dienst: Beiträge zur Geschichte und Gegenwart von Frauen im kirchlichen Leben der Schweiz*, ed. Sophia Bietenhard (Bern, 1991), 27–52, esp. 38–42. For religious officials the issue was generally a moral concern, although economic factors clearly played a role. See Neidiger, *Mendikanten*, esp. 126–32.

75. *De paupertate*, fols. 30r–34r. Nider refers to Augustine's *De opere monachorum*, probably chaps. 9–10 (*Patrologiae latinae cursus completus*, ed. J.-P. Migne, 221 vols. [Paris, 1841–64], 40: col. 555–56), and to Thomas, probably his *Contra impugnantes paupertatem* 2.4, "Utrum religio-sus propriis manibus laborare." See Aquinas, *Opera*, 3:537–39.

76. *De paupertate*, fols. 39r–46r. "Mendicitas propter Christum assumpta non solum non est reprobanda sed maxime laudanda" (fol. 42v). Nider gives no exact citation but is probably referring to *Contra impugnantes paupertatem* 2.6. See Aquinas, *Opera*, 3:543–45.

77. *De paupertate*, fols. 46v–48r. On the value of labor, Nider cited primarily Henry of Ghent, *Quodlibet* 13.17. See J. Decorte, ed., *Henrici de Gandavo quodlibet XIII*, Henrici de Gandavo opera omnia, vol. 18 (Louvain, 1985), 205–40. On alms and by extension mendicancy, he cited mainly Bernard of Clairvaux, although unfortunately he did not indicate which of Bernard's many works he was using. One wonders why Nider relied on the famous Cistercian saint rather than on some Dominican or Franciscan authority to defend mendicancy. Possibly he was attempting to circumvent objections by the secular clergy at Basel that the mendicant orders could draw only on their own rationale to defend their positions.

78. *De paupertate*, fol. 47r–v.

79. Wilts, *Beginen im Bodenseeraum*, 152–53, notes that most beguines lived exactly the sort of combination of the *vita activa* and *vita contemplativa* that Nider extolled.

80. "Ymo secta beguinarum proprie sic dictarum specialiter dampnatur De religiosis dominibus, Cum de quibusdam, in Clementinis, et ibidem excommunicantur": *De secularium religionibus*, fol. 3r.

81. *De secularium religionibus,* fol. 3r. The ruling of the Mainz council is found in Mansi, 25: col. 638. An edition of the decision of Bishop Johannes of Strassburg is found in Patschovsky, "Straßburger Beginenverfolgungen," 133–42.

82. "Que faciunt obedienciam et profitentur regulam approbatam licet, immisceant statum et ritum beguinarum, propter hoc tamen non sunt dampnate nec excommunicate quia novam religionem, etc.": *De secularium religionibus,* fol. 4v.

83. "Johannes Andreae in glossa ordinaria, et Paulus de Leazariis, et Wilhelmus Lugduni, et quasi omnes moderni tenent quod Clem., Cum de quibusdam, De relig. dom., non comprehendat sorores de tercio ordine beati Francisci": *De secularium religionibus,* fol. 5v.

84. *De secularium religionibus,* fol. 7r.

85. On *Ratio recta,* see n. 56 above. The text of *Cum de mulieribus,* issued on December 30, 1320, is found in Paul Fredericq, ed., *Corpus documentorum inquisitionis haereticae pravitatis Neerlandicae,* 5 vols. (Ghent, 1889–1902), 1:170–71.

86. Tarrant, "Clementine Decrees," as n. 47 above.

87. "Beghardos, lolhardos sive beghocos, et mulieres beguinas seu swestriones ... a iure dampnatos et dampnatas." Here Basel, ÖBU, MS E I 1i, fols. 19v–20r. Similar phrases are used in other documents contained in this miscellany. See ibid., fols. 21v–22r, 23r–v, and 25r.

88. *De paupertate,* fol. 48v. On similar arguments made by Nider in his vernacular works, see John Dahmus, "Preaching to the Laity: Johannes Nider's 'Harps,'" *Journal of Ecclesiastical History* 34 (1983): 55–68, at 56 and 67; also Margit Brand, *Studien zu Johannes Niders deutschen Schriften* (Rome, 1998), 251. For a more general discussion, see John Dahmus, "Late Medieval Preachers and Lay Perfection: The Case of Johannes Herolt, O.P.," *Medieval Perspectives* 1 (1986): 122–34.

89. Schmitt, *Mort d'une hérésie,* 195–202, in fact, wondered why attacks on beguines never involved charges of witchcraft, and proposed some not entirely satisfactory answers.

90. See n. 2 above.

91. Aside from Nider, the Zurich canon lawyer Felix Hemmerlin, for example, demonstrated this lack of connection in the opposite direction. Although a harsh critic of beguines in such works as *Contra validos mendicantes* (1438) and *Contra anachoritas, beghardos, beguinasque silvestres* (probably 1439), he was relatively unconcerned about demonic magic in such works as *De exorcismus* and *De credulitate demonibus adhibenda* (both 1456/57).

4. Reform of the Orders, Reform of the Religious Spirit

1. Johannes Meyer, *Buch der Reformacio Predigerordens,* ed. Benedictus Maria Reichert, QF, vols. 2–3 (Leipzig, 1908–9), 3:ii–vi, lists Nider as principle director of reform in St. Catherine's in Nuremberg in 1428, Basel in 1429, Tulln in Austria in 1436, and St. Catherine's in Colmar in 1438. Nider was also involved in the reform of the priory in Vienna in 1434. See Werner Tschacher, *Der Formicarius des Johannes Nider von 1437/38: Studien zu den Anfängen der europäischen Hexenverfolgungen im Spätmittelalter* (Aachen, 2000), 68. Kaspar Schieler, *Magister Johannes Nider aus dem Orden der Prediger-Brüder* (Mainz, 1885), 162–63, maintains that Nider was at least indirectly involved in every reform that occurred in southern Germany from 1428 until his death in 1438.

2. See Dirk Wassermann, *Dionysius der Kartäuser: Einführung in Werk und Gedankenwelt* (Salzburg, 1996), 202–22, and Dennis D. Martin, *Fifteenth-Century Carthusian Reform: The World of Nicholas Kempf* (Leiden, 1992), 240–43.

3. On the dating of *De reformatione,* see Appendix II. The treatise survives in over fifty known manuscript copies, a remarkable number for such a work, and was printed in Paris (1512), Toulouse (1605), and Antwerp (1611). On the relatively small number of copies in which reformist treatises generally circulated in the late Middle Ages, see Jürgen Miethke, "Kirchenreform auf den Konzilien des 15. Jahrhunderts: Motive—Methoden—Wirkungen," in *Studien zum 15. Jahrhundert: Festschrift für Erich Meuthen,* ed. Johannes Helmrath and Heribert Müller, 2 vols. (Munich, 1994), 1:13–42, at 28–31.

4. Franz Egger, *Beiträge zur Geschichte des Predigerordens: Die Reform des Basler Konvents,*

1429, und die Stellung des Ordens am Basler Konzil, 1431–1449 (Bern, 1991), 83. The founders of the Dominican reform in Germany, Master General Raymond of Capua and Prior Konrad of Prussia, established basic legislation, but neither produced any systematic theoretical works on reform. See Eugen Hillenbrand, "Die Observantenbewegung in der deutschen Ordensprovinz der Dominikaner," in *Reformbemühungen und Observanzbestrebungen im spätmittelalterlichen Ordenswesen,* ed. Kaspar Elm (Berlin, 1989), 219–71, at 226. The Dominican Heinrich of Bitterfeld wrote a brief treatise, *De formatione et reformatione Ordinis Predicatorum,* in Prague sometime shortly after the launch of the reform movement at the Vienna chapter general in 1388 (Vladimír J. Koudelka, "Heinrich von Bitterfeld [† c. 1405], Professor an der Universität Prag," *Archivum Fratrum Praedicatorum* 23 [1953]: 5–65, dating of this treatise at 19–20). While Heinrich was an important figure, however, he was not a member of the close circle around Raymond of Capua that initiated the Dominican reform, and there is no direct evidence that his treatise influenced them. Nider appears to have been aware of Heinrich's work but did not rely heavily on it while composing his own treatise (Koudelka, "Heinrich von Bitterfeld," 26 and 29). In *De reformatione* 2.16, fol. 224r, Nider writes: "Memor de hoc me legisse cuiusdam doctoris devoti ordinis predicatorum tractatum quendam et responsa notabilia, que coram me non habeo, nec memoria mea ista forte in toto retinet." Nider may well be referring to Heinrich of Bitterfeld's treatise here.

5. See Michael D. Bailey, "Abstinence and Reform at the Council of Basel: Johannes Nider's *De abstinencia esus carnium," Mediaeval Studies* 59 (1997): 225–60.

6. Elisabeth G. Gleason, "Catholic Reformation, Counterreformation, and Papal Reform in the Sixteenth Century," in *Handbook of European History, 1400–1600: Late Middle Ages, Renaissance, and Reformation,* ed. Thomas A. Brady Jr., Heiko A. Oberman, and James D. Tracy, 2 vols. (Leiden, 1994–95), 2:317–45, at 318–19, maintains that all reform within the Catholic church remained primarily "conservative and backward-looking" until at least the 1540s.

7. A convenient overview of the dominance of ideas of reform and the varieties in which they existed in the fifteenth and sixteenth centuries is Gerald Strauss, "Ideas of *Reformatio* and *Renovatio* from the Middle Ages to the Reformation," in Brady et al., *Handbook of European History,* 2:1–30; also Erika Rummel, "Voices of Reform from Hus to Erasmus," ibid., 2:61–91. For the period before the Reformation, Francis Oakley, *The Western Church in the Later Middle Ages* (Ithaca, N.Y., 1979), 213–59, remains an excellent overview. For fuller context, see Steven Ozment, *The Age of Reform: An Intellectual and Religious History of Late Medieval and Reformation Europe* (New Haven, 1980), and Heiko Oberman, *Forerunners of the Reformation: The Shape of Late Medieval Thought Illustrated by Key Documents,* 2nd ed. (Philadelphia, 1981). The basic study of the Christian idea of reform is Gerhart Ladner, *The Idea of Reform: Its Impact on Christian Thought and Action in the Age of the Fathers* (Cambridge, Mass., 1959). See also his later articles "Reformatio" and "Reform: Innovation and Tradition in Medieval Christendom," both in Ladner, *Images and Ideas in the Middle Ages: Selected Studies in History and Art,* 3 vols. (Rome, 1983), 2:519–31 and 533–58.

8. John Van Engen, "The Church in the Fifteenth Century," in Brady et al., *Handbook of European History,* 1:305–30, at 307–8.

9. Excellent overviews are found in Johannes Helmrath, "Reform als Thema der Konzilien des Spätmittelalters," in *Christian Unity: The Council of Ferrara-Florence, 1438/39–1989,* ed. Giuseppe Alberigo (Leuven, 1991), 75–152; Helmrath, "Theorie und Praxis der Kirchenreform im Spätmittelalter," *Rottenburger Jahrbuch für Kirchengeschichte* 11 (1992): 41–70; and Miethke, "Kirchenreform" (as n. 3 above). On reform activity at the Council of Constance, see Phillip H. Stump, *The Reforms of the Council of Constance (1414–1418)* (Leiden, 1994). On Basel, see Johannes Helmrath, *Das Basler Konzil: Forschungsstand und Probleme* (Cologne, 1987), 331–52.

10. On Gerson, see Louis B. Pascoe, *Jean Gerson: Principles of Church Reform* (Leiden, 1973), esp. 17–48. On d'Ailly, see Oakley, *Western Church,* 307–10. On the attitude of the council fathers at Constance, see Stump, *Reforms of the Council of Constance,* 138.

11. Best on the development of conciliarism at Basel is Werner Krämer, *Konsens und Rezeption: Verfassungsprinzipien der Kirche im Basler Konziliarismus, mit Edition ausgewählter Texte*

(Münster, 1980). For an overview, see Jürgen Miethke, "Konziliarismus—die neue Doktrin einer neuen Kirchenverfassung," in *Reform von Kirche und Reich zur Zeit der Konzilien von Konstanz (1414–1418) und Basel (1431–1449)*, ed. Ivan Hlaváček and Alexander Patschovsky (Constance, 1996), 29–59.

12. Helmrath, "Reform als Thema," 146–48; idem, "Theorie und Praxis der Kirchenreform," 66–67.

13. "Ex quibus omnibus iam liquet quam sunt quidem simplices qui ecclesiam in omni fere statu lapsam graviter putant per unum concilium generale posse reformari totaliter. Bona plura facere potest, non ambigo, generale concilium, sed non simul reformare omnia. Opus hoc est non unius concilii sed dierum plurimum": *De reformatione* 2.14, fol. 222r.

14. "Respondetur quod tunc solum velle reformari quando alii omnes reformarentur est nunquam velle reformari nisi in valle Iosaphat tempore extremi iudicii": *De reformatione* 1.8, fol. 197r.

15. *Formicarius* 1.7, p. 53. I should note here that I do not essentially disagree with Phillip Stump's conclusion that "the reforms of the Council of Constance were much more successful than past historians have admitted" (*Reforms of the Council of Constance*, 270). It is clear, however, that Constance only began the reform process; it hardly succeeded in enacting a general reform of the sort Nider was discussing.

16. The standard work is Walter Brandmüller, *Das Konzil von Pavia-Siena, 1423–1424*, 2 vols. (Münster, 1968–74).

17. *Formicarius* 1.7, p. 54.

18. *Formicarius* 1.7, p. 53.

19. On monastic reform at Basel, see Helmrath, *Basler Konzil*, 129–32, as well as Dieter Mertens, "Reformkonzilien und Ordensreform im 15. Jahrhundert," in Elm, *Reformbemühungen* (as n. 4 above), 431–57.

20. "Verum de reformacione particulari in civitate ecclesie possibili in multis statibus in religionibus non dubito": *Formicarius* 1.7, p. 55. Another prominent religious reformer in the early fifteenth century, Bernardino of Siena, also felt that a general reform was impossible but that successful partial reforms could be enacted. See Oakley, *Western Church*, 231. Oakley also draws a comparison with Nider here. On partial vs. total reform, see Helmrath, "Reform als Thema," 148–52, and idem, "Theorie und Praxis der Kirchenreform," 68–70.

21. Jürgen Miethke, "Die Konzilien als Forum der öffentlichen Meinung im 15. Jahrhundert," *Deutsches Archiv für Erforschung des Mittelalters* 37 (1981): 736–73. Exchange of ideas at the councils is also noted, particularly in regard to the spread of concern over superstition, sorcery, and witchcraft, in Tschacher, *Der Formicarius*, 329–33, and in Edward Peters, "The Medieval Church and State on Superstition, Magic, and Witchcraft," in *Witchcraft and Magic in Europe: The Middle Ages*, ed. Bengt Ankarloo and Stuart Clark (Philadelphia, 2002), 173–245, at 227.

22. Nider's own *De abstinencia esus carnium* was probably written for this purpose. See Bailey, "Abstinence and Reform," 235. More generally, see Miethke, "Konzilien als Forum," 753–55.

23. *CB*, 2:3–4.

24. "Ideo in hoc sensu est simpliciter neganda": *De abstinencia*, fol. 275r, in response to Benedict XII's bull *Summi magistri*. See C. Cocquelines, ed., *Magnum bullarium Romanum*, vol. 3.2 (1741; reprint Graz, 1964), 236.

25. On the context of *De abstinencia*, see Bailey, "Abstinence and Reform." On the response of the religious orders in general to the conflict between council and pope, see Joachim Stieber, *Pope Eugenius IV, the Council of Basel, and the Secular and Ecclesiastical Authorities in the Empire: The Conflict over Supreme Authority and Power in the Church* (Leiden, 1978), 92–113.

26. Helmrath, "Reform als Thema," 135; Petrus Becker, "Benediktinische Reformbewegung im Spätmittelalter," in *Untersuchungen zu Kloster und Stift* (Göttingen, 1980), 167–87, at 174.

27. "Tamen Alexander de Hallis dicit quod gravissime peccaverunt monachi qui abusum edendi carnes primo introduxerunt. Et eciam valde graviter hodie peccant qui illum abusum ex concupiscencia et libidine continuant scienter": *De abstinencia*, fol. 253v. Aquinas's argument is found in his *Quodlibet* 1.9.4. See Thomas Aquinas, *Quodlibetal Questions 1 and 2*, trans. Sandra Edwards (Wetterin, 1983), 66–68. Unfortunately, Nider offers no indication of which of Alexander of Hales's

works he is citing. Alexander deals generally with gluttony and drunkenness in his *Summa* (see Alexander de Hales, *Summa theologica*, 4 vols. [Quaracchi, 1924–48], 3:573–92), but Nider does not appear to be drawing directly on this work.

28. The Roman pope Leo IX and the Greek patriarch Kerullarios had formally excommunicated each other in 1054. The actual divisions between Eastern and Western Christendom extended back centuries before that date.

29. *De reformatione* 1.9, fol. 197v. In fact, although Nider denied the charge, the Dominican observant movement was essentially an order within an order, having its own priories and being governed separately under its own vicars, of whom he himself was one. See Dieter Mertens, "Monastische Reformbewegungen des 15. Jahrhunderts: Ideen—Ziele—Resultate," in Hlaváček and Patschovsky *Reform von Kirche und Reich* (as n. 11 above), 157–81, at 165.

30. Other monastic reformers shared this conviction. See Wassermann, *Dionysius der Kartäuser,* 162–63; Martin, *Fifteenth-Century Carthusian Reform,* 240–43.

31. Again, other fifteenth-century reformers shared Nider's ideas. See Wassermann, *Dionysius der Kartäuser,* 228–36; Christopher M. Bellitto, *Nicolas de Clamanges: Spirituality, Personal Reform, and Pastoral Renewal on the Eve of the Reformations* (Washington, D.C., 2001), esp. 59–90.

32. For a brief discussion of reform as return, see Strauss, "Ideas of *Reformatio* and *Renovatio*" (as n. 7 above), 4–7.

33. "Rogatus sum a te, pater mi, qui reformacionis officio in tuo collapso ordine insistis . . . materiam aliqua coligerem de sacris codicibus, per que superna assistente gracia sub sermonis stemate vel per normas alias forma tua religionis, olim pulcherrima sed heu a multis nunc perdita, possit reinduci facilius": *De reformatione,* prologue, fol. 186v.

34. "Unde reformacio est forme alicuius deperdite denua introduccio": *De reformatione* 2.2, fol. 208v.

35. Chap. 36 concerns the allowance of meat to the sick in the monastery infirmary, while chap. 39 governs the monastic diet and forbids monks to eat meat. See Timothy Fry, ed., *RB 1980: The Rule of St. Benedict in Latin and English with Notes* (Collegeville, Minn., 1981), 234–35 and 238–39.

36. "Quia omnis dispensacio petita a prelato debet fieri ad honorem Christi, in cuius persona dispensat, vel ad utilitatem ecclesie, que est corpus Christi": *De reformatione* 1.11, fol. 199v. Nider here drew on Aquinas, *Summa theologiae* 1.2.96.4. See Aquinas, *Opera,* 2:482. Dispensation as a chief cause of collapse in religious orders is discussed in *De reformatione* 2.15, fol. 224v.

37. "Deinde dico quod consuetudo transgrediendi votum castitatis paupertatis et obediencie et aliorum que sub precepto cadunt nunquam legem potest facere . . . nec consuetudo sed corruptela dicenda est. . . . Sicut contra votum valet non consuetudo sic nec contra religionem et eadem racione non est dispensacio sed dissipacio": *De reformatione* 1.5, fol. 194r–v.

38. "Nocte itaque insecuta vidit demonem locum intrantem in quo iacebant. Cumque frater qui dispensaverat quereret a demone, quid quereret respondit demon: Veni visitare fratres qui comederunt carnes": *De abstinencia,* fol. 263v. The story is from Gerald de Frachet, *Vitae fratrum ordinis praedicatorum* 4.18, ed. Benedictus Maria Reichert, MOPH, vol. 1 (Louvain, 1896), 205–6.

39. "Dispensare est cum licencia ad infernum intrare": *De reformatione* 1.11, fol. 199v.

40. Foundational here are the studies of Gerhart Ladner (as n. 7 above), who sees the idea of *reformare in melius* described as early as Tertullian, and rooted even earlier in Saint Paul's notion of personal reform through striving to return to the "likeness of God," inherent in all humans but lost through sin. See (e.g. only) Ladner, *Idea of Reform,* 62 and 134. The concept of "creative imitation" is found in Karl Morrison, *The Mimetic Tradition of Reform in the West* (Princeton, 1982).

41. *De reformatione* 1.7, fol. 196r. These passages are based, sometimes rather loosely, on Ezekiel 11:19; Mark 16:17; Psalms 95:1, 97:1, and 149:1; 1 Corinthians 5:7; Isaiah 62:2; and Hebrews 10:19–20, respectively.

42. *De reformatione* 2.14, fol. 222r.

43. *De reformatione* 2.4, fol. 211r. The idea that the entire history of monasticism was one of continual reform was centuries old. See Ladner, *Idea of Reform,* 4.

44. *De reformatione* 2.4, fol. 211r.

45. *Formicarius* 1.7, p. 52. Other reformers used this image as well. See Pascoe, *Jean Gerson* (as n. 10), 19–20. On various forms of eschatological concern in late medieval reform movements, see Mertens, "Monastische Reformbewegungen," 158–59, and Alexander Patschovsky, "Der Reformbegriff zur Zeit der Konzilien von Konstanz und Basel," in Hlaváček and Patschovsky, *Reform von Kirche und Reich* (as n. 11), 7–28, here 7.

46. *De reformatione* 1.4, fols. 192v–193r.

47. *De reformatione* 2.16, fol. 224r–v.

48. *De reformatione* 2.20, fol. 228r.

49. *De reformatione* 2.10, fol. 217v.

50. *De reformatione* 3.1, fol. 230r.

51. *De reformatione* 3.2, fols. 231v–232r, and 3.8, fols. 238v–241v, respectively.

52. "Astuti et perversi homines callidissimas obiecciones opponunt et argumenta": *De reformatione* 2.5, fol. 212v.

53. *De reformatione* 2.8, fol. 216r. Rather than the more familiar account in Exodus 32, Nider draws on the harsher description of the Israelites' idolatry in Deuteronomy 32.

54. "Melius fortassent [*sic*, probably *fortasse*] arguerent quod aput reformatos unus resuscitatur ordo, et aput deformatos nullus manet ordo, sed sempiternus horror inhabitat": *De reformatione* 1.9, fol. 198r.

55. "Ecclesiam multipliciter iuvat": *De reformatione* 2.6, fol. 212v.

56. Since the reform movement ultimately triumphed in the Dominican order, as well as in most others, most later accounts present only the victorious reformist view, and for this reason the non-reformed or conventual viewpoint has received short shrift. See Mertens, "Monastische Reformbewegungen," 157–58.

57. Emphasis on personal spiritual reform was widespread in the late Middle Ages. See Wassermann, *Dionysius der Kartäuser,* and Bellitto, *Nicolas de Clamanges* (as n. 31 above). On the importance of "spiritual interiority" during the later Reformation, particularly its connection to demonology and witchcraft, see Stuart Clark, *Thinking with Demons: The Idea of Witchcraft in Early Modern Europe* (Oxford, 1997), 440, as well as literature cited there. On the centrality of the Pauline notion of reform as a personal movement toward the divine, see Ladner, *Idea of Reform,* esp. 49–62.

58. *De reformatione* 1.8, fol. 197v.

59. *De reformatione* 2.8, fol. 215r–v.

60. In *De paupertate,* fol. 52r, Nider noted that it was often more difficult to uphold monastic vows while living as a layperson in the world than in a monastery or cloistered setting.

61. *De paupertate,* fol. 53r.

62. Margit Brand, *Studien zu Johannes Niders deutschen Schriften* (Rome, 1998), 7–9 and 251.

5. The Reform of the Christian World: Johannes Nider's Formicarius

1. "Vade ad formicam, o piger, et considera vias eius, et disce sapientiam": *Formicarius* 1.1, p. 1.

2. On the basic structure of the *Formicarius,* see Werner Tschacher, *Der Formicarius des Johannes Nider von 1437/38: Studien zu den Anfängen der europäischen Hexenverfolgungen im Spätmittelalter* (Aachen, 2000), 147–49. Although focusing particularly on witchcraft, Tschacher is also the most complete general study of the *Formicarius* available.

3. Tschacher, *Der Formicarius,* 121–24.

4. Carlo Ginzburg, *Ecstasies: Deciphering the Witches' Sabbath,* trans. Raymond Rosenthal (New York, 1991), 69.

5. Although his overall focus remains on witchcraft, Tschacher, *Der Formciarius,* 133–243, provides extended discussion of the structure and general themes of the work.

6. There has been one study of the *Formicarius* specifically in these terms: Beatrice Galbreth, "Nider and the Exemplum—A Study of the Formicarius," *Fabula: Zeitschrift für Erzählforschung* 6

(1963): 55–72. Unfortunately, it is of no value. See instead J.-Th. Welter, *L'Exemplum dans la littérature religieuse et didactique du Moyen Age* (1927; reprint Geneva, 1973), 435–36, where Nider is treated very briefly.

7. Nider's biographer Kaspar Schieler noted this early on. In his discussion of Nider's written works, he isolated the *Formicarius* at the outset, "weil es nach seinem Inhalte in keine der folgenden Klassen vollständig paßt": *Magister Johannes Nider aus dem Orden der Prediger-Brüder* (Mainz, 1885), 373.

8. R. N. Swanson, *Religion and Devotion in Western Europe, c. 1215–1515* (Cambridge, 1995), 66.

9. See Appendix II.

10. Schieler, *Magister Johannes Nider,* 372.

11. Tschacher, *Der Formicarius,* 83–107, lists and provides the provenance for all known manuscript copies.

12. *Formicarius* 5.3, p. 349.

13. On Peter, see Tschacher, *Der Formicarius,* 173–75. There are three possible identifications for this man: Peter von Greyerz, Peter Wendschatz, and Peter von Ey or Eyg, all of whom served as Bernese bailiff in the Simme valley (*L'imaginaire du sabbat,* 223–24). There is no record that any of these men was at Basel during the council, although Peter von Greyerz's son of the same name was in Basel in 1433 on a mission from the city council of Bern (*L'imaginaire du sabbat,* 228).

14. *Formicarius* 5.8, p. 387.

15. Schieler, *Magister Johannes Nider,* 379.

16. *Formicarius* 1.6, p. 46; 1.7, pp. 53–54; and 5.8, p. 388, respectively.

17. This organization is announced in *Formicarius* 1.1, pp. 3–8. See also Tschacher, *Der Formicarius,* 133–37.

18. *Formicarius* 1.1, pp. 9–10.

19. *Exempla ex vitis patrum et Gregorii dialogis collecta per Johannem Nider,* Basel, ÖBU, MS A X 129, fols. 137r–221r. The first eighty-four exempla (to fol. 157r) are drawn from Gregory. Several from other church fathers follow, most of them from Cassian's *Collationes,* which had been a key source for Nider's earlier work *Die 24 goldenen Harfen.* Beginning with no. 132 (fol. 167r), most of the remaining exempla are then drawn from the Dominican historian Vincent of Beauvais's *Speculum historiale.*

20. *Formicarius* 1.1, pp. 1–2. Thomas discusses demons mainly in *Bonum universale de apibus* 2.55–57. There is no adequate study of this work. Lynn Thorndike treats Thomas in his magisterial *History of Magic and Experimental Science,* 8 vols. (New York, 1923–58), 2:372–95, but he is mostly concerned with Thomas's *De natura rerum* and notes only briefly Thomas's "credulity" in *Bonum universale de apibus* (p. 381). Thomas also receives brief discussion in Henry Charles Lea, *Materials toward a History of Witchcraft,* ed. Arthur C. Howland, 3 vols. (Philadelphia, 1939), 1:90–91, 154–55, 174–75.

21. Nider relates only two exempla from Thomas in *Formicarius* 5.10, pp. 405–6.

22. Caesarius of Heisterbach, *Dialogus miraculorum,* ed. Joseph Strange (1851; reprint Ridgewood, N.J., 1966); *Dialogue on Miracles,* trans H. von E. Scott and C. C. Swinton Bland (London, 1929). More recently, see Fritz Wagner, "Studien zu Caesarius von Heisterbach," *Analecta Cisterciensia* 29 (1973): 79–95. Of particular use for the themes considered here is Phillip Schmidt, *Der Teufels- und Daemonenglaube in der Erzählungen des Caesarius von Heisterbach* (Basel, 1926). On Caesarius's use of exempla see Welter, *L'Exemplum,* 113–18.

23. Tschacher, *Der Formicarius,* 151–67, lists all references to earlier written sources in the *Formicarius;* reference to *Dialogus miraculorum* at 163.

24. John Dahmus, "Late Medieval Preachers and Lay Perfection: The Case of Johannes Herolt, O.P.," *Medieval Perspectives* 1 (1986): 122–34, at 130, argues that Nider also intended another of his Latin sermon collections, the *Sermones aurei,* to reach a mostly lay audience.

25. See E. Delaruelle, E.-R. Lebande, and Paul Ourliac, *L'Eglise au temps du Grand Schisme et de la crise conciliaire (1378–1449),* 2 vols., Histoire de l'Eglise depuis les origines jusqu'à nos jours,

vol. 14 (Paris, 1962–64), 2:629–36; also Swanson, *Religion and Devotion,* 64–68. An excellent study, although focusing on a slightly later period, is Larissa Taylor, *Soldiers of Christ: Preaching in Late Medieval and Reformation France* (Oxford, 1992).

26. Delaruelle et al., *L'Eglise,* 2:636–39. On Bernardino, see Franco Mormando, *The Preacher's Demons: Bernardino of Siena and the Social Underworld of Early Renaissance Italy* (Chicago, 1999); also Cynthia L. Polecritti, *Preaching Peace in Renaissance Italy: Bernardino of Siena and His Audience* (Washington, D.C., 2000). On Vincent Ferrer, see Sigismund Brettle, *San Vicente Ferrer und sein literarische Nachlass* (Münster, 1924), and Francis Oakley, *The Western Church in the Later Middle Ages* (Ithaca, N.Y., 1979), 261–70. On preaching as a basis for the Reformation, see Euan Cameron, "The Power of the Word: Renaissance and Reformation," in *Early Modern Europe: An Oxford History,* ed. Euan Cameron (Oxford, 1999), 63–101, at 87–90.

27. Swanson, *Religion and Devotion,* 68.

28. Brettle, *San Vicente Ferrer,* 29. Nider mentions Bernardino and Vincent Ferrer in *Formicarius* 4.9, pp. 311–12, and Ferrer alone at greater length in *Formicarius* 2.1, pp. 130–35.

29. Brettle, *San Vicente Ferrer,* 2, 125, 167.

30. *De reformatione* 2.14, fol. 222r; *Formicarius* 1.7, pp. 54–55. See also Chapter 4. Bernardino expressed a similar position in a sermon delivered in Florence. See Dionisio Pacetti, ed., *San Bernardino da Siena: Le prediche volgari inedite,* 2 vols. (Siena, 1935), 2:97; quoted, along with reference to Nider, in Oakley, *Western Church,* 231.

31. *Formicarius,* prologue. The biblical reference is to Psalms 73:9.

32. On the relation of wonders to witchcraft, see Stuart Clark, *Thinking with Demons: The Idea of Witchcraft in Early Modern Europe* (Oxford, 1997), 363–74. On wonders and marvels generally, see Lorraine Daston and Katharine Park, *Wonders and the Order of Nature, 1150–1750* (New York, 1998); also several of the articles collected in *Wonders, Marvels, and Monsters in Early Modern Culture,* ed. Peter G. Platt (Newark, Del., 1999).

33. Perhaps the strongest argument here has been made by Eamon Duffy in his profound book, *The Stripping of the Altars: Traditional Religion in England, 1400–1580* (New Haven, 1992), where one of his central arguments is that "no substantial gulf existed between the religion of the clergy and the educated élite on the one hand and that of the people at large on the other" (2). Thus he chooses to speak of "traditional" rather than "popular" religion (3). Richard Kieckhefer has made a similar point in *Magic in the Middle Ages* (Cambridge, 1989), 56–57, and "The Specific Rationality of Medieval Magic," *American Historical Review* 99 (1994): 813–36, at 833–36.

34. See esp. Klaus Schreiner, "Laienfrömmigkeit—Frömmigkeit von Eliten oder Frömmigkeit des Volkes? Zur sozialen Verfaßtheit laikaler Frömmigkeitspraxis im späten Mittelalter," in *Laienfrömmigkeit im späten Mittelalter: Formen, Funktionen, politisch-soziale Zusammenhänge,* ed. Klaus Schreiner (Munich, 1992), 1–78, esp. 13–26.

35. See Richard Kieckhefer, *European Witch Trials: Their Foundations in Popular and Learned Culture, 1300–1500* (Berkeley, 1976), passim; also Michael D. Bailey, "The Medieval Concept of the Witches' Sabbath," *Exemplaria* 8 (1996): 419–36, esp. 420–22, and idem, "From Sorcery to Witchcraft: Clerical Conceptions of Magic in the Later Middle Ages," *Speculum* 76 (2001): 960–90, esp. 961–63.

36. Oakley, *Western Church,* 113–14. Likewise on Bernardino of Siena's overly pessimistic worldview, see Mormando, *Preacher's Demons,* 14.

37. *Formicarius* 1.6, pp. 48–49. Nider gives further examples of good prelates in *Formicarius* 1.7, pp. 55–57; 2.2, p. 107; and 3.5, pp. 211–12.

38. *Formicarius* 1.7, p. 55. See Chapter 4 above.

39. *Formicarius* 4.9, pp. 312–13.

40. This view still retains some of its power. Witness Margaret Aston, *Faith and Fire: Popular and Unpopular Religion, 1350–1600* (London, 1993), 9, where she recognizes the widespread popular devotion of the late Middle Ages but argues that "the sheer popularity and proliferation of some of these devotional forms is indicative of instability. The late medieval church was caught in an inflationary spiral of a dangerous kind."

41. Duffy, *Stripping of the Altars*, 4. This view is also represented by Swanson, *Religion and Devotion*, where he concludes that "vocal opposition to the Church's established structures and beliefs was very much a minority affair," that there was "little sense of widespread alienation from the devotional regimes," and that "pre-Reformation religion was in fact vital and progressing" (340–42). See also Oakley, *Western Church*, esp. 15–21 and 113–30. A seminal study for German lands remains Bernd Moeller, "Frömmigkeit in Deutschland um 1500," *Archiv für Reformationsgeschichte* 56 (1965): 3–31.

42. Richard Kieckhefer, "Major Currents in Late Medieval Devotion," in *Christian Spirituality*, vol. 2, ed. Jill Raitt (London, 1987), 75–108 at 83 and 102. See also Swanson, *Religion and Devotion*, esp. 136–90, and several of the essays in André Vauchez, *The Laity in the Middle Ages: Religious Beliefs and Devotional Practices*, trans. Margery J. Schneider, ed. Daniel E. Bornstein (Notre Dame, Ind., 1993).

43. In *Formicarius* 1.1, p. 12; 1.12, pp. 91–92; 2.6, pp. 133–34; 3.1, pp. 183–84; 3.2, p. 190; 4.2, pp. 266–67; 4.11, p. 322; and 5.11, p. 416.

44. These stories are clustered together in *Formicarius* 2.12, pp. 170–77, and 4.12, pp. 325–30.

45. *Formicarius* 2.6, pp. 135–36.

46. *Formicarius* 2.8, pp. 145–46 and 149–50, respectively.

47. *Formicarius* 4.2, pp. 266–67. On Saint Barbara as a patron of the dying, see Mathilde van Dijk, "Traveling Companion in the Journey of Life: Saint Barbara of Nicomedia in a *Devotio Moderna* Context," in *Death and Dying in the Middle Ages*, ed. Edelgard E. DuBruck and Barbara I. Gusick (New York, 1999), 221–37, at 224–27.

48. *Formicarius* 3.11, pp. 252–53.

49. *Formicarius* 5.6, p. 370. Prayer to saints is also listed as a remedy for witchcraft in *Preceptorium* 1.11.x.

50. More than a dozen stories in the *Formicarius* praise chastity and virginity, and more than fifteen include visions or revelations in some important way. The entire fifth book, dealing with magic and witchcraft, is concerned with demons. Twelve more stories in the first four books focus on demons.

51. On the dichotomous clerical view of women, see Tschacher, *Der Formicarius*, 188–99, and, in preaching, Taylor, *Soldiers of Christ*, 156–58. On sexuality as a factor in a woman's moral worth, see Clarissa Atkinson, "'Precious Balsam in a Fragile Glass': The Ideology of Virginity in the Later Middle Ages," *Journal of Family History* 8 (1983): 131–43.

52. Dyan Elliott, *Fallen Bodies: Pollution, Sexuality, and Demonology in the Middle Ages* (Philadelphia, 1999), 36. On notions about women derived from Aristotle, see Prudence Allen, *The Concept of Women: The Aristotelian Revolution, 750 BC–AD 1250* (Montreal, 1985).

53. *Formicarius* 4.1, p. 263, quoting Aquinas, *In quatuor libros Sententiarum* 4.35.1.4. See Aquinas, *Opera*, 1:606.

54. "Nec me suspicetur faciliter credere hominibus quibuslibet, presertim feminis, quas, nisi sint probate plurimum, semper in talibus delirare suspicor": *Formicarius*, prologue.

55. "Si enim presenta generali concilio in Basilea in annis sex nec unum quidem fragilis sexus monasterium, cooperante eciam secularis consulatu, reformari potuit": *Formicarius* 1.7, p. 55.

56. Basel, ÖBU, MS B III 15, fol. 76r.

57. The relation of the Klingental convent to the Dominican priory in Basel is discussed briefly in Chapter 1 above.

58. The full ordinances are edited in Gabriel M. Löhr, *Die Teutonia im 15. Jahrhundert: Studien und Texte vornehmlich zur Geschichte ihrer Reform*, QF, vol. 19 (Leipzig, 1924), 53–63, here 56–57. See also Franz Egger, *Beiträge zur Geschichte des Predigerordens: Die Reform des Basler Konvents 1429 und die Stellung des Ordens am Basler Konzil 1431–1448* (Bern, 1991), 58–59 and 76–78.

59. "Duodecim radix est feminarum incauta adhesio, sive sint ille seculares sive monastice": *De reformatione* 2.18, fol. 226v.

60. *De reformatione* 2.18, fol. 226v; from Numbers 31:15–16. Nider brought up Balaam and Phogor again when he discussed women and witchcraft in *Formicarius* 5.8, p. 384.

61. Sections of two of Nider's letters to the convent of Unterlinden in Colmar are reproduced in Wilhelm Oehl, ed., *Deutsche Mystikerbriefe des Mittelalters, 1100–1550* (Munich, 1931), 516–18. Two additional writings of Nider for reformed nuns, *De commune frequente* and *Eine nützliche Lehre,* are found in Basel, ÖBU, MS A X 130, fols. 185r–v and 258v–161v. Also his *Ordinationes de visitatione monasteriam Subtilia* and *Ordinationes de visitatione monasteriam Schönensteinbach* are found in Basel, ÖBU, MS E III 13, fols. 100r–101v.

62. "Si nobis facultas scribendi et dicendi velut vobis affuisset, vicem reddidissemus dudum fidelitate vestre": *Formicarius* 3.4, p. 205. The theme of good women victimized by wicked men was fairly common in late medieval preaching. See Taylor, *Soldiers of Christ,* 167–69.

63. *Formicarius* 3.4, p. 205. Nider repeated this general idea in *Formicarius* 3.11, p. 252, and 4.1, p. 261.

64. *Formicarius* 1.1, p. 22 (on Nuremberg); 1.4, pp. 35–36, and 2.11, pp. 167–68 (on the situation around Constance and Basel); 4.9, pp. 310–11 (on Colette of Corbie).

65. "Quales predicatores revera in hoc maliciam excedunt Vigilantii heretici": *Formicarius* 1.4, p. 33.

66. *Formicarius* 1.5, p. 38.

67. Sections edited in Joseph Hansen, *Quellen und Untersuchungen zur Geschichte des Hexenwahns und der Hexenverfolgung im Mittelalter* (1901; reprint Hildesheim, 1963), 423–35.

68. Hansen, *Quellen,* 437–44. Most late medieval sermons on marriage held out total celibacy as an ideal, although preachers knew the vast majority of their audience would not attain it. See Taylor, *Soldiers of Christ,* 161–62.

69. *Formicarius* 1.5, p. 38. John W. Dahmus, "*Dormi secure:* The Lazy Preacher's Model of Holiness for His Flock," in *Models of Holiness in Medieval Sermons,* ed. Beverly Mayne Kienzle, Textes et Etudes du Moyen Age, vol. 5 (Louvain-La-Neuve, 1996), 301–16, at 311–13, notes that late medieval sermons regularly praised virginity as the highest attainable state of life. For Nider's position on marriage in his sermon collections, see Dahmus, "Late Medieval Preachers" (as n. 24 above), 124–25 and 128.

70. This distinction was fairly standard among medieval clerical authors. See Barbara Newman, *From Virile Woman to WomanChrist: Studies in Medieval Religion and Literature* (Philadelphia, 1995), 28–30 and 44.

71. *Formicarius* 2.6, pp. 134–35 (on Anna), and 2.10, pp. 161–62 (on Agnes).

72. "Quod castitatem quis, si aliter nequit, sicut vitam suo modo defendere potest": *Formicarius* 2.10, p. 162.

73. Caroline Walker Bynum, *Fragmentation and Redemption: Essays on Gender and the Human Body in Medieval Religion* (New York, 1991), 204.

74. *Formicarius* 2.10, p. 159.

75. *Formicarius* 4.4, pp. 277–81.

76. Heinrich Kramer, *Malleus maleficarum* 1.6, trans. Montague Summers (1928; reprint New York, 1971), p. 47.

77. Almost surely the result of the moral superiority attributed to the Virgin Mary by such Dominican authorities as Albertus Magnus and Thomas Aquinas. See Allen, *Concept of Women,* 363 and 376–86.

78. Identified by Barbara Newman as the "Virile Woman" model of female religiosity. See her *From Virile Woman to WomanChirst,* 3–5 and 26.

79. In regard to witchcraft specifically, see Clark, *Thinking with Demons,* 126–27.

80. See Tschacher, *Der Formicarius,* 206–13. More generally see Peter Dinzelbacher, *Vision und Visionsliteratur im Mittelalter* (Stuttgart, 1981); also the introduction to idem, ed. and trans., *Mittelalterliche Visionsliteratur: Eine Anthologie* (Darmstadt, 1989), and idem, *Revelationes,* Typologie des sources du Moyen Age occidental, vol. 57, ed. L. Genicot (Turnhout, 1991). Dinzelbacher tends to focus exclusively on mystical visionary experience. Focusing on more commonly experienced visions but limited in geographic and chronological scope is William A. Christian, Jr., *Apparitions in Late Medieval and Renaissance Spain* (Princeton, 1981). Christian suggests (25) that visionary

experience was far less widespread in the late Middle Ages than other scholars, focusing primarily on clerical sources, have believed.

81. See Nancy Caciola, "Mystics, Demoniacs, and the Physiology of Spirit Possession in Medieval Europe," *Comparative Studies in Society and History* 42 (2000): 268–306. Barbara Newman, "Possessed by the Spirit: Devout Women, Demoniacs, and the Apostolic Life in the Thirteenth Century," *Speculum* 73 (1998): 733–70, also explores parallels between mystical and demonic experience. On the relation of mysticism to witchcraft, see Richard Kieckhefer, "The Holy and the Unholy: Sainthood, Witchcraft, and Magic in Late Medieval Europe," *Journal of Medieval and Renaissance Studies* 24 (1994): 355–85.

82. *Formicarius* 2.1, p. 97. On women's propensity to visionary experience and to deception by demons see Caciola, "Mystics," 279–85; Elliott, *Fallen Bodies*, 43–44; Christian, *Apparitions*, 197.

83. *Formicarius* 2.1, pp. 99–100.

84. At n. 45 above.

85. *Formicarius* 3.1, pp. 181–82. See also Chapter 3. Nider's account is also discussed in Nancy Caciola, "Spirits Seeking Bodies: Death, Possession and Communal Memory in the Middle Ages," in *The Place of the Dead: Death and Remembrance in Late Medieval and Early Modern Europe*, ed. Bruce Gordon and Peter Marshall (Cambridge, 2000), 66–86, at 69–73.

86. *Formicarius* 3.1, pp. 182–83.

87. *Formicarius* 3.8, pp. 230–32. A more positive version of the story of Magdalena of Freiburg is found in the "Life of Magdalena" translated in Elizabeth Petroff, ed., *Medieval Women's Visionary Literature* (New York, 1986), 350–55.

88. *Formicarius* 3.11, pp. 249–50.

89. On the canon *Episcopi*, see Chapter 2, at nn. 17 and 18.

90. *Formicarius* 2.4, pp. 123–24.

91. *Formicarius* 2.4, p. 124.

92. See Norman Cohn, *Europe's Inner Demons: The Demonization of Christians in Medieval Christendom*, rev. ed. (London, 1993), 162–80.

93. On this point see esp. Newman, "Possessed by the Spirit" (as n. 81 above).

94. Swanson, *Religion and Devotion*, 292; Cohn, *Europe's Inner Demons*, 25–34; Jeffrey Burton Russell, *Lucifer: The Devil in the Middle Ages* (Ithaca, N.Y., 1984), 275–95; Peter Dinzelbacher, "Der Realität des Teufels im Mittelalter," in *Der Hexenhammer: Entstehung und Umfeld des "Malleus maleficarum" von 1487*, ed. Peter Segl (Cologne, 1988), 151–75; Brian P. Levack, "The Great Witch-Hunt," in *Handbook of European History, 1400–1600: Late Middle Ages, Renaissance, and Reformation*, ed. Thomas A. Brady Jr., Heiko A. Oberman, and James D. Tracy, 2 vols. (Leiden, 1994–95), 2:607–40, at 624–25. Mormando, *Preacher's Demons*, 85–95, discusses the religious reformer Bernardino of Siena's "acute awareness of and near obsession with this powerful demonic force" (90).

95. Russell, *Lucifer*, 295. Levack, "Great Witch-Hunt," 625, suggests that the revival of Augustinianism in fifteenth-century theology may have been an important factor behind growing fears of demonic power.

96. On common belief in demonic power, see Kieckhefer, "Specific Rationality," 832–36. Duffy, *Stripping of the Altars*, 266–69, points to the many prayers against demons in late medieval lay devotional primers as evidence for the "vivid and urgent sense of the reality of the demonic, and the Christian's need for eternal vigilance." This evidence, however, speaks only to the literate laity, who could have read such books. Furthermore, these books were ultimately produced by clerics, even if specifically for lay consumption. If they represent "popular" or "common" religion at all, it is surely only that segment of the common religion that was most influenced by the clerical elites.

97. Kieckhefer, *European Witch Trials*, esp. 36 and 74–75; Cohn, *Europe's Inner Demons*, 211–13, 218, 229–30.

98. Nider discusses demons as one of the chief causes of decline within the orders in *De reformatione* 2.4, fol. 210r. On this point, see Tschacher, *Der Formicarius*, 379–82.

99. "Sed vicit in eo Christi gratia, professus est enim, et in conventus Basiliensi reformatione postmodum effectus procurator gratiosus": *Formicarius* 1.9, pp. 68–69.

100. *Formicarius* 1.10, pp. 70 and 74–76.

101. "Sed tamen, per dei gratiam, diabolus plus perdidit hoc in ludo, quam acquisierit, quia quaedam cervicosae feminae quas ad plenum pietas reformatorum non valebat trahere, hoc phantasma adeo terruit, ut totius vitae suae facinora confiterentur sacramentaliter, vestes veteres deponerent, et novas secundum ordinis formam induerent": *Formicarius* 5.2, p. 345.

102. "Nos qui onus belli contra iras demonum portavimus": *Formicarius* 3.3, p. 195.

103. Julio Caro Baroja, *The World of the Witches*, trans. O. N. V. Glendinning (Chicago, 1964), 92, calls it "a rather muddled book."

6. Witchcraft and Reform

1. Richard Kieckhefer, *Magic in the Middle Ages* (Cambridge, 1989), 199–200.

2. Françoise Bonney, "Autour de Jean Gerson: Opinions de théologiens sur les superstitions et la sorcellerie au début du XVᵉ siècle," *Le Moyen Age* 77 (1971): 85–98; Jan R. Veenstra, *Magic and Divination at the Courts of Burgundy and France: Text and Context of Laurens Pignon's "Contre les devineurs" (1411)* (Leiden, 1998), 137–53; Werner Tschacher, *Der Formicarius des Johannes Nider von 1437/38: Studien zu den Anfängen der europäischen Hexenverfolgungen im Spätmittelalter* (Aachen, 2000), 269–91.

3. Kieckhefer, *Magic*, 184–87. For a general discussion of superstition in the Christian tradition, see Dieter Harmening, *Superstitio: Überlieferungs- und theoriegeschichtliche Untersuchungen zur kirchlich-theologischen Aberglaubensliteratur des Mittelalters* (Berlin, 1979).

4. See Introduction, n. 11.

5. Andreas Blauert, *Frühe Hexenverfolgungen: Ketzer-, Zauberei- und Hexenprozesse des 15. Jahrhunderts* (Hamburg, 1989), 118–19, draws a connection between reformers such as Mulberg, Ferrer, and Bernardino and the first witch-hunts. Pierrette Paravy, *De la Chrétienté romaine à la Réforme en Dauphiné: Evêques, fidèles et déviants (vers 1340–vers 1530)*, 2 vols. (Rome, 1993), 2:904, notes the role Ferrer and other Dominican preachers played in Dauphiné. Best on Bernardino and witchcraft is Franco Mormando, *The Preacher's Demons: Bernardino of Siena and the Social Underworld of Early Renaissance Italy* (Chicago, 1999), 52–108, esp. 54–77, on the trials at Rome and Todi.

6. Savonarola is not particularly associated with attacks on witchcraft, but he did oppose the practice of astronomy, as well as aspects of Neoplatonic and hermetic occultism common in Renaissance Florence. See D. P. Walker, *Spiritual and Demonic Magic from Ficino to Campanella* (1958; reprint University Park, Pa., 2000), 57–58; Donald Weinstein, *Savonarola and Florence: Prophecy and Patriotism in the Renaissance* (Princeton, 1970), 191 and 202–3.

7. "Vocavi ego magisterulum, id est, daemonem, qui mihi respondit quod neutrum facere posset. Habet, inquit, fidem bonam, et diligenter se signo crucis munit? Idcirco non in corpore, sed in undecima parte fructuum suorum in campo (si libet) ei nocere possum": *Formicarius* 5.4, p. 356.

8. *Formicarius* 5.7, pp. 380–81.

9. Of demons, for example, "haec multis ex causis permittit dei iustitia aut misericordia, non tamen semper ex omissione alicuius de pretactis circumstantiis, sed aliquando pro merito acquirendo patientie" (*Formicarius* 5.2, p. 341). Of witches, "septem mihi modi occurrunt quibus ex parte eorum quae sunt hominis nocere possunt, sed nunquam nisi deo permittente" (*Formicarius* 5.3, p. 348).

10. *Formicarius* 3.11, p. 248 (1 Corinthians 11:19); *Contra heresim*, fols. 388v–389r and 392v. Other reformers also stressed the need for a *via purgativa* of adversity; see Christopher M. Bellitto, *Nicolas de Clamanges: Spirituality, Personal Reform, and Pastoral Renewal on the Eve of the Reformations* (Washington, D.C., 2001), 60–73.

11. "Possunt autem per formicas istas quae stulte domum propre hostes collocant, hi homines intelligi, qui domum et habitationem propriam contra insidias diaboli ecclesiasticis caeremoniis non studiose muniunt. Nam aqua benedicta omni die dominica (prout ipse exorcismus notat) in

habitationibus fidelium adeberet spergi, et sal exorcisatum protunc fideliter sumi, se et sua mane, et saepe quisque fidelis crucis charactere insignire, et a peccatis praesertim gravibus se immunem custodire, angelumque proprium saepe pro tutela invocare cum divino auxilio": *Formicarius* 5.2, p. 340.

12. *Formicarius* 5.4, p. 356.

13. *Formicarius* 5.6, p. 370.

14. *Formicarius* 5.3, p. 350.

15. *Preceptorium* 1.11.x.

16. On Vincent and Bernardino, see Blauert, *Frühe Hexenverfolgungen,* Paravy, *De la Chrétienté romaine à la Réforme,* and Mormando, *Preacher's Demons,* as n. 5 above. On the early modern period, see Stuart Clark, *Thinking with Demons: The Idea of Witchcraft in Early Modern Europe* (Oxford, 1997), 445–56.

17. Nider discussed this practice, and approved of it, in *Preceptorium* 1.11.pp.

18. Keith Thomas, *Religion and the Decline of Magic* (New York, 1971), 32. See also Eamon Duffy, *The Stripping of the Altars: Traditional Religion in England, 1400–1580* (New Haven, 1992), 281.

19. On this "common tradition," see Kieckhefer, *Magic,* 56–94; also (although it focuses on a slightly later period) Thomas, *Religion and the Decline of Magic,* 177–252. On the overlap and to some extent competition between systems of supernatural power, see also David Gentilcore, *From Bishop to Witch: The System of the Sacred in Early Modern Terra d'Otranto* (Manchester, 1992).

20. See esp. on this point Gentilcore, *From Bishop to Witch.*

21. "Quia aut tolli potest per aliud maleficium, seu per ritus alicuius malefici illicitos; et id constat esse illicitum. Immo potius homo mori deberet, quam talia consentire": *Formicarius* 5.3, pp. 352–51 (misnumbered for 353).

22. "Et tamen si posset per maleficium remedium adhiberi nihilominus pro peccatum perpetuum reputaretur, quia nullo modo debet aliquis daemonis auxilium per maleficium invocare": *Formicarius* 5.6, p. 371.

23. "Aut non possunt tolli nisi per superstitiosum modum vel per nova maleficiorum opera, et sic est illicitum": *Preceptorium* 1.11.x.

24. *Formicarius* 5.6, pp. 371–72, and 5.11, pp. 420–21. The story is from *Dialogues* 1.10. See *Saint Gregory the Great: Dialogues,* trans. Odo John Zimmerman, *The Fathers of the Church,* vol. 39 (New York, 1959), 42–43. Gregory uses the term *malefici,* which in his day clearly meant "maleficent sorcerer" and not "witch" as understood in the fifteenth century. How Nider intended this term when he repeated it in his account is uncertain.

25. "Tunc statim infirmus curatum se sentiens, scire volvit in remedium futuorum quid carminationis virgo applicasset. Quae respondit: Vos, mala fide vel debili, divinis approbatis exercitiis ecclesiae non inheretis, et carmina ac remedia prohibita crebro vestris infirmitatibus applicatis. Idcirco raro in corpore et semper in anima per talia laedimini": *Formicarius* 5.4, p. 357.

26. This is the overriding purpose of all late medieval popular preaching, according to R. N. Swanson, *Religion and Devotion in Western Europe, c. 1215–1515* (Cambridge, 1995), 66.

27. Pierrette Paravy, "A propos de la genèse médiévale des chasses aux sorcières: Le traité de Claude Tholosan, juge dauphinois (vers 1436)," *Mélanges de l'Ecole française de Rome* 91 (1979): 333–79, here 341–42 and 367–68; or *L'imaginaire du sabbat,* 388–92 and 424.

28. "Modum autem eundem alius iuvenis maleficus captus et incineratus, tandem licet (ut credo) vere poenitens, distinctius reservavit": *Formicarius* 5.3, p. 351.

29. "Hic in saeculo existens famosissimus fuit necromanticus … [et] satis miserabiliter et dissolute vixit plurimo tempore. Habuit autem sororem virginem devotam multum de ordine poenitentium, cuius, ut puto, precibus frater a faucibus daemonis erutus est. Compunctus enim ad diversa loca diversorum reformatorum monasteriorum venit, petens sibi sanctae conversationis tradi habitum. Sed … fidem vix aliquis viro dabat. Tandem autem receptus in antedicto monasterio, in ipso ingressu nomen mutavit et vitam. Benedictus enim vocari coepit, et secundum beati patris Benedicti regulam adeo profecit, ut infra paucos annos speculum religionis effectus": *Formicarius* 5.4, p. 353.

30. See nn. 2 and 3 above.

31. Robert W. Scribner, "Magie und Aberglaube: Zur volkstümlichen sakramentalischen Denkart am Ausgang des Mittelalters," in *Volksreligion im hohen und späten Mittelalter*, ed. Peter Dinzelbacher and Dieter R. Bauer (Paderborn, 1990), 253–74, esp. 253 and 262–63, highlights the place of magic in a *zweilichtiger Grenzzone* between sanctioned belief and illicit superstition. See also Scribner, "Ritual and Popular Religion in Catholic Germany at the Time of the Reformation," *Journal of Ecclesiastical History* 35 (1984): 47–77, esp. 72.

32. On the relation of such concerns to witchcraft, although for a slightly later period, see Clark, *Thinking with Demons*, 457–88. On the presence of such concerns in sermons, see Larissa Taylor, *Soldiers of Christ: Preaching in Late Medieval and Reformation France* (Oxford, 1992), 138–39. That these preachers did not necessarily equate such activity with witchcraft, see Taylor, 118–19.

33. To some extent, this distinction reflects the nature of witchcraft persecution in England. There, far longer than on the continent, the charge against a witch continued to be simple *maleficium*, focusing on the harmful effect of magic, not on its inherently diabolic nature. Therefore, practitioners of traditional "white" magic who were not suspected of causing harm escaped association with witchcraft to a far greater extent in England than elsewhere in Europe. See Thomas, *Religion and the Decline of Magic*, 257 and 439–40.

34. Kieckhefer, *Magic*, 56–80.

35. Duffy, *Stripping of the Altars*, 266–87, quote at 283.

36. See Kieckhefer, *Magic*, 70–74, 160–61, 166–68; also Richard Kieckhefer, *Forbidden Rites: A Necromancer's Manual of the Fifteenth Century* (University Park, Pa., 1998), 3, 13–17.

37. Kieckhefer, *Magic*, 15; Richard Kieckhefer, "The Specific Rationality of Medieval Magic," *American Historical Review* 99 (1994): 813–36, at 821.

38. This belief has led many observers who take the anthropological view of magic—that is, that magic coerces supernatural powers whereas religion supplicates them—to maintain that the medieval church was an essentially magical institution; e.g., Thomas, *Religion and the Decline of Magic*, 25–50. For a cogent response to this position, see Kieckhefer, *Magic*, 14–15, and his "Specific Rationality," 815–17.

39. "Adiuro vos grandines, et ventos per tres Christi divinos clavos qui Christi manus et pedes perforarunt, et per quatuor evangelistas sanctos Matthaeum, Marcum, Lucam, et Ioannem, ut in aqua resoluti descendatis": *Formicarius* 5.4, p. 358.

40. *Preceptorium* 1.11.hh.

41. In his *Tractatus exorcismorum seu adiurationum*, written in 1451/52, the Zurich canon lawyer Felix Hemmerlin discussed Werner's case at length and concluded that his use of blessings was entirely licit. See Hemmerlin, *Varie oblectationis opuscula et tractatus* (Strassburg, after 1497), fols. 107r–111v.

42. Kieckhefer, *Magic*, 186. For a fuller account see Robert E. Lerner, "Werner di Friedberg intrappolato dalla legge," in *La parola all'accusato*, ed. Jean-Claude Maire Vigueur and Agostino Paravicini Bagliani (Palermo, 1991), 268–81.

43. "Unde si aliquis coligat herbam medicinalem cum simbolo divino vel oratione dominica, vel scribat in cartha simbolum vel dominicam orationem, et ponat super aliquem infirmum ... non reprobatur, dummodo nulla alia superstitio admisceatur": *Preceptorium* 1.9.e. Nider also wrote about the protective powers of herbs and stones against demons in *Preceptorium* 1.11.ii.

44. *Preceptorium* 1.11.gg, drawing on Aquinas, *Summa theologiae* 2.2.96.4 (see Aquinas, *Opera*, 2:651–52). Nider provides a similar list in *De lepra morali*, fol. 65r–v.

45. Duffy, *Stripping of the Altars*, 286.

46. Duffy himself writes, "It would be a mistake to see even these 'magical' prayers as standing altogether outside the framework of the official worship and teaching of the Church": *Stripping of the Altars*, 279.

47. On such rationale among the medieval clergy generally, see Kieckhefer, "Specific Rationality," passim.

48. *Preceptorium* 1.11.kk. Here Nider is drawing on Aquinas, *Summa theologiae* 2.2.105.2 (Aquinas, *Opera*, 2:662).

49. As in Matthew 12:26–28, Luke 8:29, and Luke 9:42, in which Christ casts out demons, or Matthew 10:8 and Luke 9:1, in which Christ confers power over demons on his disciples. See the discussions in Kieckhefer, *Magic*, 34–36, and Valerie J. Flint, "The Demonisation of Magic and Sorcery in Late Antiquity: Christian Redefinitions of Pagan Religions," in *Witchcraft and Magic in Europe: Ancient Greece and Rome*, ed. Bengt Ankarloo and Stuart Clark (Philadelphia, 1999), 277–348, at 296–98.

50. "Primo enim modo non licet demones adiurare, quia vident ad amicitiam et benivolentiam pertinere, que non licet ad demone uti.... Isto modo utuntur nigromantici adiurationibus demonum. Secundo autem modo adiurationis per compulsionem videlicet licet nobis aliquo uti et aliquo non … possumus demones adiurando per virtutem divini nominis tanquam inimicos repellere, ne nobis noceant vel spiritualiter vel corporaliter.... Non tamen licitum est eos adiurare ad aliquid discendum ab eis vel etiam ad aliquid per eos obtinendum, quia hoc pertineret ad societatem aliquam cum ipsis habitam": *Preceptorium* 1.11.kk. Nider makes a similar point in *Preceptorium* 2.4.f.

51. Kieckhefer, *Forbidden Rites*, 127.

52. "Questio xxxii, utrum secularibus non ordinatis ad exorcistatum licitum sit demoniacos adiurare. Respondetur secundum Thomam in iiii, di. xxiiii, q. iii, ar. i, sub ar. iii [Aquinas, *Opera*, 1:575], quod sic non tamen tanquam ex officio, sicut etiam quod maius est ministrare ad missam privatam presertim licet seculari puro candelas accendere et huiusmodi, quam accolitatus sunt ordinis. Et tamen laicus potest ea facere, sed non ex officio": *Preceptorium* 1.11.nn.

53. "Idem dicunt doctores licitum esse de applicatione exorcismorum contra potestates daemonis. Sed ibi cavendum est, ne character aliquis ignotus, aut verba ignota sint, aut aliud superstitiosum": *Formicarius* 5.6, p. 371. Nider went on to state, again, that the laity could also exorcise demons in this way, although they could not perform the official rite of exorcism: "et idem a non habentibus ordinem licite fieri potest, non ut ex officio": *Formicarius* 5.6, p. 372.

54. *L'imaginaire du sabbat*, 519.

Conclusion: Witchcraft and the World of the Late Middle Ages

1. The last officially sanctioned execution of a witch in Europe was carried out at Glarus, Switzerland, in 1782. See Brian P. Levack, *The Witch-Hunt in Early Modern Europe*, 2nd ed. (London, 1995), 251; also idem, "The Decline and End of Witchcraft Persecutions," in *Witchcraft and Magic in Europe: The Eighteenth Century*, ed. Bengt Ankarloo and Stuart Clark (Philadelphia, 1999), 1–93, at 74–78.

2. Richard Kieckhefer, *Magic in the Middle Ages* (Cambridge, 1989), 1–2. See also Stuart Clark, *Thinking with Demons: The Idea of Witchcraft in Early Modern Europe* (Oxford, 1997), viii.

3. Clark, *Thinking with Demons*, viii, and Erich Meuthen, *Das 15. Jahrhundert*, 3rd ed. (Munich, 1996), 168–69.

4. Witness the extensive analysis of the *Formicarius* in *L'imaginaire du sabbat*, 99–265; Werner Tschacher's highly detailed study, *Der Formicarius des Johannes Nider von 1437/38: Studien zu den Anfängen der europäischen Hexenverfolgungen im Spätmittelalter* (Aachen, 2000); and, not focusing on witchcraft, Margit Brand, *Studien zu Johannes Niders deutschen Schriften* (Rome, 1998).

5. Nider repeatedly stressed the need for moderation in enforcing monastic reforms in *De reformatione* 1.16, fol. 205v, and 2.13, fol. 221v. He also maintained that slow and steady progress was more effective and more readily attainable than dramatic, sweeping change in *De reformatione* 1.8, fol. 197r–v; 2.14, fol. 222r; and 2.21, fol. 228r.

6. Pierrette Paravy, "Faire croire: Quelques hypothèses de recherche basées sur l'étude des procès de sorcellerie du Dauphiné au XVᵉ siècle," in *Faire croire: Modalités de la diffusion et la réception des messages religieux du XIIᵉ au XVᵉ siècle* (Rome, 1981), 119–30, at 124. On the relative similarity between Nider's accounts and those of other authorities in the 1430s, see Michael D. Bailey, "The Medieval Concept of the Witches' Sabbath," *Exemplaria* 8 (1996): 419–39, esp. 438–39. For some salutary caution on this point, see *L'imaginaire du sabbat*, 517–19.

7. Clark, *Thinking with Demons*, viii–ix, notes that witchcraft continued to be only one among many intellectual interests of so-called demonologists throughout the early modern period.

8. As noted by Carlo Ginzburg, *Ecstasies: Deciphering the Witches' Sabbath*, trans. Raymond Rosenthal (New York, 1991), 69. Tschacher's *Formicarius* does not suffer from this problem. Although Tschacher does not draw on Nider's other writings to the extent I have done here, he does an excellent job of setting Nider's thought on witchcraft in the broader context of the time.

9. Most clearly developed in Richard Kieckhefer, *European Witch Trials: Their Foundations in Popular and Learned Culture, 1300–1500* (Berkeley, 1976).

10. Andreas Blauert, *Frühe Hexenverfolgungen: Ketzer-, Zauberei- und Hexenprozesse des 15. Jahrhunderts* (Hamburg, 1989), 37–50; Martine Ostorero, *Folâtrer avec les demons: Sabbat et chasse aux sorciers à Vevey (1448)* (Lausanne, 1995), 169–82; Gabriel Audisio, *The Waldensian Dissent: Persecution and Survival c. 1170–c. 1570*, trans. Claire Davison (Cambridge, 1999), 74–77.

11. Robert E. Lerner, *The Heresy of the Free Spirit in the Later Middle Ages*, rev. ed. (Notre Dame, Ind., 1991), writes: "By the fifteenth century, when the Church was no longer entirely on the defensive and times were getting better, the heresy [of the Free Spirit] gradually disappeared" (243).

12. On the Free Spirit, see Lerner, *Heresy of the Free Spirit*, 20–34; on the Hussites, see Malcolm Lambert, *Medieval Heresy: Popular Movements from the Gregorian Reform to the Reformation*, 2nd ed. (Oxford, 1992), 336–37.

13. See Euan Cameron, *The Reformation of the Heretics: The Waldenses of the Alps, 1480–1580* (Oxford, 1984), 107–11, and idem, *Waldenses: Rejections of Holy Church in Medieval Europe* (Oxford, 2000), 300. Ostorero, *Folâtrer avec les démons*, 5 and 175, notes that in early trials the crime of witchcraft was referred to as the "new Waldensian heresy" (*heresim illorum hereticorum modernorum Valdensium*).

14. See the cautionary note in Francis Oakley, *The Western Church in the Later Middle Ages* (Ithaca, N.Y., 1979), 113–14.

15. See Levack, *Witch-Hunt*, 103–9.

16. Levack, *Witch-Hunt*, 116–18.

17. A brief overview of the historiography of the period may be found in the introduction to *Handbook of European History, 1400–1600: Late Middle Ages, Renaissance, and Reformation*, ed. Thomas A. Brady Jr., Heiko A. Oberman, and James D. Tracy, 2 vols. (Leiden, 1994–95), 1:xiii–xxiv, esp. xiii–xvi, on the classic conceptions of Renaissance and Reformation.

18. Meuthen, *Das 15. Jahrhundert*, 113–20, provides a good overview of historiographical debates.

19. To cite only one example of the different approaches, in 1979 Francis Oakley concluded that "the continuities binding the late-medieval church with that of the earlier period are a good deal more insistent than they have been thought to be," and that there was nothing "*necessary*" about the sort of explosive breakthrough that Luther actually succeeded in sponsoring" (*Western Church*, 314, 315). Only a year later, Steven Ozment, *The Age of Reform, 1250–1550: An Intellectual and Religious History of Late Medieval and Reformation Europe* (New Haven, 1980), stated, "This effort to view the Reformation from the perspective of the Middle Ages reflects the conviction that it was both a culmination and a transcendence of medieval intellectual and religious history" (xi).

20. Jeffrey Burton Russell, *Witchcraft in the Middle Ages* (Ithaca, N.Y., 1972), links witchcraft to heresy. Norman Cohn, *Europe's Inner Demons: The Demonization of Christians in Medieval Christendom*, rev. ed. (London, 1993), links witchcraft to heresy but more strongly to magic. Edward Peters, *The Magician, the Witch, and the Law* (Philadelphia, 1978), and Kieckhefer, *Magic*, link witchcraft to magic and sorcery. Pierrette Paravy, *De la Chrétienté romaine à la Réforme en Dauphiné: Evêques, fidèles et déviants (vers 1340–vers 1530)*, 2 vols. (Rome, 1993), 2:771–905, provides an example of the Christianization thesis, as in a way does Ginzburg, *Ecstasies*. R. I. Moore, *The Formation of a Persecuting Society: Power and Deviance in Western Europe, 950–1250* (Oxford, 1987), 5, 135, and 146, suggests a connection between witch trials and a general persecuting mentality in medieval Europe.

21. Meuthen, *Das 15. Jahrhundert*, 2. Ozment, *Age of Reform*, 205–7, has with some justice described belief in witchcraft as evidence of the religious vitality of the age.

Appendix I. Chronology of Nider's Life and Datable Works

1. Margit Brand, *Studien zu Johannes Niders deutschen Schriften* (Rome, 1998), 131. See also Ulla Williams, "Schul der Weisheit: Spirituelle *artes*-Auslegung bei Johannes Nider, mit Edition der «14. Harfe»," in *Überlieferungsgeschichtliche Editionen und Studien zur deutschen Literatur des Mittelalters: Kurt Ruh zum 75. Geburtstag,* ed. Konrad Kunze et al. (Tübingen, 1989), 391–424, at 392.

2. Joseph Hansen, *Quellen und Untersuchungen zur Geschichte des Hexenwahns und der Hexenverfolgung im Mittelalter* (1901; reprint Hildesheim, 1963), 423.

3. See Appendix II, as for all other works listed below.

Appendix II. Dating of Nider's Major Works Used in This Study

1. On this debate, see František M. Bartoš, *The Hussite Revolution, 1424–1437,* ed. John M. Klassen (New York, 1986), 41.

2. Bartoš, *Hussite Revolution,* 53–54.

3. Michael D. Bailey, "Abstinence and Reform at the Council of Basel: Johannes Nider's *De abstinencia esus carnium, Mediaeval Studies* 59 (1997): 225–60, at 228–29. The slightly revised dating here supersedes the possible dates given there.

4. The text typically reads: "Ad idem, multo expressius esse videtur per plurimas questiones Johannis de Tambacho, in questionibus suis de voluntaria paupertate, sermone de beato Dominico, qui fecerit et docuerit, etc., facto anno 1434," as in *De secularium religionibus,* fol. 6v. The alternate date of 1334 is found in Basel, ÖBU, MS A VII 42, fol. 77r. Dambach's major work on poverty, *De proprietate mendicantium,* was written in 1362, but he wrote a theological work on indulgences as early as 1341, and he served as an official witness in the trial of Meister Eckhart in 1327. The *questiones* to which Nider refers could thus possibly be a previously unknown early work written in 1334.

5. *CB,* 1:109 and 227–28.

6. On this delegation, see Franz Egger, *Beiträge zur Geschichte des Predigerordens: Die Reform des Basler Konvents, 1429, und die Stellung des Ordens am Basler Konzil, 1431–1448* (Bern, 1991), 98–99. Nider is not mentioned here, nor is he listed in conciliar records as an official delegate (*MC,* 1:77), but he could have gone as a personal assistant to his fellow Dominican Johannes of Ragusa.

7. Arguments for dating are also given in *L'imaginaire du sabbat,* 107, and most completely in Werner Tschacher, *Der Formicarius des Johannes Nider von 1437/48: Studien zu den Anfängen der europäischen Hexenverfolgungen im Spätmittelalter* (Aachen, 2000), 127–31.

Appendix III. Manuscript Copies of Nider's Treatises

1. Thomas Kaeppeli, ed., *Scriptores Ordinis Praedicatorum medii aevi,* 4 vols. (Rome, 1970–93), 2:500–515 and 4:164–65. For more complete information on manuscripts of Nider's German works, see now Margit Brand, *Studien zu Johannes Niders deutschen Schriften* (Rome, 1998). For manuscripts of the *Formicarius,* see now Werner Tschacher, *Der Formicarius des Johannes Nider von 1437/38: Studien zu den Anfängen der europäischen Hexenverfolgungen im Spätmittelalter* (Aachen, 2000), 83–107.

2. See Günter Gattermann, ed., *Handschriftencensus Rheinland* (Weisbaden, 1993), 502. Discussion of this text is now found in John Van Engen, "Privileging the Devout: A Text from the Brothers at Deventer," in *Roma, magistra mundi: Itineraria culturae medievalis, mélanges offerts au Père L. E. Boyle à l'occasion de son 75e anniversaire,* ed. J. Hamesse, 3 vols. (Louvain-la-Neuve, 1998), 2:951–63.

SELECT BIBLIOGRAPHY

Since full bibliographical information is given in the notes, I list here, for ease of reference, only those works that are cited repeatedly or are particularly important for this study. Primary and secondary printed sources are listed together.

Aquinas, Thomas. *S. Thomae Aquinatis opera omnia.* Ed. Roberto Busa. 7 vols. Stuttgart, 1980.

Bailey, Michael D. "Abstinence and Reform at the Council of Basel: Johannes Nider's *De abstinencia esus carnium.*" *Mediaeval Studies* 59 (1997): 225–60.

———. "From Sorcery to Witchcraft: Clerical Conceptions of Magic in the Later Middle Ages." *Speculum* 76 (2001): 960–90.

———. "The Medieval Concept of the Witches' Sabbath." *Exemplaria* 8 (1996): 419–39.

Bartoš, František M. *The Hussite Revolution, 1424–1437.* Ed. John M. Klassen. New York, 1986.

Blauert, Andreas. *Frühe Hexenverfolgungen: Ketzer-, Zauberei- und Hexenprozesse des 15. Jahrhunderts.* Hamburg, 1989.

Borst, Arno. "The Origins of the Witch-Craze in the Alps." In Arno Borst, *Medieval Worlds: Barbarians, Heretics, and Artists in the Middle Ages,* trans. Eric Hansen, 101–22. Chicago, 1992.

Brand, Margit. *Studien zu Johannes Niders deutschen Schriften.* Rome, 1998.

Briggs, Robin. *Witches and Neighbors: The Social and Cultural Context of European Witchcraft.* New York, 1996.

Clark, Stuart. *Thinking with Demons: The Idea of Witchcraft in Early Modern Europe.* Oxford, 1997.

Cohn, Norman. *Europe's Inner Demons: The Demonization of Christians in Medieval Christendom.* Rev. ed. London, 1993.

Degler-Spengler. *Die Beginen in Basel.* Basel, 1970. First published as "Die Beginen in Basel," *Basler Zeitschrift für Geschichte und Altertumskunde* 69 (1969): 5–83 and 70 (1970): 29–118.

Duffy, Eamon. *The Stripping of the Altars: Traditional Religion in England, 1400–1580.* New Haven, 1982.

Egger, Franz. *Beiträge zur Geschichte des Predigerordens: Die Reform des Basler Konvents, 1429, und die Stellung des Ordens am Basler Konzil, 1431–1448.* Bern, 1991.

Frank, Isnard Wilhelm. *Hausstudium und Universitätsstudium der Wiener Dominikaner bis 1500.* Archiv für österreichische Geschichte, vol. 127. Vienna, 1968.

Ginzburg, Carlo. *Ecstasies: Deciphering the Witches' Sabbath.* Trans. Raymond Rosenthal. New York, 1991.

Grundmann, Herbert. *Religious Movements in the Middle Ages: The Historical Links between Heresy, the Mendicant Orders, and the Women's Religious Movement in the Twelfth and Thirteenth Century, with the Historical Foundations of German Mysticism.* Trans. Steven Rowan. Notre Dame, Ind., 1995.

Haller, Johannes, et al., eds. *Concilium Basiliense: Studien und Quellen zur Geschichte des Concils von Basel.* 8 vols. 1896–1936. Reprint Wiesbaden, 1971.

Handbook of European History: The Late Middle Ages, Renaissance, and Reformation. Ed. Thomas A. Brady Jr., Heiko A. Oberman, and James D. Tracy. 2 vols. Leiden, 1994–95.

Hansen, Joseph. *Quellen und Untersuchungen zur Geschichte des Hexenwahns und der Hexenverfolgung im Mittelalter.* 1901. Reprint Hildesheim, 1963.

Helmrath, Johannes. *Das Basler Konzil, 1431–1449: Forschungsstand und Probleme*. Cologne, 1987.

———. "Reform als Thema der Konzilien des Spätmittelalters." In *Christian Unity: The Council of Ferrara-Florence, 1438/39–1989*, ed. Giuseppe Alberigo, 75–152. Leuven, 1991.

———. "Theorie und Praxis der Kirchenreform im Spätmittelalter." *Rottenburger Jahrbuch für Kirchengeschichte* 11 (1992): 41–70.

Heusinger, Sabine von. *Johannes Mulberg OP († 1414): Ein Leben im Spannungsfeld von Dominikanerobservanz und Beginenstreit*. Berlin, 2000.

Heymann, Frederick G. *John Žižka and the Hussite Revolution*. Princeton, 1955.

Hillenbrand, Eugen. "Die Observantenbewegung in der deutschen Ordensprovinz der Dominikaner." In *Reformbemühungen und Observanzbestrebungen im spätmittelalterlichen Ordenswesen*, ed. Kaspar Elm, 219–71. Berlin, 1989.

Hinnebusch, William A. *The History of the Dominican Order*. 2 vols. New York, 1965–73.

Kaminsky, Howard. *A History of the Hussite Revolution*. Berkeley, 1967.

Kieckhefer, Richard. *European Witch Trials: Their Foundations in Popular and Learned Culture, 1300–1500*. Berkeley, 1976.

———. *Forbidden Rites: A Necromancer's Manual of the Fifteenth Century*. University Park, Pa., 1998.

———. *Magic in the Middle Ages*. Cambridge, 1989.

———. *Repression of Heresy in Medieval Germany*. Philadelphia, 1979.

———. "The Specific Rationality of Medieval Magic." *American Historical Review* 99 (1994): 813–36.

Kors, Alan, and Edward Peters, eds. *Witchcraft in Europe, 400–1700: A Documentary History*. 2nd ed. Philadelphia, 2001.

Ladner, Gerhart. *The Idea of Reform: Its Impact on Christian Thought and Action in the Age of the Fathers*. Cambridge, Mass., 1959.

Lambert, Malcolm. *Medieval Heresy: Popular Movements from the Gregorian Reform to the Reformation*. 2nd ed. Oxford, 1992.

Lazarus, Paul. *Das Basler Konzil: Seine Berufung und Leitung, seine Gliederung und seine Behördenorganisation*. 1912. Reprint Vaduz, 1965.

Leff, Gordon. *Heresy in the Later Middle Ages: The Relation of Heterodoxy to Dissent, c. 1250–c. 1450*. 2 vols. New York, 1967.

Lerner, Robert E. *The Heresy of the Free Spirit in the Later Middle Ages*. Rev. ed. Notre Dame, Ind., 1991.

Levack, Brian P. *The Witch-Hunt in Early Modern Europe*. 2nd ed. London, 1995.

Löhr, Gabriel M., *Die Teutonia im 15. Jahrhundert: Studien und Texte vornehmlich zur Geschichte ihrer Reform*. QF, vol. 19. Leipzig, 1924.

McDonnell, Ernest W. *The Beguines and Beghards in Medieval Culture, with Special Emphasis on the Belgian Scene*. New Brunswick, N.J., 1954.

Mertens, Dieter. "Monastische Reformbewegungen des 15. Jahrhunderts: Ideen—Ziele—Resultate." In *Reform von Kirche und Reich zur Zeit der Konzilien von Konztanz (1414–1418) und Basel (1431–1449)*, ed. Ivan Hlaváček and Alexander Patschovsky, 157–81. Constance, 1996.

Meuthen, Erich. *Das 15. Jahrhundert*. 3rd ed. Munich, 1996.

Meyer, Johannes. *Buch der Reformacio Predigerordens*. Ed. Benedictus Maria Reichert. QF, vols. 2–3. Leipzig, 1908–9.

Mormando, Franco. *The Preacher's Demons: Bernardino of Siena and the Social Underworld of Early Renaissance Italy*. Chicago, 1999.

Neidiger, Bernhard. *Mendikanten zwischen Ordensideal und städtischer Realität: Untersuchung zum wirtschaftlichen Verhalten der Bettelorden in Basel*. Berlin, 1981.

———. "Die Observanzbewegungen der Bettelorden in Südwestdeutschland." *Rottenburger Jahrbuch für Kirchengeschichte* 11 (1992): 175–96.

Nider, Johannes. *Formicarius*. Ed. G. Colvener. Douai, 1602.

———. *Preceptorium divine legis*. Milan, 1489.

Oakley, Francis. *The Western Church in the Later Middle Ages*. Ithaca, N.Y., 1979.

Ostorero, Martine. *Folâtrer avec les démones: Sabbat et chasse aux sorciers à Vevey (1448)*. Lausanne, 1995.

Ostorero, Martine, Agostino Paravicini Bagliani, and Kathrin Utz Tremp, eds. *L'imaginaire du sabbat: Edition critique des textes les plus anciens (1430 c.–1440 c.)*. Lausanne, 1999.

Palacky, F., et al., eds. *Monumenta conciliorum generalium saeculi decimi quinti, scriptores concilium Basileense*. 4 vols. Vienna/Basel, 1857–1935.

Paravy, Pierrette. "A propos de la genèse médiévale des chasses aux sorcières: Le traité de Claude Tholosan, juge dauphinois (vers 1436)." *Mélanges de l'Ecole française de Rome* 91 (1979): 333–79.

———. *De la Chrétienté romaine à la Réforme en Dauphiné: Evêques, fidèles et déviants (vers 1340–vers 1530)*. 2 vols. Rome, 1993.

Patschovsky, Alexander. "Beginen, Begarden und Terziaren im 14. und 15. Jahrhundert: Das Beispiel des Basler Beginenstreits (1400/04–1411)." In *Festschrift für Eduard Hlawitschka zum 65. Geburtstag*, ed. Karl Rudolf Schnith and Roland Pauler, 403–18. Munich, 1993.

———. "Straßburger Beginenverfolgungen im 14. Jahrhundert." *Deutsches Archiv für Erforschung des Mittelalters* 30 (1974): 56–198.

Peters, Edward. *The Magician, the Witch, and the Law*. Philadelphia, 1978.

———. "The Medieval Church and State on Superstition, Magic, and Witchcraft: From Augustine to the Sixteenth Century." In *Witchcraft and Magic in Europe: The Middle Ages,* ed. Bengt Ankarloo and Stuart Clark. Philadelphia, forthcoming.

Russell, Jeffrey Burton. *Witchcraft in the Middle Ages*. Ithaca, N.Y., 1972.

Schieler, Kaspar. *Magister Johannes Nider aus dem Orden der Prediger-Brüder*. Mainz, 1885.

Schmitt, Jean-Claude. *Mort d'une hérésie: L'Eglise et les clercs face aux béguines et aux béghards du Rhin supérieur du XIVᵉ au XVᵉ siècle*. Paris, 1978.

Stieber, Joachim W. *Pope Eugenius IV, the Council of Basel, and the Secular and Ecclesiastical Authorities in the Empire: The Conflict over Supreme Authority and Power in the Church*. Leiden, 1978.

Stump, Phillip H. *The Reforms of the Council of Constance (1414–1418)*. Leiden, 1994.

Swanson, R. N. *Religion and Devotion in Europe, c. 1215–c. 1515*. Cambridge, 1995.

Taylor, Larissa. *Soldiers of Christ: Preaching in Late Medieval and Reformation France*. Oxford, 1992.

Thomas, Keith. *Religion and the Decline of Magic*. New York, 1971.

Tschacher, Werner. *Der Formicarius des Johannes Nider von 1437/38: Studien zu den Anfängen der europäischen Hexenverfolgungen im Spätmittelalter*. Aachen, 2000.

Uiblein, Paul, ed. *Die Akten der Theologischen Fakultät der Universität Wien*. 2 vols. Vienna, 1978.

Van Engen, John. "Friar Johannes Nyder on Laypeople Living as Religious in the World." In *Vita Religiosa im Mittelalter: Festschrift für Kaspar Elm zum 70. Geburtstag,* ed. Franz J. Felten and Nikolas Jaspert, 583–615. Berlin, 1999.

Wassermann, Dirk. *Dionysius der Kartäuser: Einführung in Werk und Gedankenwelt*. Salzburg, 1996.

Wilts, Andreas. *Beginen im Bodenseeraum*. Sigmaringen, 1994.

INDEX